SOCIAL ADMINISTRATION
AND THE CITIZEN

This is a revised edition of Kathleen Slack's important book, first published in 1966. Designed primarily for the student of social administration, it contains much material which should be of interest and value also to those in the practice of social work, in administration and organisation whether in voluntary or statutory social agencies. It concerns itself in the first instance with the meaning of the term social administration, its relationship to the social sciences, to social research and social policy, and proceeds to outline the purpose and content of the social services in meeting human need and human misfortune.

Attention is given to the machinery of administration, to the function of commissions, councils and committees, and to the problem of staffing, of conflict within the social services and the need for proper advice and protection of the citizen in their growing complexity. Conflicting views on the Welfare State and the temporary or permanent nature of the social services are examined and the inevitability of value judgments in social welfare is recognised.

Social Administration and the Citizen

KATHLEEN M. SLACK

LONDON
MICHAEL JOSEPH

First published in Great Britain by
MICHAEL JOSEPH LIMITED
26 Bloomsbury Street
London, W.C.1
MAY 1966
Second Edition (Revised) 1969

© *1966 by Kathleen M. Slack*

7181 0427 7

Set and printed in Great Britain by
Unwin Brothers Limited at the Gresham Press, Woking,
in Imprint type, eleven-point leaded, and bound by
James Burn at Esher, Surrey

CONTENTS

CONTENTS

ACKNOWLEDGEMENTS

I wish to acknowledge and express thanks for all the help I have received in the writing of this book and for the encouragement of my colleagues both inside and outside the London School of Economics. In particular I wish to thank Professor Titmuss and Professor Donnison for their comments on the earlier chapters; Mr Greve, Mrs Cockburn, Mr Plowman, Dr Parker, Mr Bleddyn Davies, and Miss Hunter, Tutor and Adviser in Social Studies at the University of London, for reading and making suggestions on later chapters.

Especially I would like to thank Mr Huws Jones, Principal of the National Institute for Social Work Training, who spared the time to read and comment on the whole of the script. I have been helped also by Miss Becker, Secretary of the Social and Economic Affairs Committee of the Society of Friends, by her reading of many Journals on my behalf. Last but not least I thank the many students who have been both critical and honest in their comments from the point of view of the consumer for whom this book is primarily intended. They are too many to mention by name but I am grateful to each and all of them. The final outcome is of course my own responsibility. The defects of this book rest upon no one other than myself.

I acknowledge my indebtedness finally to all those publishers and authors from whose works quotations have been taken for purposes of illustration in this book. The sources of these appear in the concluding list of references and appreciation is expressed for the permission to use them which has been given in each instance.

London School of Economics   KATHLEEN M. SLACK
1965

ACKNOWLEDGEMENTS

Second Edition (Revised)

The revision of material in this book, necessitated by the march of events that inevitably caught up with and out-dated some of its original data, has been assisted both by reviews and comments on the first edition. I am grateful to the publishers and authors whose works I have been permitted to quote since they were published in or after 1965; to Professor F. Lafitte, Head of the Social Studies Department, University of Birmingham for his comments, in particular on Chapter 2, which encouraged an expansion of its contents; and to Mr Michael Ryan, Lecturer in Social Administration at University College, Swansea for drawing my attention to certain errors, both of omission and commission, which have now been rectified. The comments of students as before have been helpful. Final responsibility for the revision made remains of course my own.

London School of Economics   KATHLEEN M. SLACK
1969

CHAPTER ONE

Clarity and Confusion in Social Administration

'Social Administration' is a term in general use in University Social Studies Departments, in pre-professional and professional courses of education and training for social workers, in government departments and town halls. It forms an option in sociology and social science degree courses and is the main subject of diploma courses. Yet it remains difficult to define and it is a fact that when the question: 'What is social administration?' was put to a number of those who claim to teach it their answers differed.

For the student this is unsatisfactory. Not to appreciate what he is studying or proposing to study is akin to his driving a car in a fog with the possibility of running into one in front, following it down the wrong road, or lurching into the ditch. For example, to say no more as does Clarke than: 'Social administration is the term used in the syllabus of the Institute of Hospital Administration',[1] is simply to run into the car in front. For an applicant for a place on a diploma course in social administration to act on the incorrect advice of the Vice-Chancellor of her University that this would only qualify her for work in the field of government,* would be to follow down the wrong road. And to enter into social case work on the strength of a course in social administration only is to invite a lurch into the ditch—an invitation it must be said that not a few accept.

Difficult though it may be it is, therefore, essential to define or at least to illustrate what social administration is before one discusses any of its individual aspects. At once it is necessary to appreciate that the term is used in two ways; a fact which is the cause of a good deal of the confusion that it generates. First social administration is used to refer to a *subject of study*. Second it is used to refer to a *process* directed to the solution of social problems, the promotion of social welfare or the implementation of social policy, a process which is furthered by the use of different methods

---

* Verbal report at the time of interview.

A*

or techniques designed to reach a decision, promote some action or establish a precedent.

At this point it may be said simply that the content of the social services forms part of social administration when it refers to a subject of study and a case conference is a method used in social administration when it refers to a process directed to the promotion of social welfare. And a Principal in the Department of Education and Science who writes 'I agree' to a minute of recommendation relating to a residential school, passed to him by an Assistant Principal, who has received the papers from an Executive Officer who has had them returned with a report from one of Her Majesty's Inspectors, is using a technique in social administration when it refers to a process directed to the promotion of social policy. Unless the two ways in which the term social administration is used are kept clear the student will probably continue to drive in a fog. It is with the first of the two that he should begin. Until he has some grasp of social administration as a subject of study he cannot expect to understand or appreciate its nuances when it refers to a process, which is difficult even for the experienced observer.

Donnison's definition of social administration as a subject of study is perhaps the simplest:

'Narrowly defined, Social Administration is the study of the development, structure and practices of the social services.'[2]

This accords with other definitions which agree, when the term is used to refer to a subject of study, that it includes the social services. Thus Titmuss said:

'Social Administration may broadly be defined as the study of the social services. . . . It is concerned with the historical development of these services, both statutory and voluntary, with the moral values implicit in social action, with the roles and functions of the services, with their economic aspects, and with the part they play in meeting certain needs in the social process.'[3]

Agreement is found also in the opening question of the introduction to an earlier work on social administration where Simey asked: 'What are the social services?'[4]

Again, whilst there were variations in the answers provided in a survey of 45 University Courses which included an examination in social administration, 'the dominant impression given . . . was a set of social institutions—the social services of Britain—which formed the principal subject matter of teaching'.[5]

Parker's definition of social administration as a subject of study did not make specific mention of the social services as such but they must clearly be included. She said: '(Social administration) is a study of those aspects of policy and administration which (a) attempt to regulate standards of living and to control the distribution of income within a particular society and (b) are intended to improve the circumstances or increase the wellbeing of a particular group or of the whole community.'[6]

Even if it is agreed, however, that social administration, when it refers to a subject of study, includes a study of the social services, it is still necessary to ask what these comprise and whether it is they and they alone that are studied. There are unfortunately even greater complexities here. The meaning of social services is more confused than the meaning of social administration itself. The student need only ponder for a moment on the following to realise the difficult nature of the terrain through which he is being expected to drive.

'How far should countries go in protecting their citizens against the adversities which may beset them?', asked Cole as the opening question of one booklet surveying the field of British social services past and present.[7] This question presupposed that the social services were primarily concerned to protect the citizen against adversity. But: 'The time is passing when the term "social service" accurately describes provision rendered only to those in some sort of trouble', stated Cohen ten years earlier.[8]

'A voluntary social service', observes one handbook of the National Council of Social Service, 'is the organisation and activities of a self governing body of people, who have joined together voluntarily to study, or act, *for the betterment of the community*'.*[9] This opens the door for the inclusion, as a social service, of almost any well intentioned activity. But in a companion volume the Council says: ' . . . there have been great changes in the scope of public services provided by statutory authorities *for the needs of the individual and the family*. . . .'*[10] This is considerably less all embracing. Hagenbuch said: 'A social service provides for

* Author's italics.

those personal economic and social needs which arise out of income insecurity and the handicaps of poverty.'[11] This limiting definition excludes any services which relate to personal need not necessarily having any connection with poverty or income insecurity, for example mental illness, loss of parents, or the infirmity of age. Marsh maintained that 'the social services are those provided by the community for no other reason than that of maintaining or improving individual well-being'.[12] Here the emphasis is on motive as much as on purpose. Those who provide the service, Marsh continued, must not do so for their own benefit; profit must not be thought of as it is in commercial or industrial enterprise. Strictly speaking this may be so but not if it suggests that those who provide a social service have no thought to their own remuneration in so doing.

The widest view was taken by Titmuss when he said: ' . . . the term "social service" has come to be applied to more and more areas of collective provision for certain "needs". It has indeed acquired a most elastic quality; its expanding frontiers, formerly enclosing little besides poor relief, sanitation, and public nuisances, now embrace a multitude of heterogeneous activities'.[13]

These authorities cannot each and all be right and unless one is looking for complete unanimity that could easily become rigidity perhaps this is as well. Despite the gallant effort of Political and Economic Planning to define the public social services precisely as: 'Those services which have as their object the enhancement of the personal welfare of individual citizens in the community',[14] it is probably wiser to accept Hall's view that 'there is no general agreement as to which services should be classified as "social"'.[15] Titmuss agreed with this when he said: 'No consistent principle seems to obtain in the definition of what is a "social service"'.[16] A particularly confusing view is that of Macleod and Powell that a service is a social service only if 'the individuals or families who avail themselves of it are receiving more than they give', and that for those who 'pay more in rates and taxes towards the social services than the benefits which they derive from them are worth', the services are not in fact social services at all.[17] This is as though to argue that because a ratepayer does not often use a public library it is not for him a public library, or that a fire brigade is only for him a fire brigade if his own house is burning down. This is not so. Whether or not a person has need himself to use a service does not decide its social nature. It merely decides the extent to which he derives direct benefit from it immediately or over a period of time.

In view of all that has been said the wise student will admit defeat and abandon any attempt to define precisely so Humpty Dumpty a term as 'social services' has become. He will recognise also that the problem is not peculiar to social administration. Social work theory, sociology, social psychology, are all areas of study in which the difficulty of definition arises and it is one that cannot be avoided. It may be that so far as social administration is concerned, until and unless a final definition does emerge, the student will find it most helpful to look at some examination papers and discover empirically what are regarded there as social services. He will then, in all probability, discover that the following comprise his area of study—national insurance, social security and family allowances, health services, physical and mental, education, housing which must be linked with town and country planning, maternity and child welfare, care of the deprived and the delinquent child and of the adult offender, youth employment, youth work and community welfare, welfare of the family, the disabled, the aged and the homeless, legal aid, advice and information services. Objections could be raised to some of the inclusions or exclusions from this list but it is neither profitable nor interesting to continue the discussion *ad nauseam*. It cannot be concluded, however, without pointing out that private pension or superannuation schemes, industrial or employers' welfare, and fiscal policy in the form of income tax rebates in respect of dependent children, aged parents or education costs, have not, judged on the empirical basis of examination papers, crept far as yet into the social service fold. But a strong case has been made for their inclusion by Titmuss on the ground that it is the aim of a service, not the administrative method or the institutional devices employed to achieve the aim, which justifies its being regarded as 'social',[18] and Young in effect supported this view by examining social services in British industry; regarding the dual motive of these services, protecting the more helpless and being concerned with the total human factor, as justifying their description if not a definition in those terms.[19]

Having decided, on an empirical basis, what the social services can include it follows that their purpose or intention, their historical development, their content and finance, the national and local statutory and voluntary bodies responsible for their provision and administration, their staffing and structure, and the problems of individual understanding, citizen participation, objection, and protection, are all included in social administration when referring to a subject of study. It might be thought that this would be enough but it is clear that the subject can be stretched even further.

Examination papers on social administration have included such questions as: 'Consider the meaning of poverty, now and over the past sixty years.' 'Sentencing is becoming a more complex task. Examine and discuss the implications of this statement.' 'Discuss the view that the concept of illness expands continually at the expense of the concept of moral failure.'

It might plausibly be argued that those who set such questions had either exhausted their stock of relevant questions or let their special interests run away with them, and that it would have been better to transfer them to papers on social economics, criminology or philosophy. On the other hand it is not unreasonable to suggest that without asking questions of this nature it is not possible to evaluate the content, purpose and worth of the services studied. Be that as it may the student of social administration must be aware of and appreciate the relationship between the content of the subject social administration and that of social history, psychology, economics, sociology, political science, philosophy and ethics; a relationship which will be examined in the next chapter.

Having outlined briefly what is covered by social administration when the term is used to refer to a subject of study, there can now be some expansion on social administration when it is used to refer to a process directed to the solution of a social problem, the promotion of social welfare, or the implementation of social policy.

Earlier in this chapter a case conference was offered as one example of a method in social administration when using the term to refer to a process directed to the promotion of social welfare. What is seen there is a group of people who are all concerned in one way or another with the welfare of a particular person, let us say a child in the setting of his family. His physical, mental and emotional health, his safety, moral or otherwise, his home environment, education, out of school activities, or any other aspect of his life, may be the concern of one or other of the members of this group. They have met together in the hope and intention, by a process of discussion and mutual assistance, to promote and further the child's welfare, in unity, not in competition, with simplification and not complication of the issues involved. The fact that these objectives may not easily or entirely be achieved, or that good intentions may be blocked by misunderstandings or personal failures, does not invalidate the claim that a process directed to the promotion of social welfare is in fact going on.

The people who are met together are all connected with one social service or another. They probably comprise a health visitor, a child welfare officer, a housing officer, a school welfare officer, possibly an officer of the National Society for the Prevention of Cruelty to Children, a family case worker, a probation officer, and a representative of the Department of Health and Social Security. Individually each will be concerned primarily with a particular aspect of the child's life and individually and corporately they should be generally concerned with his wellbeing and that of his family as a whole. Thus it may be that the danger of eviction for non-payment of rent of a council house will enter into the discussion, or the fact that the child has been truanting from school, that his brother is on probation, his father is unemployed and his mother is expecting her sixth baby, although incapable of caring properly for the other five, one of whom has already been committed to the care of the local authority as being in need of care, protection or control.

As the discussion at the case conference proceeds agreement may be reached to make use of another part of the health service, for example the home help service, or there is an agreed withdrawal of one of the workers already involved, let us say the N.S.P.C.C. officer, or alternatively the *status quo* of all concerned is maintained. As the weeks or months go by the family situation will be kept under review, one or more workers will continue to visit and support or advise, and any changes or developments, for better or worse, will be reported.

In other words an operation is under way which may affect not merely the present but the whole future of the child's and the family's life. The text book study of the social services, their purpose, content, staffing and structure, is now to be seen as the framework of a living, human situation, in which the hopes, fears, failures and sorrows of individuals are involved. In short social administration—a subject of study—has merged into social administration—a process directed to the promotion of social welfare.*

Many other illustrations of social administration when it refers to a process directed to the promotion of social welfare could be given; the meeting together, for example, of a local authority welfare officer, a social worker on the staff of an old people's welfare committee, a health visitor, and a public health inspector, to consider whether or when an old person should go into a residential home and if so who should take the first step necessary to this end, or their consideration of the solution to the problems that will be faced if he stays alone in his own home.

How smoothly, effectively, quickly and successfully such processes, whether they are in relation to the old, the young, the disabled, the homeless, the sick, the widowed, or any other persons in need, are or are not completed, depends upon a variety of factors. These include the personality and attitudes of individual councillors, social workers, administrative officers or committee members, good or bad relationships between people, interdepartmental or organisational co-operation or rivalries, understanding or misunderstanding between field and office workers, professional attitudes or preoccupations, personal imagination or apathy, and the availability of the necessary resources. It is rarely possible when studying social administration at this point to forecast events with certainty or to explain beyond peradventure what caused a particular line of action to be rejected or accepted. That there has to be some concomitance of ideas, knowledge, energy, willingness, means and co-operation, if movement is to take place, is clear. But the presence or lack of just which of these factors it is, in what proportions, and exerted by whom, that promotes or blocks progress is often difficult to discern or beyond the bounds of diplomacy to reveal. Unlike social administration

* For a detailed account of a case illustrating this process see: F. M. G. Willson, *Administrators in Action*, Vol. 1. Case V. Allen and Unwin Ltd.,1961.

when it is confined to academic study, which can be pursued relatively objectively and calmly in the confines of a library or lecture hall, social administration when it proceeds to the promotion of social welfare is liable to be charged with emotion and affected by human frailty. It is no less important and interesting for this reason but it is considerably more complex and difficult to understand.

Of social administration, when the technique of the civil servant is concerned, it could be said that there is in fact no need for the inclusion of the word 'social' before administration at all, except to indicate that one is thinking of the use of a technique in a particular field; that of social policy or social welfare. The technique itself is not one used only in the social services. It is no different from that used in any of the public services, in which case it may be called public administration. In large business organisations it may be referred to as business administration. In short the attachment here of 'social' to 'administration' does not indicate a difference in technique, but only its application to one area of work.

Social administration then, using the technique under consideration, is that of a body of persons, forming the hierarchical structure of an organisation, in which someone begins a process of collection or consideration of ideas, information or evidence relating to particular policies, persons, services or problems, about whom or which some decision has sooner or later to be reached. Such a decision may relate for example to the approval by the Home Office of a school for delinquent boys, or of the Department of Education and Science of a local education authority's plans for the building of a comprehensive school, or the Department of Health and Social Security on a letter from a widow who is not satisfied with the pension she has been awarded. It may be a decision of a county borough council to build a residential home for elderly people, or compulsorily acquire land for housing purposes, or set up a youth service sub-committee of its education committee. It may be a decision by the Department of Employment and Productivity to raise the grants payable to injured workmen undergoing courses of rehabilitation and training.

The correspondence, reports and minutes relating to the particular issue will pass upwards and downwards in the different grades of the hierarchy, out via executive officers to inspectors or others in the field for their observations, back into the department, possibly referred *en route* for comment or advice to a specialist in medicine, law, architecture or finance, to be returned in due course to the official by whom they were started. In the course of this procedure each letter, telephone call, conference, interview, report, recommendation or memorandum, will or should be minuted and added to the file, until the picture is as complete as it can be and the final decision is made by the officer on whom ultimate responsibility rests. It must not be forgotten that a decision when reached can be a negative one; a decision, that is to say, to do nothing, or to say 'No.' If, however, a positive decision is reached action will be initiated by an official letter, circular, or other means, to the interested persons or organisations, or the order to begin work will be given. If a precedent has been established by the decision it will be noted for future reference as and when necessary.

This technique is rational, purposeful, consistent and orderly. It is intended to be objective, careful, just and impartial. It involves established procedures, recognised degrees of authority, and where it relates to government departments, public accountability. It would be foolish to claim that it is never affected by internal politics, pressure of events or personal failing, or that it has no weaknesses. But it has become highly developed, operating with trained personnel, and is a characteristic and lasting feature of modern social and economic life.*

Clearly, different methods or techniques in social administration, when referring to a process directed to the promotion of social policy or welfare, will in some cases be used at one and the same time. The affairs of homeless families, for example, are likely to involve not only social workers, who also use particular methods in their part in the process of social administration, but also civil servants and local government officers concerned with housing policy, town planning, or the development of a number of related services. Case conferences, committee meetings, the passing of minutes and policy decisions in relation to the same persons or the same set of problems may all be taking place together. They are not mutually exclusive.

* For a study illustrating this technique see F. M. G. Willson, *op. cit.*, Vol. 1. Case 1.

Before leaving the two uses of the term social administration one further point may be made. It is essential to ask three questions in relation to any aspect of social administration, whether it relates to the introduction, contraction or expansion of social services, the making of social policy, the solution of a social or personal problem, or the promotion of social welfare. These questions are: 'Why?', 'What?' and 'How?'.

Why, for example, do men wish, whether as individuals, groups or a society, to do or provide something for the community as a whole, for one section of it, or for one person or family within it? What is it they wish or require to do or provide? And how or by what means can they achieve its doing or provision? Unless these three questions are asked and answered social administration, whether referring to a subject of study, or to a process directed to the promotion of social welfare will remain incomplete. Its purpose and progress will be obscure. This is true whether the issue is one of ensuring economic security for all citizens, or the planning of a new town or housing estate, or easing the burdens of mental infirmity or physical disability of one person. Why people wish to do such things, what it is necessary to provide in order to do them, and in what ways they may be achieved, should be as clear as knowledge, reason and time allow before the first steps are taken to achieve the goal in view.

In a wholly logical world 'Why?' would precede 'What?' and 'How?'. In the real world it is far more common for people to decide what they want to do and how they are going to set about doing it before they formulate clearly, if at all, why they want to act in that way. Although ideals and values do in fact lie behind actions aimed at solving social problems or reducing suffering, they are not always, or even often precisely formulated. It is more frequently the case that a problem or unpalatable fact is recognised before social values or ideals are explicitly evoked. Men do not normally clarify their ideas of social justice, for example, and then ask themselves if these ideas are realised in fact. They stigmatise something as socially unjust and decide to do something about it, justifying their actions subsequently if pressed to do so, with reference to principles of justice hitherto undefined or dimly realised.

To consider first the possible answer or answers to the question

'Why?', is neat and logical but largely unrealistic, and it is done first here for purposes of clarification only. Any student who expects to find this order of things in life as it really is is living in cloud cuckoo land.

It is also the case that one can rarely, if ever, start with a clean sheet and decide what to do and how to do it without being affected or limited by an existing situation which is the outcome of a long historical process. All that may be possible is addition, modification or rectification. It is for this reason that some of the benefits of the Welfare State were said by Neill in 1958 to be capricious because of a dependence 'on a system of local government designed for a horse and buggy age'.[20] The provision of good standard housing for all families, to take but one problem, even if it were now pursued with continuous vision and energy, would still be delayed by the existence of slums, overcrowded towns and the growth of population; by the lack of inter-war planning and continuous changes in housing and town and country planning policies. In other words social legacies of the past and existing situations may prevent both immediate and adequate provision.

Providing these realities are borne in mind it can, however, be said now that the answer or answers to the question 'Why?' may ultimately be found only by resort to philosophy, ethics or religion. Why a person wishes, for instance, to promote the comfort, safety, and wellbeing of infirm and ageing persons, whose mental and physical activities are drawing to a close, may be because he is a Humanist who holds all people to be of importance by virtue merely of their being human. Or it may be because he holds religious beliefs claiming the moral worth of every man as created in the image of God, or because he is a Utilitarian who regards the promotion of individual welfare as furthering the greatest happiness of the greatest number. Such answers to the question 'Why?' cannot be put to any scientific test. They are held only by virtue of the holder's conviction that they are right.

Other answers to the question 'Why?' or 'For what reasons or purpose?' may be for self-protection or the protection of others, as in the case of custodial care of those suffering from a mental illness involving violent behaviour. Or it may be to promote the security and economic prosperity of the nation which call for an educated populace, or to further social equality which demands the extension of opportunity in education, employment, environment or home life. It may well be, as is more often than not the case in real life, that there is more than one answer to the question 'Why?'; that motives are mixed in other words. It may be decided, for example, that it is right to pursue a policy of keeping old people in their own homes with or near to their families rather than caring for them in Homes; first because one believes love is a human necessity and no substitute can take the place of love of home and family; second because it is expensive to provide residential care and cost cannot be disregarded; and third because a recognition of human rights includes the right to choose independence even if it involves dirt, discomfort or danger for an old person.

It is self-evident, however, that even if one is clear why one wishes to do something, that is not by itself enough to achieve the end in view. It is necessary also to answer the question 'What?'. What service or services or what opportunities are required in order that problems may be solved, objectives reached or suffering relieved? The religious, philosophical, ethical, or humanitarian view that every aged and infirm, or mentally subnormal person should receive care, attention and protection, will not alone ensure that these are given. Such a view or intention must be translated into reality by the provision and maintenance of services which promote the desired end. Either some piece of social legislation must be passed to provide the answer to the question 'What?' or services must be provided by voluntary organisations on their own initiative, or an individual philanthropist or reformer must step in and make provision. To put it thus and say no more fails of course to bring out the frequent complexity of, or difficulty in arriving at the answers to the question 'What?'. That children should not be neglected or cruelly treated may be regarded as axiomatic and protective legislation be passed intending to prevent that taking place. But as Marjory Fry said: 'You cannot give children love by Act of Parliament.' So what to do is not fully answered by any number of Children Acts. What to do to right a wrong, protect the weak, or promote the good is often far from simple and sometimes no satisfactory answer is forthcoming. Nevertheless the student should remain aware that the question 'What?' must continually be asked.

Effective social administration remains incomplete, however, even if 'What?' is answered until the third question, 'How, or by what means?' has also been satisfactorily answered. 'How?' in fact, is the most practical of the three questions. It is concerned with buildings, equipment, money, manpower, knowledge, skill, administrative machinery and organisation. Without these policy cannot be translated into practice and it is, therefore, rightly said that 'he who wills the ends must will the means'.

Legislation must include the means to ensure that the law is kept. Social administrators must be clear that the decisions they reach are capable of being and will be put into practice. Social workers must consider by what means they are to further the welfare of those who are their concern; means which may include their own personalities. Every effort should be made to think out clearly and precisely the answer or answers to 'How?', and they must be practical and realistic. Unless this is so intention will remain a chimera, policy be ineffective and objective an unrealised goal. In brief, 'Why?', 'What?', and 'How?' together comprise the essential questions that lie behind principles, policies and practice in social administration. The reformer and politician, the government and legislator, and the administrator and organiser must pay attention to each in turn.

The study of social administration may often appear to be of a practical, prosaic nature but behind the powers and duties of central and local social service departments and of the civil servants and local authority officers who staff them, or the fumbling trials and errors of often understaffed, ill financed organisations, there lie ethical, political, philosophical or religious values even if these are at times vague or unformulated. If this could always be borne in mind more interest might be generated in the study of the more factual aspects of social administration than is perhaps sometimes the case.

With this, the attempt to clarify the two uses of the term social administration is concluded. If the student who on the one hand has been implicitly led to believe that social administration can be taught, otherwise it would not presumably be in his curriculum, but on the other may have been led to doubt it by the question, posed by Donnison: 'Can Administration Be Taught?',[21] is now clearer how to resolve the apparent paradox the effort to assist him will not have been in vain. The explanation, as this chapter should have shown, is that there are two uses of the same term and it is not always made clear which a speaker has in mind. Once it is decided whether the reference is to social administration as a subject of study, which covers all aspects of the social services, or whether it is to social administration as a process directed towards solving a social problem, promoting social welfare or implementing social policy, all of which are furthered by a variety of means or techniques, then the road should be clear.

CHAPTER TWO

Orientation in the Social Sciences

One question which the student of social administration frequently raises, at least in the early if not the later stages of his learning, is the relevance of a number of subjects which are required of him. These generally, or frequently, include social history, economics, psychology and some aspects of sociology, possibly presented as 'social structure' or 'social analysis'. They may also include as separate subjects of study, political science, or what used to be called politics, and social philosophy or ethics. If challenged on the ground that no subject can be studied intelligently in isolation the student will readily agree. Nevertheless he may, as a potential child care officer perhaps, continue to question the necessity, for example, of understanding supply and demand curves. The development of the trade union movement in the nineteenth century does not always appear relevant to the prospective medical social worker. The would be citizen's advice bureau organiser may not immediately appreciate the value of considering types of ethical theory. The future secretary of a council of social service, or present executive officer in a welfare department, may recognise the utility of studying the influence of heredity and environment on human behaviour, but is not persuaded that so much attention as is given, let us say, to theories of learning is really necessary.

One objection to such points of view is that any student who is concerned solely with his present or future employment is taking so narrow and utilitarian view of his studies that he should not be in an institution, or pursuing a course of liberal studies, in the first place. Probably the majority, if not all, students accept this criticism but they may still complain that insufficient effort is made by their teachers or their text books to demonstrate the relationship between the subjects with which they are faced. They suggest that if this were done at the beginning of their course they would find their studies more profitable and would avoid unnecessary and frustrating floundering at the outset. They are in fact seeking what is popularly called an orientation course. This chapter is an attempt to assist those who feel this need.

First, the element common to all the social sciences should be clear. This, of course, is their concern with human behaviour. If the student of social administration can view all his work in this light he should find his study more meaningful. In the final resort it is the behaviour of the individual person, or the corporate behaviour of the family, group, community or society that forms the basis of all that he studies. The emphasis or selectivity of one of the social sciences may be different from that of another but each is concerned with human behaviour in some way.

Behaviour in this context, needless to say, means more than overt, outwardly observable action. It includes internal emotional responses to events and situations, political and religious beliefs, economic and social ambitions or aspirations, negative or positive reactions to the opportunities or limitations of the entire framework of living; in short the whole complex of behaviour that characterises man and distinguishes him from animals and other organisms. It is possible, of course, that the concern with human behaviour of the social sciences may not always be immediately apparent. But if this cannot be discerned at all, even with the most imaginative and rigorous searching, then either the teacher, the text book, or the student is at fault.

Perhaps the common concern with human behaviour can best be illustrated by attempting a brief examination of the broad area of study of the social sciences mentioned and of the particular goals each pursues. In attempting this one is open to criticism on two counts. On the one hand because the particular aspects of the totality of human behaviour which each of the sciences studies can never be precisely defined. It is often difficult to decide into which a particular study falls. There is too much overlap and interpenetration at many points to allow this. 'It has even seemed at times', Hicks said, 'that the great efforts which have been made to get a clear idea of [those] boundaries have merely revealed unsuperable difficulties.'[1] On the other hand criticism can stem from the fact that there is as Simpson pointed out 'continuing dispute as to the relation of the individual social sciences to each other and whether or not there is or can be an inter-disciplinary approach'.[2] The effort made here to demarcate the areas and indicate the aims of different social sciences is thus justified only by the intention of assisting those in the early stages of study. With this in mind one can turn first to social history which Rowse claimed, 'is a study in which you are dealing with human nature all the time'.[3]

History is concerned with human behaviour in relation to particular or concrete past events, both isolated and recurrent. It is an examination and analysis of the material conditions and the occurrences that have affected men's lives and, in turn, of the influence of men's ideas and actions upon the conditions and the course of their lives. Put in another way it is an attempt to discern, reconstruct and appreciate events, and the ideas, ideals, principles and purposes that have lain behind those events or have been generated by them. Without such an attempt no period of time or the lives of people in it can be understood or explained.

History involves discovery of evidence, enquiry into causes, description of events and an interpretation of each, seeing the individual within the whole and the whole in relation to the individual. It is concerned with men and women as political, economic and social beings. Trevelyan put this more imaginatively when he wrote:

'The scope [of social history] may be defined as the daily life of the inhabitants of the land in past ages: this includes the human as well as the economic relation of different classes to one another, the character of family and household life, the conditions of labour and leisure, the attitude of man to nature, the culture of each age as it arose out of these general conditions of life, and took over changing forms in religion, literature and music, architecture, learning and thought.'

And again

'Our effort is not only to get what few glimpses we can of [man's] intimate personality but to reconstruct the whole fabric of each passing age, and see how it affected him; to get to know more in some respects than the dweller in the past himself knew about the conditions that enveloped and controlled his life.'[4]

There is no doubt that human behaviour forms the heart of the matter here and that an understanding of how it is fashioned is the goal in view.

The importance of a study of history to the student of social administration, apart from an interest in the subject for its own sake, is clear. He cannot understand the policies, problems and procedures of his own time without some knowledge and appreciation of the ideas and events of the times in which contemporary provisions and practices were born and matured, or in which they were noticeable by their absence.

It is impossible, for example, to understand the development of public health or education in this country without an awareness of the influence of war—the Crimean War, the Boer War, the 1914–1918 War, and the World War of 1939—on economic and social conditions and policies. The growth of central and local government activities and the part they play in social welfare today can be understood only in the light of social and economic development of the past hundred years, and of the pressures exerted upon and charging men's minds with new ideas.

One might as well try to explain why a man of middle years is what he is without paying regard to the influences of his childhood and adolescence, or why a town has the population and shape it has without regard to the development of trade and transport, as to try to explain why the services of the second half of the twentieth century are what they are, without paying regard to the conditions from which they sprang. In short as Donnison said: 'To study the development of the social services in isolation from the history of their times is to tear a meaningless shred from the fabric of the past.'[5] History declared Rowse; 'enables you to understand . . . the public events, affairs and trends of your time. . . . If you do not understand the world you live in you are merely its sport, and apt to become its victim.'[6] This is particularly apposite for the student of social administration.

If one turns now to economics a similar concern with human behaviour is to be found. Robbins defined economics as 'the science which studies human behaviour as a relationship between ends and scarce means which have alternative uses'.[7] This definition may, it is true, lead to confusion as to what are ends and what are means. The market mechanism, for example, is a means whereby the production and distribution of goods and services are achieved, but some economists appear to treat it almost as an end, that is to say as desirable in itself for its own sake. Nevertheless, despite this limitation, the definition does show that economics is concerned with human behaviour, for it involves an appreciation of what men both need and want, both to use and to enjoy, and an examination of the ways and means they set about satisfying their needs and wants and choosing between the scarce resources that are at their disposal.

At a primitive level needs may be for but the basic necessities of life itself; food, clothing and shelter. At a less primitive level needs may call for means by which men not only feed, clothe, and shelter themselves, but develop their physical prowess, move from place to place, worship a deity, or wage a war. At a sophisticated level needs and wants comprise all the desires of man in the twentieth century, which include not only mundane articles such as refrigerators, washing machines, tables and chairs, but the means to enjoy music, art, poetry, sport, travel, forecast the weather, or explore space.

Men have to choose one means of satisfying their needs and wants rather than another because the resources available to them are limited in supply. Few things other than air, and that only above ground and below high altitudes, are in free or plentiful supply in relation to the population wishing to use them. Efforts to obtain and increase them and choice between them must, therefore, be made. It is this effort to obtain and increase, and this choice between scarce resources to satisfy man that fashion human behaviour in an economic sense.

It follows that economics is concerned with how, where, and with what resources men make a living, with the nature and conditions of their employment or alternatively why they are unemployed. It is concerned with the outcome or reward of their efforts and with the sharing, equal or otherwise, of the fruits of their labour. It concerns itself with how and where things are made or grown, how they get a price, are offered for sale, and why prices change. It examines national as well as individual production, income, saving and investment, and international as well as national trading and exchange. It explains the banking and monetary systems and all kinds of financial institutions. It examines the nature and influence of trade unions and the structure of industry, government ownership or control, taxation and fiscal policy. All these constitute the complexities of human behaviour whereby men in a developed economy gain control over their environment, obtain a livelihood, increase their area of enjoyment and compete or co-operate with their fellow men to further their selfish or mutual material interests.

It should, therefore, be clear to the student of social administration why an understanding of economics is necessary for him, whether he intends to enter the field of social work, social research, the civil service, local government, or the employ of a voluntary organisation. He cannot intelligently do any of these things if, for example, he has no understanding of prices, wage levels, employment or unemployment possibilities, the location of industry, population projections and life expectancies. His clients, field of research, or the ultimate target of his administrative or organising activities will consist of or include people who are wage earners, spenders of housekeeping money, young people with cash in their pockets for the first time, those deprived of an income because of illness or old age, householders hoping for a mortgage or bank loan, those facing increases in rent, rates, taxes or interest charges. To understand their situation the research worker, social worker, administrator or organiser must call on his knowledge of economic theory. This is necessary also to enable him to judge the accuracy of such a statement as that of Schwarz when he said: 'If you stopped drinking, smoking and gambling the finances of the Welfare State would break down.'[8] Would they?

The matter does not end there, however. Social economics—in so far as this is distinguishable from economic theory—is an important part of this area of study. Social economics includes in its scope tax-raising for public expenditure, spending on and financing the social services, the nature, causes and prevention of poverty, housing shortages and subsidies, exchequer grants to local authorities, and alternative methods of providing family allowances or retirement pensions. It studies the incidence of taxation and the benefits derived from the social services; whether they who recieve the benefits are those who need* them most or whether they receive them proportionately to need,* or apparent need.* It is concerned with standards of living, the distribution of claims on limited resources, the employment of married women and questions of equal pay for equal work; with whether or how far public services should be paid for out of taxation, and whether they should be available for all or only on proof of need* and test of means.

* The meaning and nature of human 'need' are discussed in Chapter Six.

It is here that the relevance of economics for the student of social administration is most clearly shown. Social policy and the provision of services may be determined, not by what is regarded as humanly desirable, but by what is recognised as economically possible. Social ends may be limited by economic means. A decision to raise or not to raise the school leaving age may be taken, not because children would or would not benefit by another year at school, but because the government maintains that the nation has or has not the means to build and equip schools and pay teachers' salaries, or because it chooses to spend its means in other ways.

As Powell said: ' . . . the modern social services find their place in the modern economic structure of the nation, and their problems in the wider unsolved problems of its economic life. They are seen to be one aspect of the increase, the distribution and the application of its resources. Our system of taxation, in the widest and truest sense which covers all the channels through which those resources are made available for public purposes, and our economic and monetary policy, which regulates the application of those resources, cannot in future be held apart from social service policy. Unless we reconcile and combine all three we can succeed in none.'[9]

It is clear, in short, that an understanding of economics is necessary if the question 'How?', posed in the last chapter, is to be realistically answered. And the economist has given some particular help here by developing the role of measurement, and evolving techniques of manipulating figures; for example of the national income, the cost of living, the level of production. These concepts have indeed crept into everyday language, seeping into the very culture of our society. Without them it would be impossible, for instance, to estimate how much is likely to be available for expenditure on the expansion of this service or that in any given period of time, or how to maintain the income of any particular group at a level commensurate with expenditure necessary for the maintenance of a reasonable standard of living.

It is at this point that 'choice' is emphasised again as the underlying reality of economics. Choice is the very nature or stuff of man's economic behaviour—choice between using scarce resources in one way rather than another, for the production of particular goods and services—choice by the consumer in the expenditure of his personal income—choice in spending more on the social services or the defence services of a country. Economics is always concerned with what men choose in the making of their living, faced as they always are with the necessity of choice by reason of the scarcity of resources at their disposal.

This concept of choice in economics is clearly no simple one but neither is it one that can be ignored because of its complexity. It is essential in life to make choices at some point and those that relate to expenditure in one area can have a profound affect upon policy in another. For example the decision to implement the recommendations of the Committee on Higher Education (the Robbins Committee), involving in 1980–1981 a total public expenditure on full-time higher education of £742 million,[10] must affect the possibility of raising the statutory school leaving age for everyone to sixteen or over. For, as the Committee pointed out: 'In the last analysis, the real cost of anything is what has to be foregone in order to have it.'[11] This concept of cost is different from that of the accountant which relates only to the money costs of an administrative organisation. Choice in economics involves a recognition that those who choose must go without or sacrifice something, as well as have or enjoy something. The second can be had only at the cost of the first.

Economics does not, however, explain *why* men choose as they do. It does not explain what their motives are. This is the province in part of psychology, which is the third of the social sciences to which attention is now turned. It is of course not only in the matter of choice that there is interconnection between economics and psychology. Another example is afforded in the recognition that in pursuing a policy of taxation governments should pay regard not only to the progressive or regressive nature of a tax, but also to psychological attitudes towards different forms of taxation, which may affect people's willingness to pay.

Psychology is often defined as the systematic study of behaviour, but as all the sciences are, or should be, systematic and as the common concern of the social sciences is human behaviour, this definition does not go far enough, though it does indicate the characteristic use of experiment in this science as others. Perhaps the student of social administration may look upon psychology as the systematic study of the cycle of human growth, of the working of the human mind and of human feelings or emotions, of the ways in which human beings function in relation or response to human experiences as a whole.

The use in psychology of experimental and statistical methods has provided much of the evidence about thinking, memory, language, attitudes, perception and communication which the psychologist is concerned to understand. He makes use of the scientific method in the same way as any other social scientist; that is systematic observation, formulation of hypotheses arising from this observation, their experimental testing and the formulation of a resulting theory or statement of law, making possible the prediction of like occurrences or behaviour in like circumstances.

Psychology is concerned with the nature or existence of innate or acquired drives and intelligence. It examines both the individual and the group and the concept of personality, or sum total of the components of any one human being. Particular areas or stages of human behaviour or development may be looked at. These include family life and parental relationships, child rearing and development, adolescence, education, and occupation. The emphasis varies according to whether the field is that of developmental, educational, or industrial psychology. Attention may also be centred in illness, crime, sex, or religion. Psychology is concerned with the rational and the irrational, with the normal and the abnormal, and with the political and social aspects of human behaviour. In short it is concerned with increasing understanding of why as well as how men or groups of men act, interact, and react to their environment, their fellow men and society as a whole. It is concerned with predicting behaviour, or establishing universal laws or characteristics of human behaviour in any society. Its study should enable one to assess the validity of observations such as those of Seldon when he said:

'Some of the things that went on in the war-time economy and in the post-war economy . . . suggested that the badges of citizenship worn by some were very tarnished. The badge was frequently dishonoured because it rests on faulty human psychology.'

'Their teachings [of the Classical Economists] endure because their psychology was realistic.'[12]

It should quickly be appreciated by the student also that without a knowledge of psychology he is unlikely fully to understand why decisions are reached, policies decided upon, or problems solved. Human beings are both the source of all administrative processes and social policies, and the target of those processes and policies. They can, therefore, whether they are the source or the target, pour oil on troubled waters, or fan the flames of discord. They can set cats among pigeons or step in where angels fear to tread. They may have the faith to remove mountains or fall at the first sound of the trumpet. They can overlook or distort facts, be blinded by prejudice, suffer failure of memory and lack initiative, or proceed with precision, accuracy, energy and objectivity. Their emotions, motives, learning, habits, memories, perceptions, prejudices, drives, desires, consciences and intelligence all enter into the formulation of policy and the practice of administration, and one or more of these may run counter to or support conscious wishes and intentions to be objective, impartial and just.

It is clear, therefore, why the notion of choice is of equal importance in psychology as in economics, for choice implies a motive as well as a means. It implies a process of learning and selecting. It is related to habit, convention and social training and to the ability or inability to tolerate insecurity, uncertainty or risk. The choice or behaviour of man must thus be explained in psychological as well as economic terms. An excellent example of how the psychological condition or emotional state of mind of the social administrator can account for what occurs is to be found in the following observation derived from the personal experience of a County Alderman, Margaret Cole:

'In local government at all events, if you examine what are supposed to be shocking cases of "red tape", you will find very often that the cause is not "red tape" . . . at all, but the simple failure of the human element. Somebody did not read the papers carefully enough; somebody was feeling ill, had toothache or had just received a piece of very bad personal news which affected his work; somebody found an applicant peculiarly irritating and allowed himself to dictate a harsh scolding instead of a courteous reply; somebody couldn't find the file and didn't like to confess its loss; in the extreme case somebody . . . may have lost his temper completely with somebody else, dug his toes in and refused to budge, quite oblivious of the public waiting outside, in all ignorance, until the administrators should be pleased to return to their senses.'[13]

The matter does not end with economics and psychology, how-

B

ever. Sociology also examines and has explanations to offer about human behaviour and man's choices. The subject matter or nature of sociology has long been a matter of discussion amongst sociologists themselves and the brief examination given to it here in no way does justice to the nature and variety of their arguments. It is no more than an initial assistance to students of social administration who find themselves required for the first time to appreciate the meaning and scope of sociology, and its relationship to the other subjects of their study.

Sociology has been defined in a variety of ways of which the widest is that it is 'the science of society'. So wide is this, however, that it may serve only to confuse and a breakdown is required. Three definitions of a more precise nature have been suggested by Ginsberg. Sociology, he said is: 'The comparative study of social institutions using as a guiding idea the concept of the development of humanity'—'Sociology in the broadest sense is the study of human interactions and interrelations, their conditions and consequences'—'Sociology is the science of social institutions, that is the forms or modes of social relationships exhibited in culture, or the activities of men as members of society'.[14] Ginsberg identified four principal problems of sociology; social structure, social function, social control, and social change[15] (whose opposite is social persistence). If the student looks in turn at these he should gain the initial insight necessary for him to appreciate what sociology is about.

Social structure includes the economic system of a society and its demographic or population structure; that is to say the quantity, quality, and distribution of the population, its age and sex groups, birth and death rates and family size. It is composed also of the major social institutions or areas of organised social life; marriage and the family, education and the school, religion and the church, law and the administration of justice, property and the distribution of wealth, politics and the machinery of government. It is influenced by the urban or rural nature of a society, its method of production, system of communication, industrial and occupational groups and social stratification. In short social structure comprises all the principal elements or parts which go to make up society, including the relationships between them and their impact on human behaviour.

Social function may be defined as the contribution that a social institution makes to the maintenance of a society or, to put it another way, the purpose it serves to maintain one or other of the prerequisites necessary for the continuance of society. For example, the functions of the family and kinship system include procreation, or recruitment of the members of the society, and the care and maintenance of the dependent young. The functions of education include the transmission of culture and the furtherance of communication, whether in speech or writing. The function of the law is to contain or control disruptive elements, or arbitrate between conflicting parties. The function of the military order is to provide measures of defence if attacked, or of conquest for economic or other reason.

Social control can be described as the process of restraining the impulses and actions of any who may threaten the values, order or safety of a society or of any individual or group within it. It is furthered by reward and punishment; in the first instance through parental discipline, at a later stage through the supervision and command of others in authority, and in the final resort by legal sanction and prohibition. In a less obvious way social control is exercised by group pressures, moral and religious sanctions, fashions, conventions, public opinion, attitudes of ridicule, ostracism or hostility. It is part of the process of socialisation whereby group norms and values are transmitted and acceptance of appropriate social roles encouraged.

Social change refers to the developments, arrest or decay which, in the course of time, may come about in the structure of a society, in social roles, or in the functions of social institutions. The processes of industrialisation and urbanisation are two such changes. Secularisation and the diminution of religious beliefs and sanctions comprise a third. The development of bureaucracy and of large scale industry are others. Alterations in the form and functions of the family and the role of the father or mother form another. The sociologist is concerned to note what changes take place, for what reasons, with what consequences or implications, and to consider whether these further stability or are the cause of conflict in society.

In addition to the above four problems of sociology there is also that of social pathology which refers to the disturbances or maladjustments in society. These include crime and delinquency, industrial dispute, racial and religious persecution, and war. The sociologist tries to identify and analyse the conflicts and behaviour which society regards as anti-social and may suggest remedies for them.

In looking at the broad divisions of the subject-matter of sociology—social structure—social function—social control—social change—social pathology—the sociologist makes use of certain basic concepts; culture, community, association, group, class, institution, role and status. He finds in these both the springs and the regularities, or recurrent patterns of human behaviour.

It can now be seen that whereas psychology is primarily concerned with or emphasises the individual nature of personality and its development through life phases and through person to person or group influences and relationships, sociology emphasises the influence of culture, of socialisation, the structure of society, and its pressure on an individual or a group. It is concerned with the influential nature of social customs, traditions, and established ways of behaviour. Marshall said that it 'is curious to discover how social systems work and how they change . . . [It] directs its questions towards the understanding of social phenomena as wholes, towards synthesis of different lines of interest, towards seeing things in the round.'[16]

Whereas the psychologist, to take one example, will examine the behaviour patterns or the personality changes of old age; the crisis periods of later life; and the effect of ageing on family life; the sociologist will be concerned with ageing in different societies; with the social role and status of the older person; changes in the age distribution and the impact of ageing on the social structure as a whole; with the contribution made towards the wellbeing of the old by the family, social group or residential institution. Both the disciplines will contribute, therefore, to knowledge that will further an informed policy in making provision for the aged. Or, to take another example, the psychologist will study the emotional factors in delinquency; the significance of family relationships; personality disorder and crime; delinquency as a symptom of deprivation, frustration or aggression; the effect of different forms of treatment on the offender; and the sociologist will examine the connection between delinquency and social class; of environmental or educational opportunity; delinquent sub-cultures; the peak periods of law breaking; the nature and frequency of different offences; and the prison or borstal as an institution. Each has a different contribution to make to an understanding of the causes of crime, the prevention of delinquency, and the treatment of the offender.

A recent introduction to social work has acknowledged how both the study of psychology and sociology has assisted the case worker:

'Case workers were for a long time puzzled by the irrational behaviour of many of their clients. Then psycho-analysis began to throw a light on aspects of human behaviour which before had been inexplicable. . . . Social workers have now recaptured some of their earlier emphasis on the importance of the social environment and are borrowing concepts from the field of sociology, in particular they are now using some aspects of role theory. . . . The study of society has shown that individual people's behaviour is very largely determined by cultural beliefs and rules of behaviour—what is "done" or "not done" in their particular set or neighbourhood group.'[17]

In putting forward their case for the concern of the family doctor in the social problems of his patients the Standing Medical Advisory Committee of the Central Health Services Council also paid tribute to the contribution which sociology and psychology can make to their understanding. 'Education in sociology and normal psychology is as important', they said, 'as in other pre-clinical subjects.'[18]

To turn now to political science: This has been defined as the science of government or, more recently, as the study of power. The first—political science as the science of government—involves the organisation of government as such, whether centrally, locally, or through other public bodies. It compares different systems of government. It is concerned with the various processes of legislation carried out by the legislature, that is to say by the Queen in Council in Parliament, the House of Lords and House of Commons. It examines the role of the executive or administrative function of the Government carried out by its civil servants in various central departments. And it includes the function of the judiciary, or courts of law, which hear and determine disputes whether between individuals or between individuals and the State.

In short, political science defined as the science of government seeks to examine and understand in what ways men are governed and how they behave whether as those who govern or those who are governed. In a modern state the functions and machinery of government are extensive and complex and they impinge upon the citizen in all aspects of his life. It is clear, therefore, that political science as the science of government is no abstract subject divorced from the realities of life. It is intimately concerned with daily living and the behaviour of man within the society in which he lives, which must be based upon some degree of order, and in which he has to have regard to the duties, rights and freedom of others as well as to his own.

Political science as the study of power is not different in essence from political science as the science of government but it is perhaps more sophisticated in its approach. Since it conceives government as the achievement and use of power it studies the different forms of power that exist, the various ways in which power is obtained and exerted and it compares different systems of power in different societies or at different periods of time.

This concept is not of necessity sinister as is sometimes suggested, although the love or unwise use of power may well be. It is essential in society that man's behaviour must, to some degree at least, be orderly, and to achieve that degree of order government must be effective. To be effective government must of necessity in the last resort be coercive. That is to say it must be backed by power. Government is the final authority vested in the State. Thus the party 'in power' forms the government, and this government exercises the power it holds to promote the particular policies it supports. If it falls it loses power which passes, in a democracy, to the party elected in its stead.

Behind this process which is a continuous one, unless broken by the disruption of bloody revolution or the catastrophe of war, goes the formation of policy, the reaching of decisions, the framing of laws, the promotion of justice, and the procedure of administration. Attempting to influence these will be pressure groups, voluntary bodies, citizen associations, and the like, which seek to exercise some degree of control or influence over the extent or direction of power which is exerted by those in authority. All these, political science as a study of power is concerned to analyse and understand and in doing so it is clearly involved with the behaviour of man.

Finally, there is philosophy and ethics, the last of the social sciences to which reference is now made. These differ from those others which have been briefly examined in that they are normative, that is to say they seek to discover or lay down norms or standards of correct behaviour. They cannot rest with the observation and recording of facts but must interpret these by reference to that which is regarded as right or proper in a social or moral sense.

Philosophy, (excluding linguistic philosophy), has been defined briefly as the pursuit of wisdom, and ethics as the science concerned with moral principles. With these definitions there enter questions of value as distinct from questions of fact. Since the student of social administration will inevitably find himself concerned, as will be seen shortly, with values and value judgements he cannot avoid philosophical and ethical considerations whether or not the subjects are included as such in his curriculum.

It is not possible in the limited opportunity available here in any way to do justice to the whole range of questions which philosophy or ethics may examine. It must suffice to point out that basically they are concerned with the nature or character of the world, persisting or changing, and of man's social and moral behaviour in it. They include consideration of the problem of right and wrong and whether these are natural and permanent or merely conventional and temporal. They consider the dependence or independence of morality upon or from religious precept or the intervention or revelation of the supernatural. They are concerned with whether man is possessed of free will or whether his behaviour is determined by his environment. They are concerned not only with the ends to be achieved in life but the means to be used to reach them. They direct attention to the meaning and promotion of justice, liberty and equality and to men's attitudes towards pleasure or happiness, suffering or pain. They are involved with the rights and duties of men as individuals in society and with the proper nature of government.

The student of social administration will inevitably find himself constantly asking questions that relate to such issues, (or if he does not there will be something seriously the matter with him). But it may well be—indeed it probably will be—that he will be unable to find easy answers and some answers will elude him not only during his course of studies but long after. Nevertheless the problems that philosophy and ethics pose must be faced because man is a being whose behaviour cannot be separated from moral concepts of some kind. And everyone, but particularly those who are employed in situations involving personal relationships, sooner or later, come face to face with this fact.

To sum up this brief examination of the areas of study and the goals of the social sciences: It may be said that the social historian is concerned with human behaviour in relation to the events of the past, the economist in relation to the making of a living and pursuit of material satisfactions, the psychologist in relation to the thoughts, feelings and attitudes of the individual and his relation to the group, the sociologist in relation to the social structure, institutions and development of different societies, and the social philosopher and moralist in relation to the rightness or ethical nature of that behaviour in the context in which it takes place. Each is concerned, in his own sphere, to identify the sources or springs of human behaviour, to find causal connections between social and economic events, to account for solidarity or breakdown, to predict and frame general laws of behaviour, to clarify individual and social problems, and to build up a body of knowledge to serve the interests and welfare of man.

In these ways all are clearly of importance to social administration whether in the making of social policy, the promotion of social welfare, the solution of social problems, or the building of effective machinery of government. The student of social administration must be prepared and ready, therefore, to profit from each of the social sciences and benefit from the light it can shed on his particular field of work. It may sometimes appear that one is less important to one worker than another. For instance, economics may seem less important to the social worker or psychology to the administrator, but each has a valuable contribution to make to both. The erstwhile National Assistance Board and its successor the Ministry of Social Security, now one part of the Department of Health and Social Security, may serve as an illustration of the importance of all the social sciences in the study and practice of social administration.

It is impossible, first, to appreciate why in 1948 an independent Board was charged with the administration of National Assistance when one Ministry could well have undertaken the task together with that of administering National Insurance, as was recommended by Beveridge in 1942 and as was in fact established in 1966, without a knowledge of the history of the Poor Law and attitudes towards it, particularly in the economic circumstances of the 1930s. Hence the need for a study of social history.

In the second place it is impossible amongst other things to decide whether the rate of grant or benefit paid was or is adequate without knowing about the cost of living and how it is arrived at. Hence the need for an understanding of social economics. In the third place a right regard on the part of officers of the Board, or their successors at the Ministry of Social Security, towards those applying for, or in receipt of grant or benefit, is likely only if they have an understanding of attitudes, their own and those of others, and appreciate what asking for money and being different from other people in this respect means to an applicant. Here lies the contribution of social psychology. Fourthly, it is not possible to assess the importance of national assistance, which has now become supplementary benefit or allowance, without knowing the nature and extent of the need met from year to year, the age, sex, and social class of recipients, the number of persons who and the length of time they were or are in receipt of help, and the impact on the life of a person or family largely or solely dependent upon such help for income. Hence the need for sociological analysis. Finally, there arise questions relating to whether and if so why it is right and proper that those who are in employment and good health should be ready and willing financially to support those who are not, and whether this should be a voluntary act of generosity or a legal requirement shared by all out of common funds. Thus the payment of grant or benefit involves philosophical or ethical considerations.

In conclusion it is as well to state explicitly what has been implicit throughout; that social administration is not one more social science with its own theory and body of knowledge. It makes use of the findings of any of the social sciences which are relevant to its sphere; a sphere which includes, as seen in Chapter One, the identification of and solving of social problems, the making and

B*

implementation of social policy, and the promotion of social welfare. Social administration may focus attention on one area or synthesise various areas of knowledge of social institutions and human behaviour and thereby increase understanding, but its distinctive character is that it combines and benefits from any of the conclusions of the social sciences which assist it and uses them as tools in the performance of the functions which are its particular concern. In other words the student must see social administration as benefiting from the social sciences, not as one more. He must not contrast it with them as if it were itself a discipline but recognise its purposes and appreciate that the knowledge which enables it to pursue those purposes comes to a considerable extent from the subjects he sometimes queries as necessary to his field of work or interest.

Finally it must be recognised that social administration, like philosophy and ethics, is not free from making judgements about social or human values. History, economics, psychology or sociology can analyse, account for, and possibly predict human behaviour without necessarily passing moral judgement on it; without, that is to say, presuming or concluding that one form of behaviour is good and another bad. The historian, economist, psychologist, or sociologist can of course, and often does do this, expressly or otherwise. 'Many, perhaps most, social scientists even up to our own time were originally led to the social sciences because of their interest in social reform', said Myrdal, and: 'The social sciences have all received their impetus much more from the urge to improve society than from simple curiosity about its working.'[19] But these social scientists are not compelled to concern themselves with reform or improvement.

The social administrator, social worker, or social policy maker, on the other hand, is obliged to do so. The very purpose of their administration, work, or policy, is to produce the conditions of what is regarded as a good life; to prevent or alleviate hardship; to promote opportunity; to guide or control those who threaten the wellbeing of themselves or others. Social administration is value centred throughout. It rests and is built on ethical judgements. The social services which form its content as a subject of a study amply illustrate this. Education is provided because knowledge is believed to be a good and ignorance a bad thing.

Disease is treated because health is looked upon as more desirable than sickness. Income is maintained because poverty is regarded as an evil. Housing and towns are built because homelessness and overcrowding are held to be damaging to human beings. And so on. Likewise social administration, when the term is used to refer to a process directed to the solution of social problems, or the promotion of social welfare, tacitly assumes that the solution of social problems and the achievement of social welfare are things it is right to further.

Works on social administration inevitably speak of 'ought' or 'should', as well as of 'was' or 'is'. They are normative and prescriptive as well as descriptive. For example:*

'To keep the family together as long as possible . . . *should* become an essential aim of social policy.'[20]

'To raise the quality of environment of all our people *should* be at the very centre of social policy.'[21]

' "Social policy" is directly concerned with what *ought* to be done, or at any rate with the choice of what is in some sense the *best* among possible alternative ways of collective action.'[22]

'In the last resort, our appraisal of the Welfare State will depend on our scale of *values*—it will be a value judgement.'[23]

'We need to emphasise that social policy involves asserting the primacy of a whole set of *values*—non economic values—which may conflict, about which there is no unanimity and which are seldom expressed save in imprecise catchwords—justice, fairness, equity, social equality, fellowship, freedom, welfare state.'[24]

These examples of the 'oughts' and 'shoulds' of social administration concern both principles and practice. They show that behind the importance placed upon family unity or environmental provision there lie fundamental values about human life, and individual importance. The successful pursuit of these fundamental values has to be translated into precise terms and thus to be practical is not to be unimaginative. Great ends have often to be achieved by prosaic means.

The view that ethical considerations lie at the heart of social administration is in fact shared by many if not all of those who teach it. As Donnison said: 'The deliberate introduction of value

* Author's italics in the quotations that follow.

judgements and critical appraisals appears to be one of the distinctive features of social administration as taught in many Universities.'[25] From this agreement about values in social administration one can proceed to a consideration of social policy and what it is.

For further examination of the social sciences see: *The Social Sciences—An Outline for the Intending Student*, Editor, David C. Marsh, Routledge and Kegan Paul Ltd., 1965.

For an examination of some basic values in social casework see: *Social Casework and Administration*, XI.—Anthony Forder, Faber and Faber, 1966.

CHAPTER THREE

Theory and Practice in Social Policy

Were human behaviour always prompted by reason and foresight it would be logical to accompany a discussion of social policy by a consideration of the contribution of social research to its making. But what men do, or cause to be done, is not always or necessarily based upon an informed assessment of a situation or on an impartial judgement of need or merit. In a democratic society men are free also to make decisions without being bound by the rules of scientific method, even if this includes the freedom to make mistakes.

Since these things are so social policy is at times, although of course not necessarily or most frequently, settled without first obtaining evidence to support its wisdom. It may be based on expressions of opinion or commonly held beliefs, the validity of which has never been put to the test. That poverty was the fault of the individual was one such belief which lay behind the deterrent principle of the Poor Law in the nineteenth century. Policy today based on Seldon's view that there are 'unprincipled people who use family allowances to buy luxuries' and that new services may have to be devised because of the neglect of children arising, 'not through poverty but through the desire to earn for luxuries',[1] would be based on contemporary assumptions the truth of which is supported only by hearsay.

A policy may arise from the exigencies of a particular situation, such as war, or be designed on an *ad hoc* basis to meet what is believed to be only a short term need. The fixing of the minimum age for drawing statutory retirement pension at sixty-five in 1925 (reduced for women to sixty in 1940) illustrates, for example, the employment situation at that time rather than the needs of older persons. But the ages of sixty and sixty-five have remained in spite of the economic and social hardships these now often cause. It is also the case that it is not always possible for social policy to wait upon social research. If speed is a necessary element in social provision faith and hope may have to take precedence over fact finding.

For all these reasons it is in keeping with social administration in real life in a free society to examine social policy before social research, particularly as the second should be the servant and not the master of the first and also because it is frequently concerned with one particular place or point of time whereas social policy is more often concerned with long-term and general situations. Policy makers can be criticised only if they have had the opportunity—that is to say the time, the skill and the means have been at their disposal—but they have made no effort to understand causes, identify and measure need, or examine results. How far social research has been used in policy making is examined in Chapter Five. Here it is asked first, what is meant by social policy?

'Policy', as defined in the *Concise Oxford Dictionary*, is a 'course of action adopted by government, party, etc.' Social policy then includes government or party action relating to the social aspects of life, as compared, for example, to agricultural policy, economic policy or defence policy. To particularise: 'Social policy', said Beales, 'is a collective term for the public provisions through which we attack insecurity and correct the debilitating tendencies of our "capitalist" inheritance.'[2] This is the view of a social historian. It is a statement that can be challenged but it illustrates the necessity for the student of social administration to have a knowledge of history. He cannot otherwise appreciate what Beales meant by 'our "capitalist" inheritance', nor judge whether or not this has 'debilitating tendencies'.

Continuing, Beales presented the view (shortly to be questioned) that social policy is progressive and that in our own time it has been continuous, increasingly purposeful and beneficent. It is not merely to attack industrial evils, but to declare civic minima which condition the lives of all age groups. The various branches of social policy are not mere sweeteners of the harshness of a system of individualised compulsions. They represent positive social provision against waste of life, resources, and inefficiency in a world of public as well as private enterprise. Twentieth-century social policy contributes to the totality of our wellbeing, it represents a policy of freedom through organisation.

Titmuss, speaking of time of war, referred to social policy as: 'Those acts of Governments deliberately designed and taken to improve the welfare of the civil population.'[3] He also said: 'By the end of the Second World War the Government had, through the agency of newly established or existing services, assumed and developed a measure of direct concern for the health and wellbeing of the population. . . . It was increasingly regarded as a proper function or even obligation of Government to ward off distress and strain among not only the poor but almost all classes of society.'[4] And the standard of the service, he claimed, was more flexible and higher than was thought sufficient for those in receipt of poor relief. The welfare policies were free of social discrimination and indignity, and their universal character ensured their acceptance and success. At least as far as wartime was concerned Titmuss thus supported Beales' view that social policy is purposeful and beneficent in nature.

Macbeath, who spoke of social policies rather than social policy, regarded them as being 'concerned with the right ordering of the network of relationships between men and women who live together in societies, or with principles which govern the activities of individuals and groups so far as they affect the lives and interests of other people'.[5] Whilst this is a much wider view it too can be regarded as benevolent in intent. Milhaud also supported the beneficent school of thought when he said: 'Social policy enunciates the objectives to be reached in the social field to secure and improve the welfare of populations.'[6]

The same is true of Hagenbuch's more limited view: 'Stated in general terms, the mainspring of social policy' (which he also said was human sympathy) 'may be said to be the desire to ensure every member of the community certain minimum standards and certain opportunities.'[7] Milhaud and Hagenbuch thus both allow aim or objective to be included as social policy; not only that which is actually adopted or provided. In other words intention as well as achievement is part of the process of policy making.

Lafitte took an extensive view of social policy when he said: ' . . . social policy treats of the distribution of power and opportunities among citizens outside the political sphere: relations between rich and poor, masters and servants, trade unionists and non-unionists, landlords and tenants, men and women, parents and children, courts and criminals, the normal and the abnormal in body and mind. On this view the whole quality of social life and human relations is of interest to social policy. . . .'[8]

More recently Marshall stated that 'social policy' is not a technical term with an exact meaning. He used it to refer to the policy of governments regarding action which has a direct impact on the welfare of the citizens by providing them with services or income. The central core of social policy, he said, consists of social insurance, public or national assistance, the health and welfare services and education.[9] Again social policy is seen to be benevolent. It serves the welfare of citizens.

Despite this consensus of opinion it must, however, be recognised—and this is of no small importance—that social policy is not *of necessity* positive or beneficent, nor need it spring from human sympathy. These may merely be characteristic of social policy or policies in one place or at one time, and not be inherent in social policy as such. It is quite possible, for example, for a government deliberately to follow a policy of doing nothing, or at least as little as possible, for the welfare of the citizen, short perhaps of letting him starve if this can be prevented. The 'course of action' adopted by the government in such a case is a negative one. Such was the laissez-faire policy of the nineteenth century in its heyday. The Nazi social policy, aimed at the extermination of the Jews, was certainly positive in the sense that it had a conscious and defined objective that was persistently and actively pursued, but it can scarcely be regarded as beneficent, nor as springing from human sympathy.

The view that social policy is progressive also presents difficulties, for what is 'progressive'? Continuously moving in one direction and if so in the direction of providing more or of providing less out of public funds? Continuously expanding to include ever more areas of social life? Persistently endeavouring to promote independent provision by the individual for himself and his family? 'Progressive' implies a change for the better; but who is to decide and on what criteria what is better?

What is progressive in social policy is accepted only by those who are agreed where they want to go and how they wish to get there, or, in other words, who are agreed on the answers to the questions 'What?' and 'How?' referred to in Chapter One. Since this is unlikely to be an all inclusive group it is wiser to use a more neutral word than progressive; for example, altering—developing—expanding—contracting. These can take account of social and economic change and allow for objective measurement or comparisons over time. They avoid the difficult concept of progress, at least until full consideration has been given to the different possibilities and problems involved in the making and implementing of social policy.

It is also the case that the conclusions of those writing in or about the general climate of opinion and social expectations at the end of the Second World War gave rise to less disagreement than is the case today. The desirability of social policy 'conditioning the lives of all citizens', or its 'universal character', is not now acceptable to everyone. This is shown, for example, in Howe's view that: 'We must ensure that the existing services have built into them the mechanism that is necessary to enable them to contract.'[10] The idea of selective rather than universal benefits, that is benefits provided only or to a greater extent for those in proven need, has gained increasing support.*

It is clear that in the 1950s a period of reappraisal of post-war social policy began; on the part of some at least in this country. Whilst it is probable that all would agree that a positive social policy of some sort is an essential element in the social and economic structure of every developed or developing country, it is less likely that Milhaud's view that 'it will be called to play an ever increasing role',[11] will now command universal consent. For this reason 'social policy' should be defined in a way which allows for contraction as well as expansion; for minimum as well as maximum provision; and for the withdrawal as well as the advance of the State in ordering or safeguarding the social wellbeing of the citizen.

The opposition to expansion and universalism has of course been recognised by those whose views have been quoted. Titmuss, for instance, himself pointed out: 'The public services are increasingly seen, as Galbraith says,† as an incubus; an unnecessary, doctrinaire burden on private enterprise.'[12] And he recognised,

---

* For detailed consideration of selectivity versus universality see: Richard M. Titmuss, *Commitment to Welfare*, Chapter X. George Allen and Unwin, Ltd., 1968 and: *Social Services for All?* Parts one and two, Fabian Society, Tracts 382, and 383, June 1968.

† In *The Affluent Society*.

although he has not accepted, the criticism that the extension of State services is harmful to the economic and moral wellbeing of the nation.[13] Because of the inevitable differences of opinion about the nature of social policy Lafitte's neutral observation: 'In the main social policy is an attempt to steer the life of society along channels it would not follow if left to itself',[14] is useful, although he later expanded this, and in doing so the neutrality of his first observation was at the end lost. " . . . social policy", he said, "is the judgement that, if left alone by political authority, the state of society would rapidly become intolerable. Through collective action, in particular by imposing the State's directing power on the forces of the market, we work to steer society, along paths it would not naturally follow, towards accepted goals unattainable without public organisation. . . . Through social policy we assert the primacy of our belief that the way of life matters more than ways of getting a living." '[15]

But consideration of social policy must not begin and end with the part played by the State in steering society. A place must be given to individual reformers and voluntary organisations also, for it is frequently with them that the promotion of a positive social policy begins, or a service is first provided. Or they can successfully raise objections to a State social policy; as for instance when the Charity Organisation Society, the predecessor to the Family Welfare Association, successfully opposed provision of free school meals for necessitous children in 1887 on the ground that it would undermine the solidarity of the family and risk permanently demoralising large numbers of the population. This constitutes another example of a social policy—in this instance a negative one—based upon commonly held beliefs which, when put to the test, were shown to be invalid. It illustrates too that what may be thought to be for the good of the individual or for the community as a whole is not necessarily the same as that which is protective or benevolent. It also supports the contention that to do or provide nothing is as much social policy as to do or provide something. Only if a government has given no thought to the social good of the citizen or the community, and consequently made no decisions or provisions, can it be said that it has no social policy at all. If it has given thought but has rejected protection or provision then its social policy is negative, not absent.

It is quite possible deliberately to pursue a policy of delay, of putting off till tomorrow what need not be done today. The setting up of a committee of enquiry to examine and report on a particular problem about which the government is being hard pressed but about which it is reluctant, for some reason, to take action, may be part of such a policy. An administrator who leaves a file on his desk for a time without taking action on it may be purposefully pursuing a policy of 'masterly inactivity'. He is not simply doing nothing. He is acting in the hope or expectation that later rather than immediate intervention will be more effective, or that given time the problem will solve itself and his intervention will not be necessary at all. This, in his view, may be the best for everyone concerned.

If a social policy is followed which some people, whether at the time or of a later generation, regard as wrong or retrograde it is nevertheless social policy. What is regarded at different points of time or by different people as necessary or good for the individual or the community, will derive from concrete environmental, economic, political or military situations, and from philosophies of justice, equality, liberty, human rights and duties. Social policy will reflect contemporary knowledge, understanding and sympathy about human needs, relationships and behaviour. As neither situations, philosophies nor knowledge are static, so neither is social policy. It will change with changing ideas, events and circumstances. Whether the change is for better or worse each must decide for himself.

In contrast to this view of social policy as the outcome of conscious thought and deliberation about actual situations in the light of contemporary knowledge and ideas, there is the view that holds that it will evolve gradually, even imperceptibly, from decisions taken on particular cases which set precedents that ultimately become generally applied. Such may be regarded as the formulation of social policy by tacit consent; the policy itself being recognised after, not before it has taken shape, by which time it may have become so familiar and accepted a part of the social scene that it remains unchallenged or unchanged. Donnison went so far as to suggest that the policies of a social service are what it does, which may or may not coincide with its official aims.[16] This view is supported by Rodgers who said that social policies were only interesting and worth studying if they were real policies (not mere paper plans); policies which were being actively pursued and had already gone some way towards achieving their objectives.[17] This is contrary to the view of Milhaud and Hagenbuch quoted earlier but elsewhere Donnison said that an 'organisation's "policies" include its aims (realised and unrealised) and its functions (what it is believed to do and what it actually does)'.[18] There may appear to be some contradiction here but one can avoid confusion by recognising that social policy has a two-fold aspect—first the aim or objective of a course of action, and second the outcome of that action. The aim may be said to be social policy in intent, whereas the outcome is social policy in practice. Another useful distinction was made by Jones when she referred to: 'The gap between social policy (the optimal service we would like to provide) and social provision (the often minimal service which is all that can be offered within existing services)', which she added 'is a very wide one'.[19] Here the optimal service is the social policy in intent; the minimal service is the social policy in practice.

An example of unconscious development or change of policy, from intent to practice, may be taken from the work of a voluntary organisation. The end of the last war was accompanied by the setting up of a network of local old people's welfare committees. A model constitution, framed by the National Old People's Welfare Council, set out five objects of such committees. In summary form these were to promote and assist the general good of old people by assisting the work of statutory authorities and voluntary organisations; to promote and organise co-operation in the achievement of that purpose; to assist any charitable body financially or otherwise to that end; to promote, carry out or assist in carrying out surveys of the needs of old people; and to arrange or provide for or assist the holding of exhibitions, meetings, lectures and classes to further these objects. Nothing was included in the model constitution which covered the provision of any personal service by an old people's welfare committee itself.

Over the years, however, the committees, or many of them, did in fact begin to provide and organise personal services themselves, which they gradually expanded in variety and extent. This they did little by little, one service and then another, without reference to any explicit or agreed constitutional principles, beyond that of assisting the old, and they did it because no one else seemed able or willing at the time to do so. When in due course the constitutional position was questioned legal opinion was sought and expressed the view that 'to promote and assist' included 'to provide', although it is clear the position was not thought of in that way in the first instance. Ultimately in 1964, the Chairman's Preface to the Annual Report of the National Old People's Welfare Council observed: 'The primary function of an old people's welfare committee is to provide personal service.' This did not preclude other functions of an old people's welfare committee as set out in the Council's literature but it showed an expansion of purpose or policy from that with which the movement began. It is unlikely anyone could say just when the change took place. It is apparent that strong precedents were being established, altering the focus of policy, without a realisation at the time that this was happening. The example is given only to illustrate how policy can change without any accompanying awareness that this is so, not in criticism of the change itself which may well have been desirable in the circumstances of the time.

It would be a mistake to ignore the intent of social policy even if it fails to materialise or becomes twisted by pressure of circumstance. Once a policy has been formulated and expressed it is there for future reference, if no more. And it may have a long term or gradual, even if not an immediate effect. All policies of intent serve as guides or goads to action even if their realisation is delayed or diverted, or even if ideals founder for a time on the rocks of reality. At the same time it is important that those who decide social policy in practice, by a process of establishing precedent, whether they be administrators or social workers, should recognise what they are doing and its significance. They may be fixing procedures which will have a long life affecting a large number of people and this should not be done in casual unawareness of the responsibility involved.

It is quite possible that policy in intent of one department or organisation may be thwarted by policy in practice of another. It was, for example, the policy of the Ministry of Health in intent, following an amendment in 1962 of Section 31 of the National Assistance Act, 1948, that local authorities should make the fullest use of voluntary bodies in the promotion of the welfare of old people even though the amendment had given the authorities power to provide a meals and recreation service themselves. The policy in practice, however, of several London Metropolitan Boroughs (as they then were), within a few months of the amendment of the Act, was to withdraw all grant aid from the voluntary old people's welfare committee in their area, resulting in the extinction or substantial curtailment of the services those committees provided. This was the precise opposite of what the Ministry intended. Many a voluntary body has known too the bitterness of being unable to implement a policy of intent owing to the difficulty of raising sufficient funds to render possible that policy in practice.

It is not necessarily the case, where there is a difference of opinion, that the department or organisation which has a policy in intent, that is to say which is the architect of a policy, is right and that which changes policy in practice is wrong. There can be and are genuine and sincere disagreements about the nature or urgency of a social problem or need and consequently about the appropriateness of an intended social policy. It is clear that appraisal of present or of past social policy is affected by a number of factors—differences in social values—differences in degree of foresight possessed—differences in tolerance of judgement based on hindsight—differences in attitude towards economic and social changes. What is relevant or acceptable at one point of time or by one body of persons is not or would not necessarily have been so at or by another. Harshly to criticise a past generation for lack of sympathy, sensitivity, or wisdom in social policy may be merely to overlook the fact that change in public opinion or understanding only comes about gradually, that it has not only to be accepted but absorbed into common practice, and that administrative procedures may lag behind social requirements. The policy and practice of any period should be evaluated only in the light of the conditions, opinions and knowledge of that time.

It may be asked now whether it is better to speak of social policy or social policies. The answer is that each is appropriate in different contexts. As Titmuss said: 'There is no single or simple pattern of social policy, but a variegated mosaic of services, detailed, dispersed and complex, all varying in character and importance.'[20]

The parts of the mosaic are the particular positive social policies related to different areas of social life or individual needs; for example social policy in relation to housing, child care, mental health, old age, the blind, and so on.* These are individual social policies.

It is quite possible, unfortunately, for a policy wholly beneficial in intent to have an entirely unexpected and unhappy outcome as well as the outcome desired. This, for instance, was the case when compulsory schooling was introduced in the 1870s. This was beneficial from the point of the educational needs of the child but it added to the poverty of the parents bereft of his earnings. More recently the post-war policy of rent control, intended to protect tenants against major increases in rents arising from the housing shortage, resulted not only in such protection but also in the neglect by owners of working class property because restriction in income rendered it impossible even for good landlords to meet the cost of maintenance and repairs. Thus deterioration in housing conditions was actually encouraged by a social policy entirely benevolent in its intent.

The policy of equal rights to free treatment under the national health service, combined with rapid advances in medical knowledge, has resulted in growing problems of caring for those who would previously have died. A clear illustration of this is in a publication of the Invalid Children's Aid Association.[21] This points out not only that large numbers of children who would once have died now live, but that they do so with long-lasting or chronic defects and that this can dislocate the homes and the lives of the families concerned. There is consequently a call for a new appreciation of the need of parents for advice, guidance and support, particularly in view of the current policy of caring for children in their own homes rather than in institutions, which may lay a heavy burden, emotional and domestic, on those concerned. The good intentions embodied both in the policy of the national health service and of care at home have thus resulted in this instance in an increasing number of families being beset by acute problems of child care not faced by them before.

* For consideration of social policy in different areas see the publications of the Library of Social Policy and Administration, General Editor Kathleen Jones, Routledge and Kegan Paul Limited.

If a social policy does produce such unintended and unfortunate results as these three examples show, it then becomes important that another step be taken to right the unintended wrong. In other words existing policy needs to be changed, modified, extended or supported.

As well as individual social policies relating to particular areas of life or individual need there can be a general social policy relating to social welfare as a whole. That all citizens should have equal right to make use of the social services regardless of their income or occupation, is one such policy in practice at the present time in this country, although its wisdom has been questioned by some. For instance the Bow Group have said: 'Public opinion is instinctively affronted, by the fact that family allowances . . . can find their way into the most prosperous professional home. Equally disturbing is that fact that retirement pensions . . . may be drawn by people with substantial private means.'[22] Another general current social policy—in intent at least—is that local authorities should use voluntary organisations in the planning and implementation of their arrangements for their health and welfare services.* Whether, or to what extent, this becomes or continues to be social policy in practice in all local authority areas remains to be seen.

Social policy or policies in intent become social policy or policies in practice as and when they are rendered effective, either by means of social legislation embodying and implementing the objectives in view, or by voluntary organisations obtaining the means to put their programmes into effect. Historically statutory social policy in this country began in the sixteenth century with, and was limited until the nineteenth century to the Poor Law, which was concerned with the problem of poverty and the treatment of the pauper. It expanded slowly in the nineteenth century until it encompassed—although to an extent that would be regarded as very limited today—public health, education, housing, protection of women and children, workmen's compensation and conditions of employment. It was a piece by piece, trial and error process.

The slow, *ad hoc* development continued in the twentieth century up to the Second World War. This, in its later stages, was accompanied and followed in the 1940s by the extension or

* See Ministry of Health Circulars to Local Authorities 2/62 7/621 2/62 18/62.

introduction of social legislation which could be regarded as the most rapid expansion of social policy in British social history, with the possible exception of the years 1902–1911. Both were periods in which some at least may be said to have approached social policy as a connected whole rather than in a piecemeal manner. The earlier period included those responsible for the Minority Report of the Royal Commission on the Poor Laws and Relief of Distress, 1905–1909. This report divided persons into the non-ablebodied and the ablebodied. It recommended that local authorities should deal with the needs of children of school age by education committees; with the needs of the sick, permanently incapacitated, infants under school age, and the aged needing institutional care by health committees; with the needs of mentally defectives by asylum committees; and of the aged in receipt of pensions by pensions committees. Each committee was to be supervised by an appropriate government department and a Ministry of Labour was to be set up to organise the labour market to prevent or minimise unemployment. Provision was to be made for the maintenance of those who were still unemployed and colonies were to be provided for the reform of vagrants, mendicants or those failing to maintain their families. A Registrar of Public Assistance was to co-ordinate all these activities and keep a register of persons in the care of different authorities.

The second occasion of an approach to social policy as a connected whole is to be found in 1942 in the report of the Committee on Social Insurance and Allied Services (the Beveridge Committee), with its assumption that 'organisation of social insurance should be treated as one part only of a comprehensive policy of social progress',[23] and its recognition of the need to conquer the giants of want, disease, ignorance, squalor and idleness. The Minority Poor Law Commissioners did not see the achievement of their objectives, Beveridge did. His report was accepted and followed by the Education Act, 1944, the Family Allowances Act, 1945, the Housing and the New Towns Acts, 1946, the Town and Country Planning Act, 1946, the National Health Service Act, 1946, the National Insurance, and the National Insurance (Industrial Injuries) Acts, 1946, the National Assistance Act, 1948, the Children Act, 1948, the Criminal Justice Act, 1948, and the Legal Aid and Advice Act, 1949.

This period was thus one of great expectations and achievements so far as a positive social policy was concerned, but the fat years were followed by lean ones. The demands of rearmament, the problem of inflation, and a change of Government resulted in a brake being put upon further expansion, and in the failure in some instances to implement in practice the policy of intent. County colleges and health centres, with some exceptions, failed to materialise. The community centre, nursery school, and youth service programmes were curtailed. The school leaving age was not raised to sixteen. Finally, the expansion of the 1940s gave place to the reappraisal and retrenchment of the 1950s and the 1960s.

Precisely what it is that causes a particular social policy to be formulated, implemented, or rejected, at a particular point of time, it is often difficult and sometimes impossible to say. But it is clear that success in social policy requires a political party sympathetic to the policy in principle, in power at the right time, which must be a time that combines a favourable climate of opinion with the means available to express and implement such opinion, together with circumstances in which action is possible, and the right person to act as architect or protagonist. Lacking one or other of these, social policy may remain unformulated, unaccepted, unimplemented or unchanged. Given all, on the other hand, a policy may be offered and accepted with speed and unanimity. The causes that may deter or delay a change or development in social policy can include concentration on other matters such as a threat of war; economic depression or inflation which limits the availability of resources or requires limitation of public expenditure; control by a government unsympathetic to State intervention; a general climate of opinion uninformed or unfavourable to change; or even an overall increase in affluence encouraging a complacent feeling that all is well as it is.

It is reasonable to claim that the ready acceptance of the recommendations contained in the Beveridge Report, and the policy it involved, was due to the general climate of opinion at the time, combined with a government committed to an expansionist social policy, allied with confidence in the architect of the plan himself. Marshall referred in this connection to the 'dramatic presentation of the programme and the deep emotions it roused'; 'plus the quite exceptional national spirit bred by the war and the situation that followed it'.[24]

To the questions 'Why?' and 'How?', referred to in Chapter One, therefore, there must be added 'When?' and 'By whom?', if social policy is to be presented with a reasonable chance of success.* It may have to face the opposition of contrary political philosophies; of personal ambitions or opportunism; of vested interests; of arguments based on economy or expediency; or of sheer lack of imagination. The path of the supporter of social change—and any new policy involves some measure of change—whether he be private citizen, civil servant, minister of the Crown, or a combination of persons in pressure or interest groups, is one which requires diplomacy as well as enthusiasm, patience as well as persuasiveness, and tact as well as energy. A policy can be wrecked by wrong timing or the wrong support. The same policy offered at an opportune moment can succeed in the hands of a skilful or forceful advocate. The more a situation is charged with human emotions the more difficult it may be successfully to pursue a particular social policy. This accounts, to take some varied examples, for the one time vehement opposition to women's suffrage, to reform of the divorce laws, the laws relating to male homosexuality, or Sunday observance.

The long history of development in social policy relating to children, including compulsory education, limitation of hours of work, health measures and protection against neglect, cruelty or exploitation in their own homes by their own parents, reveals a continuous fight against the deeply held, emotionally charged belief in the sanctity of the family and parental rights. Opposition to free school meals for necessitous children on these grounds has already been referred to. Another instance was the view expressed by an authority on the factory system, in a discussion on the employment of mothers: 'But let the State step in between the mother and her child . . . domestic confidence is dissolved, family privacy invaded and maternal responsibility assailed. For the tender care of the mother is substituted the tender mercies of the

---

* For examples of the influence of individuals on social policy see: Sir Henry Bunbury (Ed.), *Lloyd George's Ambulance Wagon*, Methuen, 1957. Asa Briggs, *Seebohm Rowntree, 1871–1954*, Longmans, 1961. T. S. and M. B. Simey, *Charles Booth—Social Scientist*, Oxford University Press, 1960.

State, for the security of natural affection, the securities of an unnatural law. Better by far that many another infant should perish in its innocence and unconsciousness than to be the victim of such a state of things.'*

The work of the N.S.P.C.C. in its early days was opposed because its protective intentions were regarded as inevitably involving interference between parent and child. This opposition diminished with the passing of time but only in the last twenty years can it be said that the policy of giving equal consideration to the welfare of the child as to the rights of the parents, if a clash between the two occurs, has prevailed.

One final point remains. There may be instances in which social policy is affected by those who are not accountable to Parliament. Titmuss instanced, for example, the influence of insurance, financial, and commercial interests, in the direction and use of resources for profitable enterprises rather than for relieving the squalor of slum areas. Of such direction he said: 'Social policies will be imposed without democratic discussion; without consideration of the local consequences which may result from them.' . . . 'What we can only call "social policy decisions" are continually being made, without any proper awareness or public discussion of what is involved in terms of the common good, and what consequences may flow from the choices made.'[25] This use of the term social policy or policies is, however, extending its meaning beyond that suggested in this chapter. It must be remembered that insurance companies and the like do not have and do not claim to have social aims or objectives. What they do may affect social policy which suggests the necessity of government intervention, but they are not themselves direct or deliberate makers of social policy.

It should be clear from all that has now been said that the formulation and implementation of social policy—social policy in intent and social policy in practice—is a complex process raising fundamental questions. Lafitte asked, for example, whether: 'One compulsory method of meeting a given social need [is] always to be preferred to several different methods freely chosen by groups of people for themselves?' And whether 'we prefer

* Quoted in The Victorian Family, H. L. Beales, in Ideas and Beliefs of the Victorians, Sylvan Press Ltd., 1949.

a varied and pluralistic social order, where responsibility and initiative are as widely diffused as possible, or a uniform and concentrated order in which good government is rated more highly than self-government?'[26] Policy makers must consider and answer such questions but the student should not look for finality in the decisions they reach. He must not expect unanimity of view or of value, and he must not be surprised if a movement in one direction or at one time is followed by reverse at another. This does not mean he has no need to make up his own mind about what is right or wrong, wise or foolish, in social policy and to support conservation or change accordingly. Indeed, unless he does this at some point he will merely be a tailor's dummy gazing lifelessly through glass, ever separated from the real world outside.*

* For examination of the factors affecting the development of social policy in education, health, and social security, see the relevant chapters in: Morris Ginsberg (Ed.), *Law and Opinion in England in the Twentieth Century*, Stevens, 1959.
   For a brief consideration of other issues in the nature, scope and intent of social policy see: Joan L. M. Eyden, *Social Policy in Action*, Routledge and Kegan Paul Ltd., 1969.

CHAPTER FOUR

Concepts of the Welfare State

' "Welfare State" is a term for which I have developed a strong dislike.'[1] In saying this Marshall possibly gave expression to a view already held by a number of people. Marsh likewise 'felt dubious about the concept', and 'increasingly bewildered by the vague way in which the words have come to be used'.[2] If teachers of social administration have come to feel this way the student may well be forgiven if he also is confused. But Marshall continued: 'One can hardly avoid using a term like the "Welfare State". . . . It would be a great pity to discard it. Any catchword which has been widely used by people speaking about their own society must tell us something about that society.'[3] The term—the origin of which is somewhat obscure—has in fact been in general use since the middle 1940s and it seems likely to remain a permanent part of the language of politics and the jargon of social administration. It is impossible to ignore it and impossible likewise to leave consideration of social policy without examining the concept. For it is in the Welfare State—however this be defined—that a positive and inclusive social policy has found its fullest expression. This is true even if such a policy has been slowed down and even if it were to be reversed; if, for example, Peacock's goal that 'the true object of the Welfare State, . . . is to teach people how to do without it',[4] were to be actively pursued.

A major problem in the controversy about the Welfare State is that, like the social services, there is no general agreement as to what it is and no consensus of opinion about its precise aims, or characteristics. It is clear that antagonist and protagonist have not the same concept in mind. The Welfare State means or conveys different things to different people. In these circumstances agreement about the value or disvalue of the Welfare State cannot easily, if ever, be reached. The student can but examine what has been said and done and make up his own mind. What follows, therefore, is in part a résumé of representative opinions of the Welfare State which the student must be aware of in order to make up his mind.

The literature on the Welfare State is now extensive and even a cursory examination of only part of it shows how distant agreement is. The concept has swung from the extreme view of Goldman that it was 'a mechanism for distributing golden eggs',[5] through the purely economic concept of Abrams that the Welfare State was essentially 'one where State power is used deliberately to modify the consequences of the normal play of economic forces in order to obtain a more equal distribution of income earning property and skills'.[6]

A somewhat wider view was that of Bruce who regarded the Welfare State as being 'the sum of efforts over many years to remedy the practical social difficulties and evils of a modern system of economic organisation which grew with but little regard for the majority of those who became involved in it. . . . [It] is organised to ensure the well-being of its citizens and to use their resources to that end.'[7] Then there was the political idealism of the view that the Welfare State was one in which social security and social services were the birthright of every citizen, normally speaking without test of means, in which the development of social services are democratically organised to meet the essential needs of the whole community and in which the whole community participated as a matter of course.[8]

Others who have set out the principles, aims, or characteristics of the Welfare State as they have seen them include Martin who referred to two principles of the Welfare State; the right of everyone to a job, and a guaranteed social minimum of health, wealth, and leisure. The Welfare State, he said, was the sum-total of the reforms achieved by the fight for shorter hours and better pay, jobs for all, good housing, educational opportunity, abolition of poverty and the provision of cultural opportunities, and the chance of a full and dignified life.[9]

Marshall saw the Welfare State characterised in five ways—by intense individualism; the claim of the individual to welfare being sacred and irrefutable, partaking of the character of a natural right—by collectivism; the State being the responsible promoter and guardian of the welfare of the whole community—by a belief in equality; equal opportunity meaning an equal chance to reveal differences some of which are superiorities—by personal liberty; relying on individual choice and motivation in the fulfilment of the

State's purposes in all their details—and by a democratic form of society opposed to rigid class divisions; in particular to a governing class and to anything which favoured sharply distinguished culture patterns at different social levels.[10]

Later Marshall said that the Welfare State in Britain was unique because it was born as the culmination of a long process beginning in the nineteenth century, in Britain's peculiar war and post-war circumstances which continued without a break from resistance to attack, victory, scarcity and reconstruction, the mutual service society of the war merging into the mutual benefit society of the peace.[11]

Cormack spoke of the Welfare State as characterised by the provision of a basic minimum—the essentials of life for those who could not provide for themselves—and of a basic optimum—the best standard of life that the country could afford for its citizens without distinction of cash or class.[12]

Hobman described the Welfare State as a compromise between the two extremes of communism on the one hand and unbridled individualism on the other and as such, in spite of all its imperfections, setting a pattern for any humane and progressive society. It guaranteed a minimum standard of subsistence without removing incentives to personal enterprise and brought about a limited redistribution of income without pretending to establish economic equality among its citizens. It assured adequate help to all in need, giving assistance as of right not as a charity nor with the stigma of pauperism. It was paternal and benevolent in intention but over-burdened with officials with a little brief authority and an outlook usually strictly departmentalised.[13]

Robson saw the Welfare State originating in the nineteenth century in the initiation of the State services of public health, education and factory regulation, and in the action in the twentieth century to relieve or prevent destitution. He included as essential the distribution of the national income in such a way as to secure adequate rewards to all forms of social service which the community desired to continue or to call into being. It involved also equality of opportunity, liberty, social services, social security, nationalisation if necessary to attain welfare objectives, and a public policy, positive and preventive, predominantly concerned with the welfare of all members of the State.[14] Seldon, on the other hand, stigmatised the Welfare State as having degenerated into a Universal Aunt.[15]

Neill spoke of the Welfare State as having three basic responsibilities—the modification of the normal play of economic forces in a market economy to assist the needs of under-privileged groups and individuals by providing every citizen with a basic real income adequate for subsistence irrespective of the market value of his work—compensation for existing inequalities in the distribution of income and property so that at least every child and young person, if not also every adult, had an approximately equal opportunity to develop mind and body to their fullest potentiality —and alteration of the physical and social environment of work and living to remove the 'blighted' areas of industrial society. He saw the Welfare State as being born of a process of trial and error whereby groups of philosophers and politicians, social reformers and social workers developed ideas and practices to compensate the individual for consequences of social disorganisation brought about by urbanisation and industrialism.[16]

Peacock claimed that justification for the Welfare State was based on either the necessity for paternalism because people in the main could not look after themselves, or the necessity for nationalised social services because nationalisation was the most efficient way of providing them; and that if people acted in an ideally responsible way there would be no need for a Welfare State.[17] Raison expressed the view that the Welfare State should concentrate on providing a net to catch those who fell into hardship.[18]

Finally, so far as this discussion is concerned, Titmuss said that four main categories of services were largely responsible for Britain being described as a Welfare State—education, medical care, social security and housing—with a fifth comprising a number of smaller services—child care, juvenile delinquency, employment bureaux and financial grants to many voluntary bodies The aim of full employment could be regarded as an integral part of a Welfare State only in some senses.[19]

What now can be discerned from these different conceptions of the Welfare State and its purposes? First, although this is by way of a digression, they offer useful examples of the necessity for the student of social administration to study both history and

c

economics. How otherwise can he appreciate what Martin was referring to when he spoke of reforms achieved by the fight for shorter hours and better pay, and what Marshall had in mind when he spoke of the culmination of a long process beginning in the nineteenth century? How otherwise can he appreciate the full implications of Abrams' reference to 'the normal play of economic forces', or the meaning of Robson's reference to 'the distribution of the national income', or of Neill's to a 'basic real income'? Unless he has a knowledge of history and of economics not only will much of the meaning ascribed to the Welfare State inevitably pass over his head, but he will be unable to separate the straw from the chaff in the argument and counter-argument with which he is faced.

Secondly, a contrast can be made between those who see the Welfare State characterised by the provision of a basic minimum below which none should fall and those who see it characterised by optimum provision. There is a substantial difference in the social and economic implications of these two views and they cannot, therefore, simply be noted as differences of opinion. The second involves substantially higher, possibly limitless, State expenditure than the first and presents additional problems of administration and of recruitment, training and employment of personnel of a very wide variety; teachers, doctors, social workers, clerical officers, administrators and others. Those who elect to follow the advocates of optimum provision must be aware of these implications and be ready and able to answer the question 'How?' as well as the question 'What?', so far as social policy in practice is concerned.

Thirdly, there can be discerned more than once the recognition that the social policy of a Welfare State ties the nation's social and economic affairs irrevocably together, that wealth and welfare march hand in hand, not alone. This leads to a recognition of the contrast between those who see the Welfare State only in terms of the material advantages it aims to provide—full employment—economic security—health—education—and so on, and those who see it also as furthering cultural opportunities, aesthetic environment and the enhancement of individual personality. For the second it is not true, as Schwarz claimed, that 'as far as practical politics are concerned, "welfare" has only one significance and that is "material welfare".[20] This view is not justified even on the limited evidence so far provided. What is significant, however, is that it is often the view of the critics of the Welfare State who define and measure welfare entirely in money or material terms and see the possibility of the decease of the Welfare State as and when productivity increases, with the country and the individual becoming increasingly well-to-do.

This was clear when Peacock said that if people, as they grow richer, were to act in an ideally responsible way there would be no need for a Welfare State. This argument incidentally could be applied to the defence services, all forms of punishment, taxation, and compulsions of any kind and is not a very realistic one. It was clear also, however, when he referred to teaching people how to do without the Welfare State. Seen in money terms only that objective might be possible, although it overlooked the fact that with continuously rising standards in such things as health, education, and housing, costs as well as incomes rise and the citizen, like Alice with the Red Queen, has to run as hard as he can to stay where he is. This is not merely a problem of inflation. It is the outcome also of new medical knowledge and skills, expensive medical equipment, the demand for better equipped schools, universities, technicians and scientists, and an appreciation of the need for improved living conditions for a healthy community.

But the conception of welfare in material terms only is too narrow. How, it may be asked, can an orphaned child act in an ideally responsible way so that there would be no need of a child care service? How can an aged and infirm old person be taught to do without the care, even limited as it is at the present time, which the State provides? How can a severely mentally ill person act in an ideally responsible way so that hospital treatment or other provision becomes unnecessary? How can an unemployed man be taught to do without a system of employment exchanges, or a disabled workman to do without a rehabilitation service, or a blind person without training facilities? And can one really see a time when there will be no offenders against or breakers of the law and thus no need of a probation or prison welfare service?

These are only a few of the questions that can be asked to illustrate that welfare is not merely a matter of money and material things; required only because people act irresponsibly or lack wise teaching. How the services of a Welfare State should be paid for is a proper and necessary question to ask, but payment is only one part of the whole issue of State responsibility. It is reasonable to argue that people might be asked to make more direct payments for welfare services but not logical to conclude that a Welfare State could then be dismantled.

A final contrast that can be made is between those who view the Welfare State as mischievous and misconceived and those who, although they recognise flaws and limitations in it, are generally in sympathy with what they regard as its policy and objectives. To the first it involves or encourages certain undesirable qualities—paternalism—irresponsibility—false assumptions—decadence—degeneration. To the second it denotes certain political, philosophical and social values—democracy—individualism—collectivism—balance—liberty—equality—the avoidance of class distinctions. In these differing views is a clear example of the moral or ethical values that lie at the heart of social administration.

For sympathisers and critics alike, however, the proof of the pudding must be in the eating. If the policies and provisions of the Welfare State withstand the onslaughts made upon them it may be possible by the end of the century to judge whether or not they lead to the desirable or the undesirable results anticipated. Even then, however, it will be difficult to disentangle cause and effect and to judge what is the outcome of the Welfare State and what of other factors. Many of the ills of society today are blamed by the critics upon the Welfare State when it is clear that their cause lies elsewhere. Old people in residential institutions, for example, are not generally there because their families neglect them and leave them to be cared for by the Welfare State, as is often said. The majority in institutional care are in fact unmarried, have no children, or are separated from them physically by long distances or by death.

There is no certainty that the Welfare State will continue until the end of the century, however, or any other point of time, even in an attenuated form. Already in 1955 Finer referred to the Welfare State being ground away by the twin millstones of increased armaments and inflation.[21] And in the same year it was said: 'The social task of our time is to find a path that leads onwards through and beyond the Welfare State, to a less bureaucratic, freer, more creative social order, which for lack of a better term, we may describe as a Welfare Society.'[22]

Three years previously the same observer, in asking for a major review of the whole social security system, had said: 'This can be done with general consent, so long as it is made clear that there is no intention of undermining the structure or departing from the broad purposes of the Welfare State. No element of doubt must be left in the public mind on these grave issues because today, under existing world conditions, it is a prerequisite for the survival of the British way of life that it finds expression in terms of a well-conceived, firm and progressive social policy.'[23] The changing attitude towards the Welfare State is clearly demonstrated in these contrasting views expressed by the same person.

In 1961 the phrase 'post Welfare State' was actually used by Howell, not merely as a desirable but as a certain state of affairs.[24] And Marshall, who was not one of the adverse critics of the Welfare State in principle, went further and said that as the situation which gave rise to the Welfare State in the transition from war to peace changed, so the Welfare State passed away. Its institutions, practices, procedures and expertise were still with us but they were operating in a different setting and without the original consensus which welded them into a social system with a distinctive spirit of its own.[25] In other words there was the machinery but not the common impetus to direct or drive it in such a way as to entitle the State today to be called a Welfare State.

Marshall made the interesting point that the Welfare State was born and welcomed into a world of shortages, rationing, controls and restrictions, or what he called the Austerity Society, but that this world had passed away by the middle of the 1950s and the Affluent Society had taken its place. It was then, he said, that the attack upon the Welfare State began, in particular the principles of universality and free services, and as a consequence though welfare measures remained the Welfare Model did not. The Welfare State and its rival the Affluent Society became 'engaged in a drama', and the Welfare State was at a disadvantage, Marshall suggested, for six reasons.

First, because of its association in people's minds with the austerity of the post-war years. Second, because inflation prevented the achievement of a subsistence level for all and required the growth of national assistance, or poor relief under another name. Third, because the rise in the standard of living made the principle of universality appear rather silly. Fourth, because the expansion of the Affluent Society caused not only a loss of value but a loss of dignity in the benefits the Welfare State provided. Fifth, because public provision of welfare shifted to private schemes, assisted by tax concessions. And sixth and last, because the contributory device (in national insurance) began to appear cumbersome, illogical and pointless.

A last instance of the evident belief in the past nature of the Welfare State was to be found in the 44th Annual Report for 1962–1963 of the National Council of Social Service. In this it was said that the most significant post-war concept was that of the Welfare State which (although reshaped on numerous occasions) had a profound influence on the life of the country, until the Welfare Society emerged as a logical successor. The 'Welfare Society' is thus referred to a second time as succeeding the Welfare State. On this occasion it was characterised as a society dependent for its fulfilment upon 'general participation' never to be wholly satisfied by the payment of taxes or by legislative action however sensitive and humane.

At the same time as the supposed passing of the Welfare State has been noted or welcomed by some, it is clear that others continue to look upon it as a reality. The term, therefore, still tells us something about how people view the society in which they live. The 1960s were marked by repeated references to the Welfare State. The sixth and last edition of Hall's book *The Social Services of Modern England*[26] closed with a chapter entitled 'The Welfare State'. This was written in terms of current not past issues. The Fabian Society published a Tract in 1960 on *Casualties of the Welfare State*, by one who introduced herself not as an expert in any aspect of the Welfare State, but as a worker in it, in an office dealing with personal enquiries nearly all of which, it was said, involved Welfare State rights and obligations.[27] In 1961 the Birmingham Council of Christian Churches published a study of relationships between the social services and the churches in a city suburb, with the title 'Responsibility in the Welfare State?'. This referred throughout to the Welfare State as a living reality.[28] In 1961 also Political and Economic Planning published a survey in which 734 mothers, to test whether the issues were live ones in the minds of the ordinary public, were asked whether they had heard people talking about the Welfare State and what they thought it meant. Fifty per cent gave a positive reply.[29] In 1964 an argument on 'Freedom in the Welfare State' was published by The Fabian Society.[30] As noted at the outset of this chapter, Marsh considered its future and this too was in 1964. In 1967 Gregg published an economic and social history of Great Britain from 1945 onwards entitled *The Welfare State*.[31]

Questions relating to the Welfare State are still being asked of students in examination papers and these are concerned not merely with its historical, but with its present significance also. The term is constantly used in newspapers, social service journals, and on wireless and television programmes. In short, it is clear that the Welfare State cannot be written off as something that has played its part in Britain's social history but has no relevance to present-day thought or issues. It is still of importance in people's social thinking and their ideas about social policy, even if these are at times somewhat muddled. But since the concept has become both confused and complex the student must not expect to find the issues easy to clarify. This is particularly the case since behind much of the discussion about change, continuation, or disappearance of the Welfare State, its meaning, merits, or demerits, there lies a considerable degree of ignorance about who benefits or has benefited from it and to what extent, and how far human needs still remain unmet.

On the one hand there are those who point out that there are still a substantial number of people, even if a minority, who fall below the standard of living enjoyed by the majority; many of the retired or widowed; those living on social security allowances; the slum dweller; the homeless; those educated in sub-standard schools, or treated in sub-standard hospitals; those in overcrowded prisons and out of date Homes; the chronically sick or disabled. As long as such under-privileged groups exist, those who have them in mind hold that to talk of abolishing or dismantling the Welfare State is certainly premature, if not mischievous. That there is still a long way to go in abolishing poverty, or squalor in large cities, or out of date schools particularly in rural districts, or in abolishing overcrowding and homelessness in areas of population growth is clear. The view that the Welfare State is something appropriate only to the past would appear on these facts to be at least unrealistic, if it is not unjust. On the other hand there are those who believe such social ills as are still to be seen, which they do not deny, will automatically pass with increasing prosperity without requiring the machinery of a Welfare State which they regard not only as very costly but as cumbersome and outdated.

It is easier to decide on the merits of these two views, which are at least related to facts, than on the merits of different philosophies that support or reject the Welfare State, for here one is faced with the values and value judgements that are an intrinsic part of social administration but have no yardstick by which they can be objectively measured and judged.

Who is to decide and on what criteria whether to answer 'Yes' or 'No' to the question 'Am I my brother's keeper?' and if 'Yes' whether it follows that protection against common dangers and disablements is to be provided out of common funds and services? Or on the other hand if the answer is 'No' is each man an island unto himself, to be discouraged from thinking in terms of corporate provision which merely degrades him?

Who can judge finally whether it is in fact the case that 'giving to anybody and everybody deprives the act of grace and makes it the sport of spongers', or that 'in a mature community it should be a badge of pride that we receive no favours from the State?'[32] Or is the injunction to 'bear one another's burdens' as applicable in a rich society as in a poor one, referring to all areas of life, material and non-material; State participation being but a corporate recognition of an ethical principle denoting neither immaturity nor sponging?

Who can bring evidence to show which, if either, of the two following incompatible views is correct? 'The Welfare State . . . will appeal to those who dislike the sight of great poverty or of great inequalities of wealth; to whom it matters much that everyone shall be decently fed, housed and clothed, who ardently desire that all children shall have a genuine chance of realising their abilities to the utmost extent; who obtain positive satisfaction from a sense of social purpose permeating the community, and of solidarity knitting together the whole body of citizens.'[33] Or: 'One of the overall results of the individually attractive programmes of our political opponents has been to make the people of this country ever more and more dependent on the universal provider and ever further from a sense of responsibility for its actions.'[34]

These and similar issues are resolved to the mutual satisfaction only of like-minded individuals or groups, by virtue of the common ethical and social considerations to which they give weight. Whereas they may find it possible to persuade some others to follow their reasoning and accept their conclusions it is clear they will never persuade everyone to do so. Equally good men can and do differ about principles and in so far as the Welfare State embodies principles, which it clearly does, it will be open to support or attack from good men, as well as from those who support or attack it by reason of prejudice, selfishness or ignorance and without recourse to principles at all.

To sum up, and at the risk of over-simplification, it may be said that the issues involved in the consideration of concepts of the Welfare State are fivefold: Whether the citizen should be expected to make more or less provision for himself out of his own pocket, or whether statutory services, free or at less than cost, should be expanded, maintained or contracted: Whether people should have freedom to choose which services they will use or enjoy, or whether they should be protected against unwise choice, their own ignorance and mistakes or those of others: Whether organised State responsibility can and should give way entirely to spontaneous community responsibility of neighbour for neighbour, or whether State provision should continue regardless of the extent of citizen participation: Whether universal corporate provision is more of a burden than a benefit to the community, either economically or socially, and whether the concept of the Welfare State is based on reality or on sentimentality.

What is clear is that social policy in a Welfare State, whatever view is taken of the desirability of such a State, must be beneficent in intent. In this it accords with the views on social policy presented in the earlier part of the last chapter. No one could hold that Welfare State social policy is harsh or negative, or springs other than from benevolent even if misguided intentions. Its policy may be mistaken in that it will not achieve, or is not the best way of achieving what it sets out to do; namely to advance and secure the welfare and wellbeing of the citizen in particular

c*

or general respects. But it cannot be argued that those who hold the power to fashion and implement its social policy are motivated solely by self-seeking or self-protective goals. They may be misguided, over-protective, or lovers of popularity but they are not tyrannical nor lacking in concern for the health and wellbeing of the individual and the society in which he lives.

As is the case with social policy in any State, however, the student must eventually make up his own mind and act on his own convictions. Even if the term 'Welfare State' were to pass out of common usage he would still find himself discussing 'The Good Society', for the debate is in fact about the meaning and conditions of the good life, always to be sought, never finally attained.

CHAPTER FIVE

Social Research and Social Policy

In the light of Chapter One on the meaning of social administration it may be said that social research can be regarded in the
first place as one method used in the process of solving social
problems or promoting social welfare. In other words its primary
purpose is to produce factual evidence on which social policy,
action, or reform may be based or evaluated. It could as rightly
be said of social research workers as Cole said of sociologists that
their task is 'to strengthen the case [for reform] by fuller investigation of the evils needed to be overcome, and to present their
results in such a way as to secure greater public attention'.[1] This
is part of the process of promoting social welfare. In the second
place the evidence which social research produces comes to form
part of the body of knowledge contained in social administration
as a subject of study with which the student must become familiar.
He will learn about the social services from the social research
worker as well as from the textbook. The student, the social
worker, and the social administrator will or should all find that
at one and the same time they are asking questions about policy
and practice that demand fresh research, and making themselves
familiar with the results of completed research.

In Chapter Three social policy and social research were linked
as necessary the one to the other. The view was expressed that
whenever time and circumstance permit the formulation of the
first should wait upon the outcome of the second. But it was
suggested this had often been overlooked by policy makers. The
time is now ripe to pursue this further and to consider the value
of social research and the use made of it or not, as the case may be.

First, by way of introduction, it may be said that research of
any kind is an effort to discover or verify facts, new facts or old
facts (if such an expression may be used), through a scientific
study of a subject, involving systematic analysis, critical examination and interpretation of what the study reveals. The research

may relate, *inter alia*, to medicine, to the marketing or consumption of goods or services, to public opinion or preferences, to physical or psychical phenomena, or a whole range of social problems and provisions. In the last instance the study can be included under the wide umbrella of social research, of which social surveys are a part.

The methodology of research includes the experimental under the controlled conditions of a laboratory; the observational using one or other of the physical senses, not necessarily under controlled conditions but possibly involving active participation in the life of a neighbourhood or reading the case studies of social workers; the historical with the study of minutes, records, diaries, biographies or other data relating to past events; the exploratory in a particular area or relating to a certain phenomenon; the interrogational through the interview and the questionnaire; the statistical in the counting and measuring of quantifiable data; and the comparative whether between persons, times or places. Clearly these methods are not mutually exclusive. It is possible and often essential both to observe and to question, to experiment and to study records, to explore and to measure or compare, or to combine more than two of these approaches.

It is easy to see that the application of some methods is more difficult in the social than in the natural sciences. The natural sciences can control laboratory conditions in a way, or to an extent, not possible to the social sciences, concerned as they always are with human behaviour. Man cannot be the subject of experiment for purposes of observation, or to test hypotheses, as can inanimate matter, plants or, within limits, animals. This does not exclude any experiments in the laboratory, as many experiments in psychology show, but it does exclude—other than in such inhuman conditions as were found in Nazi concentration camps—pressing a test to the point of endangering growth or life, damaging personality, or producing an irreversible condition that may prove to be less desirable than the original.

Even if men agree to be the subject of an experiment, or it is one that involves no risk, repetition under identical and controlled conditions by any number of research workers, to confirm results for themselves, is not always possible in the social sciences as it is in the natural sciences. The mixing of two parts of hydrogen with one part of oxygen under given temperature and pressure will always result in the production of water and this can be tested and observed by any number of persons in the laboratory. The result of mixing two social classes on a number of housing estates, although it can be carefully observed, cannot be repeated *ad infinitum*. Even where conditions are broadly the same they will not be identical on each estate and behaviour, although it may be similar, will not, therefore, be as unvaried as the result of mixing gases. Hence a rule of human behaviour cannot be formulated as precisely as can a rule of gaseous behaviour; on which future results can be predicted. But Moser pointed out that:

'It is altogether false to imagine that research divides neatly into two categories—experimental and others—and that only the former can lead to valid causative inferences. Rather should one view research as being ranged along a scale, with the most completely controlled experiment at one end and uncontrolled observation at the other.'[2]

Another problem in the social sciences is that the subject of study—man—is indivisible. He cannot, when alive, be physically separated into parts for the purposes of examination as can a botanical specimen. Nor can one part of a human society be separated and isolated from the rest to observe how men behave as can a clutch of new-born chicks. Also emotional response as well as physical response is part of man's nature and this applies to both observer and observed. Neither are outside the society under investigation. They are both part of it and this renders complete objectivity difficult. Emotions may influence response to different situations or processes, including the process of being observed, questioned or experimented on; or there may be a refusal to co-operate at all. Such response or refusal may well colour results. The social scientist faces too the problem that social situations, opinions and life are constantly changing in ways not met with in the natural sciences. Also single causes of social phenomena are rare. They are many and complex and thus difficult to separate.

Whilst all these obstacles lead to Huxley's conclusion that social science could never become fully and rigorously scientific,[3] awareness of the problems, coupled with trained observation and skilled interviewing, could reduce the dangers. Modern techniques of the social survey, of sampling, questionnaire design, statistical measurement, and mathematical correlation, do not refine social research to the same degree of precision as research in the natural sciences, but they can be used to increase knowledge of human behaviour, to make comparisons, estimate degree of need, demand or opinion, and thus contribute to informed policy making.

In some instances the primary motive of research may be aesthetic; to discover and enjoy the art or literature of another society or age. In another instance it may be to extend the frontiers of knowledge; about the meaning of dreams or the customs of primitive peoples. In another it may be curiosity; to know more about the unexplored areas of the universe. In another it may be utilitarian; to improve health, living or working conditions, reduce the cost of education or the incidence of delinquency. Social research as a general rule can be placed in the last, the utilitarian category. This is not to say that it is never undertaken to extend knowledge nor out of curiosity, but it is not generally so and it should never be pursued for reason of curiosity alone.* Social research involves people's lives, often intimately, and as the Prayer Book similarly advises those contemplating marriage, it ought not to be undertaken unadvisedly, lightly or wantonly. It is scarcely necessary to say that to discern or verify facts is much more difficult in practice than in theory. It is particularly difficult to distinguish what are 'the facts of the case' in social affairs. Two people can and frequently do describe one and the same event in different ways. They can report what they both observe in front of them in contradictory fashion. Not only is this the case but 'facts' may become lost or obscured by the passage of time, the confusion of events, the forgetfulness of people, the desire, possibly unconscious, to conceal or reveal only in part.

Feelings are also facts which can affect situations. What, for example, are the true facts if a patient says, 'I can't move my arm doctor'; when examination reveals nothing organically the matter. Is the patient malingering? Is he mentally ill? Has some morbid condition been overlooked? What are the facts when an old person tells a student who is assisting in a piece of research attempting to measure social contacts amongst the old, that no one ever comes to see her, when her landlady could report that she herself fre-

* See: *Research in the Personal Social Services—Proposals for a Code of Practice*, The National Institute for Social Work Training 1965. National Council of Social Service, Reference No. 700.

quently goes in and that a son calls each weekend. Is the old lady losing her memory? Is she seeking sympathy? Is she suspicious, proud, or unwilling to reveal her affairs to a stranger? Is she just perverse? Anyone who tries to get 'the facts' from an old person has to be aware of a host of difficulties that cloud the issue. It may be that one has to live, day in day out, with a particular person before knowing whether what is presented as fact, *is* fact or fantasy.

Bearing all the difficulties of getting the facts in mind it is still the case that without them none of the purposes of research can satisfactorily be achieved. To attempt to relate, explain, describe, measure, estimate, assess, treat, change, cure, predict, reject or decide, all of which research may be designed to do, without the facts or some facts, is at best inspired guesswork, at worst blindly foolish. The outcome of guesswork may be successful but it may equally well be ineffective, dubious, wasteful, or even fatal. And the more closely the matter is concerned with human life and welfare the more important is it to be aware of these dangers. Whereas a false account of a long-ended battle may do no more than imperil the reputation of a scholar, or an incorrect explanation of an unusual phenomenon do no more than add to the disrepute of a quack, wrong treatment of a disease may kill the patient or a failure to estimate numbers result in a gross shortage of an essential commodity.

The second happened in the early days of the national health service when the initial demand for spectacles and teeth was far greater than the supply. This occasioned Abrams' observation: 'To those accustomed to using social surveys it was a surprise and a disappointment that the actuarial and administrative calculations for the national health scheme were not based on preliminary surveys of the population's needs for medical care.'[4] A greater effort was made in the case of hearing aids when the need and demand arising out of deafness were estimated by the use of the Social Survey,[5] further reference to which is made shortly.

Since ascertaining the facts, in so far as this is possible, is manifestly so important in the intelligent planning and efficient promotion of social policy and provision, it was unfortunate that a member of the House of Lords could say in a debate on the welfare services:

'I am not one of those people who are keen on social studies; I prefer the practical application, and I rather dislike the idea that on a specimen number of people you can get an answer on which it is completely possible to act.'[6]

The question that arises from this observation is, the practical application of what to what and how, if one has no information on which to base action. And a judgement on the reliability of random sampling should rest, not upon a personal dislike of the method, but upon the proven success or otherwise of its use.

If but little attention is paid to social welfare, and the area of State responsibility is narrow, correspondingly little need will be felt for social research, other than to encourage the State to extend its area of responsibility. But as Glass said: 'The larger the area of government responsibility in the field of social policy, the greater the urgency for governmental action to be based on and tested by social research. . . . [It] is particularly required, first, in the formulation of policy, and secondly, in testing and advancing the implementation of policy.'[7]

The fact that social research is necessary for informed action does not of course mean that it is the panacea for all social ills. To gain knowledge and understanding is a first and necessary step towards the solution of a social problem or success in social policy, but these ends also require energetic pursuit, wise leadership, concerned personnel, acceptance by interested parties and the public generally. Medical research has shown, for example, that heavy smoking is an important factor in the production of lung cancer and has estimated the probability of such a smoker contracting the disease. This, however, has not solved the problem of the rising death rate from cancer of the lung. This would require vigorous propaganda, social education and training, absence or at least reduction of advertising, parental example and discouragement, as well as legislation prohibiting the sale of tobacco to the young; and possibly other measures as well. To achieve these it would be necessary to have a strong lead from a government at present drawing considerable revenue from tobacco tax, and from municipal councils benefiting from rate payments from local tobacco firms. Such a lead would have to be allied also with the co-operation of a trade enjoying substantial profits, and of men dependent for their living on cigarette manufacture. Finally, a major change on the part of the public of a long-established social habit would be necessary. Until these five things occur the facts revealed by research seem likely to remain unheeded by the majority. This does not mean that the research has been wasted but only that its application to the solution of the problem is neither automatic nor inevitable.

It is clear also that facts revealed by research may sometimes prove less effective than a graphic description by a novelist, poet or journalist: the Kingsleys, Hoods, and Dickens of this world. Research can reveal the numbers of persons affected by and the nature of certain living or economic conditions, and account for or estimate the resulting disease, disability or death. Literary work, although it may not provide complete or even accurate data, may, however, arouse more concern about the problem and result more quickly in reform. It is nevertheless foolish to place faith in isolated, possibly inaccurate descriptive or imaginative work. Wise social policy requires knowledge about the nature, the cause, the extent, the whereabouts, the similarities and the differences of human needs, which the novel or the newspaper cannot provide unaided. Literary work may rouse the conscience and the energy of a nation. Research is necessary if conscience and energy are to be harnessed to efficient, effective, and economic effort.

Whilst social research is no substitute for qualities of mind or person, for political or social vision, or ethical commitment, fortunately 'there is no incompatibility between drawing upon spiritual strength or moral courage and also upon the findings of empirical research'.[8] Neither good will alone, nor knowledge alone can solve the social problems of the time. The two must be allies, the one warming, the other illuminating progress towards socially desired ends.

Since this is so the person who undertakes social research can rightly have his own set of values. In other words social research can be as value centred as any other aspect of social administration. But this is not to say that the social research worker fails to recognise the necessity of impartiality in the examination of his results, nor of intellectual integrity and reliability. He can have practical ends in mind and a desire to contribute towards the solution of a social problem but this should not jeopardise a scientific approach to his work. That is to say the social research

worker can be a committed person, provided he is equally prepared to abandon an hypothesis if the evidence requires this, as
to frame one. Indeed it is arguable that successful social research
requires sympathy, imagination, sensitivity and concern as much
as absence of bias and prejudice. It is difficult, for example, to
imagine that Howard, Booth, and Townsend would have spent
so much effort and time on their researches into the conditions of
the prisons, the poor and the aged, if they had not at the outset
been concerned about what they believed to be the evil nature of
the conditions and anxious that something should be done to
alter them. They were in short committed men engaged in social
research. These views on the compatibility of committal and
objectivity are supported by Cole who was himself an experienced
social investigator:

'Because I hold strong subjective views on social questions, and have
always taken part and interest in social investigations primarily for the
purpose of furthering causes in which I believe, I have always rejected
the appellation of "social scientist". . . . This does not mean that I
reject, or seek to minimise the importance of studying as impartially as
possible all the relevant "social facts" on the presence of which any
effective action for change must needs rest to a very great extent. . . .
    'Evidently the investigator ought not to allow his beliefs or sympathies
to lead him into falsifying facts; but in many fields of study sympathy is
essential to understanding, and the investigator who remains coldly
aloof will never discover some of the most essential facts—especially
the facts about the value-judgments of the persons whose conditions
and mutual relations he is setting out to study.'[9]

Clearly if committal does give rise to prejudice or intellectual
blindness then the value of the research will be undermined and
possibly nullified. The fact, as Glass said, that 'policy may be
founded in part on value judgements does not in any way reduce
the need to scrutinise its assumptions in the light of objective
research'.[10] It is wise to point out here that neither a high intelligence, a good education, nor a professional qualification, are in
themselves guarantees of objectivity, impartiality or detachment.
The Editor of Case Conference rightly expressed concern when two
correspondents, responsible for recruiting and training voluntary
workers, concluded a letter with the observation that these voluntary workers included 'members of all the professions, people with

executive and managerial experience in business and women who graduated before marriage. With such backgrounds we find there are no obstacles of prejudice to be overcome'.[11] This is extremely unlikely, indeed one could say it is almost certainly untrue. What is probable is that trainers and trainees shared the same prejudices and consequently failed to recognise them as such. That there are difficulties in avoiding this and clear dangers in value centred social research is evident as Wootton pointed out:

'In social research generally constant vigilance is necessary against the risk of prejudice . . . the social scientist has constantly to extricate himself from a tangle of social and ethical value-judgments . . . there is a risk that such judgments may have an undesirable influence upon choice of hypotheses, and that the latter will be derived from irrelevant moral and social attitudes rather than from careful scrutiny of the available evidence.'[12]

But to extricate oneself from a tangle does not require one thereafter to throw away the rope. Risk is an inevitable part of life, including social research; first to be recognised, then to be guarded against.

Social investigators are all liable to err and must be ever alert to this possibility. The more important the area of the investigation and the more far reaching any resultant legislation the more important is it that bias and prejudice be avoided. The 1832–34 Royal Commission for Inquiring into the Administration and Practical Operation of the Poor Laws offers an excellent illustration of what can happen when this fundamental point is overlooked. Of this Commission McGregor said: 'Of all the empirical investigations before the fifties that which preceded the Act of 1834 was the least open-minded, the most concerned to validate the dogmatic presuppositions of political economy.'[13] And the result was social misery for a large number of innocent people.

It may be well now to consider what can properly be included under the umbrella of social research and what must be excluded. First, the mere expression of opinion about a social situation or problem, or the random gathering together and presentation of expressions of opinion, in however impressive a form, cannot be included. Opinion may bear little or no relation to the facts of the case and it is with the discovery or verification of facts that research is concerned. It is because certain royal commissions and committees of enquiry have delivered themselves of, and based their conclusions on expressions of opinion only, excluding any discovery, verification or analysis of facts, that they have been open to criticism. These must be excluded from under the social research umbrella. Two examples of such are to be found in the report of the Consultative Committee on the Education of the Adolescent, 1927 (the Hadow Committee), and in the report of the Royal Commission on Marriage and Divorce, 1956 (the Morton Commission). The major terms of reference of the first were:

'to consider and report upon the organisation, objective and curriculum of courses of study suitable for children who will remain in full-time attendance at schools, other than Secondary Schools, up to the age of 15, regard being had on the one hand to the requirements of a good general education and the desirability of providing a reasonable variety of curriculum, so far as is practicable, for children of varying tastes and abilities, and on the other to the probable occupations of the pupils in commerce, industry and agriculture'.[14]

In the introduction to its report the Committee delivered itself of the opinion that 'there is a tide which begins to rise in the veins of youth at the age of eleven and twelve'. On the basis of this unsubstantiated observation they recommended that all children should be transferred at eleven or twelve from primary schools to a type of secondary education, whether grammar or modern, or to senior classes moving on into junior technical schools, designed to suit the different abilities believed to be apparent in different types of children at that age. These recommendations were supported in due course by equally unsubstantiated observations contained in the report of a Special Committee on Curriculum and Examinations in Secondary Schools (the Norwood Committee). This categorised children as those who are 'interested in learning for its own sake, who can grasp an argument or follow a piece of connected reasoning. . . .' those whose 'interests lie markedly in the field of applied science or applied art . . . (who often have) an uncanny insight into the intricacies of mechanism, (but for whom) the subtleties of language construction are too delicate'; and those who deal 'more easily with concrete things than with ideas'.[15] From this random categorisation there arose the concept of secondary grammar, secondary technical and secondary modern schools. The recommendations shaped the structure of secondary education following the 1944 Education Act. Thus without any research to show whether the hypotheses, supported only by the expression of opinion of interested parties, were correct, transfer at 11-plus and selection on an examination for particular types of schools became general educational policy and standard practice for the best part of twenty years, until growing dissatisfaction amongst teachers and educationists demanded change.

In the second case instanced the Morton Commission was required to undertake an enquiry into and to consider matters which had an important bearing on a wide and delicate area of social policy. It had:

'To enquire into the law of England and the law of Scotland concerning divorce and other matrimonial causes and into the powers of courts of inferior jurisdiction on matters affecting relations between husband and wife, and to consider whether any changes should be made in the law or its administration, including the law relating to the property rights of husband and wife, both during marriage and after its termination (except by death), having in mind the need to promote and maintain healthy and happy married life and to safeguard the interests and wellbeing of children; and to consider whether any alteration should be made in the law prohibiting marriage with certain relations by kindred or affinity.'[16]

With so major a task, having long term and substantial implications, the failure to include any empirical investigation into marriage breakdown, its causes, or accompanying social problems and effects, was a major and serious omission on the part of the Commission. It had less excuse than the Hadow Committee in this for in the thirty years between the setting up of the two bodies social research experience and techniques had been both improved and publicised. There was a greater awareness of the need for research and a larger body of knowledge and persons to call upon for advice and assistance. Nevertheless McGregor felt justified in saying:

'The Morton Commission's search for evidence has produced one of the most impressive collections of unsupported cliché ever subsidised by the taxpayer. . . . No Commissioner possessed expert knowledge of the considerable body of modern sociological research . . . or was equipped with an understanding of the techniques and potentialities of social investigation developed during the last twenty years.'[17]

In contrast to the two foregoing instances royal commissions and committees of enquiry can and have undertaken social research as part of their investigations. Examples of this are to be found in the report of the Royal Commission on Population, 1949 (the Simon Commission), and the report of the Central Advisory Council for Education (England) '15 to 18', 1959 (the Crowther Report). The Simon Commission began its work by setting up three specialist committees—statistics—economics—and biological and medical—to investigate the scientific aspect of the problem and to advise, in order that expert knowledge would be available and used. Special investigations were conducted including a family census, a fertility enquiry, and one on the cost of bringing up children. The Commission thus had the benefit of the services of specialists provided by the medical profession, statisticians and social scientists, who were also represented amongst the Commissioners. The conclusions and recommendations of the Commission were, therefore, based not only on what they referred to as 'the formal evidence' of 78 bodies and individuals but on social research in the whole area of their study. In view of the fact that the Commission's terms of reference included the duty:

'to consider what measures, if any, should be taken in the national interest to influence the future trend of population; and to make recommendations,'[18]

this was clearly of the greatest importance.

The task of the Central Advisory Council for Education was:

'to consider in relation to the changing social and industrial needs of our society, and the needs of its individual citizens, the education of boys and girls between 15 and 18, and in particular to consider the balance at various levels of general and specialised studies between these ages and to examine the interrelationship of the various stages of education'.[19]

The Council did not confine itself to consideration of 'evidence' offered by a substantial number of organisations and individuals but sponsored three surveys; one, the Social Survey, undertaken by the Central Office of Information, the second, the National Service Survey, undertaken by the Army War Office and the R.A.F. Air Ministry, and the third, the Technical Courses Survey, undertaken by Technical Colleges. The Council was thus supplied not only with reliable figures but relevant and necessary information about social factors affecting the issues they had to consider, and on which they could reliably base their conclusions and recommendations.

Whether or not the reports of commissions or committees of enquiry can be regarded as constituting social research is seen, from the examples given above, to depend on whether they have used scientific method to ascertain and analyse the facts of a case and based their conclusions on those facts. If what is referred to as 'evidence' is solely opinion then it is not social research and should not be regarded as such. It may have a value in indicating the strength or variety of views on a particular issue and it allows opportunity for the experience and judgment of the expert to be considered and given weight to in any final assessment, but this is different from and must not be confused with the fact-finding of research.

Confusion can easily arise here, particularly for the student who is unfamiliar with the jargon used, from the frequent practice of commissions and committees of enquiry of inviting interested persons or parties to submit to them what they call 'evidence', whether in writing or orally. This 'evidence' is generally no more than the expression of the opinions or beliefs of the person or body holding them, the validity of which has not necessarily been put to any test. Or it is 'evidence' in the sense that it does relate to an observed and actual situation or problem but is insufficient in itself to be regarded as typical—that is to say common to the majority. It may, if tested, be found to relate only to a minority or unrepresentative group. Evidence proper is that which pertains to established facts, or that which is admissible not only as relevant but as reliable.

Students can be warned here that if they are asked in an examination 'to consider the evidence', for example of the adequacy or otherwise of welfare services for the disabled, it is not an open invitation to produce all they have ever read, seen, heard or thought about the subject. Such questions require answers that refer to facts revealed by social research, surveys, reports, or investigations that show—in the example suggested—whether or not the need for home helps is matched by their supply; whether the number of specially designed and equipped houses accords with the numbers of disabled persons needing and wishing to live in them; how many social clubs are available and whether these are sufficient to satisfy requirements and so on. Isolated horror stories, unsubstantiated press reports, and general hearsay, do not constitute evidence. Facts alone provide evidence: facts about the nature and extent of need, about the objective situation in which people are living, about the way in which services are administered, about the attitudes people have towards themselves and others, or towards asking for and using services available to them. Not until opinions and beliefs have been put to the test and verified as factually correct can they be regarded as evidence; other of course than evidence as to some people's opinions.

Some who perhaps ought to know better use the word 're- search' when they mean informed discussion and they are in danger of adding to the confusion. For example, there are Fabian Society Research Series pamphlets as distinct from Fabian Tracts. The The first are intended to be of a more factual objective nature than the second which are permitted to have a political bias. But whereas some of them may, not all of them can be regarded as research. For example Fabian Research Series 224 *The Housing Problem*[20] can be so regarded, but Fabian Research Series 231 *The Ingleby Report*[21] cannot. This was composed of three critical essays none of which involved research. This is not to say, of course, that they did not make a useful contribution to social thinking on child care and juvenile delinquency. The student must not get the idea that only research is valuable to this end.

As well as what is clear territory of research or empirical investi- gation in social administration, there may also be something of a no man's land or twilight area. In this it is arguable whether or not the work undertaken can be regarded as research. One example was the report of the Care of Children Committee, 1946 (the Curtis Committee).[22] In so far as this Committee obtained factual evidence of the conditions under which deprived children were living at the time and based their conclusions thereon, their work could be regarded as research. Such evidence the Committee did obtain in respect of 41 counties, but they gave no indication in what way they selected those counties, nor why in them they selected particular workhouses, schools, Homes and foster homes to visit. Nor did they reveal their frame of reference in looking at those institutions or questioning any of the staff or children. There was no way, therefore, of judging whether such research as there was resulted in statistically significant data.

The same observation may be made of the report of the Committee on Maladjusted Children, 1955 (the Underwood Committee); the members of which 'visited, individually or in small groups, a selection of the establishments providing treatment for maladjusted children'.[23] How many establishments, of what nature, how selected, where and to what end, the report did not state. In short it was, in the main, historical and descriptive, not evidential.

To sum up: It may be said that it can only be decided whether the work of any particular committee can be regarded as constituting social research, in part or in whole, by a study of its report and an examination of the nature and method of its deliberations. The student can exercise his judgement in this matter, in the field of social policy and administration, by looking at some, or better still all the reports of the royal commissions and committees of enquiry given in Chapter Nine.

Two American observers once expressed the view that social research in England had resulted in the formulation of social policy and the introduction of social legislation in this country to a far greater degree than in the U.S.A.[24] The reason for this was said by them to lie not in the nature or methods of the research but in the different historical and philosophical backgrounds of the two countries; including concepts of freedom and individual responsibility. England had been more willing, they said, to accept State reforms and public services than the U.S.A. which had put its faith in rugged individualism and the moral virtue of personal effort and initiative to overcome the evils revealed by social research. This suggested that attitudes of mind constitute one factor in encouraging the use of evidence that such research reveals.

There is no reasons why if the Government in this country has a mind to it that the full facts on which policy in any area of social welfare should be based, should not be collected as often as is necessary. In 1941 the Government Social Survey was organised as a Division of the Central Office of Information to undertake surveys on behalf of any government department at its request, or on behalf of bodies such as departmental committees of enquiry. Mention has already been made of the use of the Social Survey in 1948 to estimate the demand for hearing aids and of its use in 1959 by the Central Advisory Council for Education (England). It has also been employed in medical research, research into food consumption, London housing, the employment of women in industry, domiciliary meals services for the old, the home help service, and in many other areas of social welfare. In April 1967 the Social Survey became a separate department with its own Controller reporting directly to Treasury Ministers.

The tide is clearly turning towards more government social research and of departmental committees of enquiry. The three most recent reports on education support this view. The report on those between the ages of 13 and 16 of average or less than average ability who are or will be following full-time courses either at school or in establishments of further education (the Newsom Committee Report), 1963;[25] that on full-time higher education in Great Britain (the Robbins Committee Report), 1963,[26] and that on children and their primary schools (the Plowden Committee Report), 1968;[27] all show appreciation of the necessity for research before reaching conclusions and making recommendations about education policy.

The Home Office, concerned about the continuing problem of delinquency, established a research unit in 1957 and has since then financially assisted a number of research projects into causation of crime and the results of treatment of offenders. Further to this the Home Secretary informed the House of Commons in February 1967 that the Home Office Advisory Council on the Penal System had set up a standing sub-committee on criminological research which had taken the place of the existing Home Office Research Advisory Committee. The sub-committee was intended to provide a forum for advice on the make-up of criminological research programmes and to inform the department about research generally.

In March 1964 the Home Secretary announced that he and the

Secretary of State for Education and Science had commissioned the National Foundation for Education Research to undertake a research project into the factors in the organisation and life of a school that might affect the attitudes, behaviour and attainments of school children, with the hope of discovering how variations in these factors might exert a positive influence on educational attainment and personal development and social adjustment.

More recent departmental research included the needs of the old[28] and the problem of poverty.[29] Both these projects followed similar research undertaken by other persons but though late in the day they constituted signs of growing appreciation by government of the need for information about continuing social problems upon which action could be based.

Having been very critical of the Ministry of Housing and Local Government for its lack until recently of research on housing problems Donnison observed in 1967: 'Times have changed.' He pointed out that the Ministry now had a competent statistical staff, a sociological survey unit, a consultant economist, and that its staff were collaborating with an expanding circle of research workers in universities and elsewhere.[30]

The Government announced a decision in May 1963 to set up a Committee on Social Studies (the Heyworth Committee) to review research in the field of social studies and look into the question of establishing a Social Science Research Council. The need for such an enquiry was first raised in Parliament in 1960 and the delay in taking positive action did not suggest any great sense of urgency. But when the Heyworth Committee finally made its report in June 1965 the Government agreed in principle to the setting up of a Social Science Research Council, under the aegis of the Secretary of State for Education and Science, to provide stronger support and better co-ordination of research in the field of social studies. Such a Council was set up in December 1965 with terms of reference covering the social sciences, defined as demography, economics and econometrics, political science and international relations, social psychology, social anthropology, industrial relations, sociology and social administration and social and economic statistics.

The initial expenditure of the Council was estimated as £600,000 in its first year rising to £2,250,000 in its fourth year. This expenditure was to be in respect of research grants at universities and postgraduate training in relevant subjects, but it was to include awards then administered by the Department of Industrial and Social Research. Thus not all the estimated expenditure was to be additional to existing sums and only a very substantial real increase can give reality to the Government's verbal recognition of the important role of the social scientist in the formation and execution of social policy. Otherwise too much will still be left to individual effort; to universities; or independent institutions of social research; with or without financial aid from private trusts. Since it is government that will reach final decisions on matters of social policy, concern will remain until acceptance of public responsibility in social welfare is fully matched by acceptance of public responsibility in obtaining the facts on which that policy should be based.

Power to undertake research is written into many pieces of social legislation. Section 82 of the Education Act, 1944, gives power to a local education authority, with the approval of the Minister of Education (now Secretary of State for Education and Science) to make provision for conducting or assisting the conduct of research as appears to the authority to be desirable, for the purpose of improving the educational facilities provided for their area. Section 16 of the National Health Service Act, 1946, empowers the Minister of Health to conduct, or assist by grants or otherwise, any person to conduct research into any matters relating to the causation, prevention, diagnosis or treatment of illness, and boards of governors of teaching hospitals, regional hospital boards and hospital management committees are likewise empowered to conduct such research. Section 73 of the National Insurance (Industrial Injuries) Act, 1946, empowers the Minister of Pensions and National Insurance, later the Minister of Social Security, to promote or conduct research, or assist financially or otherwise others engaged in research into the causes and incidence of and methods of prevention of accident, injuries and disease against which persons are insured under the Act.

Sections 2 and 3 of the Health Visiting and Social Work (Training) Act, 1962, gives to the Council for the Training of Health Visitors and to the Council for Training in Social Work powers to carry out, or assist other persons in carrying out, research into matters relating to the training of health visitors or for social work in the health and welfare services. And Section 5 of the Act empowers the Minister of Health and the Secretary of State for the Home Department to promote research into any matter relating to the functions of local authorities under Part III of the National Assistance Act and to participate with or assist other persons in conducting such research. Local welfare authorities are also empowered to conduct or assist other persons in conducting similar research. But the explanatory memorandum which preceded this Act included a statement that additional expenditure on research would be very small, an observation that led to much criticism.

Section 77 of the Criminal Justice Act, 1948, authorises public expenditure on the conduct of research into the causes of delinquency and the treatment of offenders. Section 45 of the Children and Young Persons Act, 1963, empowers the Secretary of State to conduct, or assist other persons in conducting, research into any matter connected with his functions or the functions of local authorities under that Act, or the Children and Young Persons Acts, 1933 to 1956, the Children Acts, 1948 and 1958, or any matter connected with the adoption of children. Clause 71 (1) of the London Government Act, 1963, goes further than merely making possible conduct of research and requires that the Greater London Council shall run a research and information department for the collection of information relating to any matter affecting Greater London; such information to be made available to any authority concerned with local government, any government department or the public. The Greater London Council now has a Research and Intelligence Unit under a Director of Research and Intelligence, to carry out the statutory duty laid upon it.

It is clear in all these instances that if there is the will there is the way for research necessary for the formulation or re-formulation of social policy to be undertaken. At the same time the difficulties of instituting effective social research to these ends, which Glass enumerated in 1950, remain—that policy given expression at a particular point of time is often intended to serve for an undefined period—that those who make social policy are seldom fully explicit as to their objectives or assumptions—that policy is never single-minded but results from the struggle between competing demands

—that there are irrational, self-satisfying and ignorant elements in policy making.[31]

To these may be added the fact that social research may reveal such a volume of unmet need that for political reasons it is either not undertaken or its results are not published. Nevertheless it is true to say that there is growing appreciation of the importance of social research on the part of statutory and voluntary bodies alike and this chapter can well be closed with a paragraph from the report of the Committee on Local Authority Personal and Allied Services (the Seebohm Committee), referred to in Chapter Six, which stands even though that Committee did not hold that reorganisation of local government personal social services should wait until after research and experiment had taken place.

'We cannot emphasise too strongly', the Committee said, 'the part which research must play in the creation and maintenance of an effective family service. Social planning is an illusion without adequate facts; and the adequacy of services mere speculation without evaluation. Nor is it sufficient for research to be done spasmodically however good it be. It must be a continuing process accepted as a familiar and permanent feature of any department or agency concerned with social provision.'[32]

The student interested, but not experienced in social research may find the following short studies on planning and method useful:

The National Old People's Welfare Council, *A Short Guide to Social Survey Methods*, National Council of Social Service, 1960, Reference No. 579.

Ralph Berry, *How to write a research paper*, Pergamon Press Ltd., 1966.

K. M. Evans, *Planning Small Scale Research*, National Foundation for Educational Research in England and Wales, 1968.

CHAPTER SIX

Human Needs and the Social Services

Consideration has been given now to the meaning of social administration, to social administration and the social sciences, to social policy and the Welfare State, and to the wisdom of social research accompanying the making of social policy. It is to the social services, which are the embodiment of positive social policy in practice, to which attention is now turned. Whilst the student should have a full knowledge of the administrative structure and the content of the social services, it is not intended to examine these in detail here. This has already been done elsewhere and it is possible to turn to existing sources of information for the fuller knowledge which is essential.* Nor is more said about the meaning of 'social services'. The difficulty of definition has already been discussed in Chapter One. Attention is centred rather in the purpose of the services commonly regarded as social. Indeed more light may be shed on what they are by an examination of what they do—or are intended to do—than by seeking further for definition.

* See (i) *Penelope Hall's Social Services of England and Wales*, Ed. Anthony Forder, Routledge and Kegan Paul Ltd., 1969.

(ii) *An Introduction to the Study of Social Administration*, Ed. David C. Marsh, Routledge and Kegan Paul Ltd., 1965.

(iii) *Local Health and Welfare Services*, Julia Parker, George Allen & Unwin, 1965.

(iv) *Consumer's Guide to the British Social Services*, Phyllis Willmott, Penguin Books Ltd., 1967.

The following Reference Pamphlets (available from H.M.S.O.) and Reference Papers (available from C.O.I.) also serve as useful guides:

Reference Pamphlet No. 1. Local Government in Britain
No. 3. Social Services in Britain
No. 9. Town and Country Planning in Britain
No. 20. Health Services in Britain
No. 34. Children in Britain
No. 35. The Treatment of Offenders in Britain
No. 40. The Central Government of Britain
No. 44. The New Towns of Britain
Reference Paper R5506 Youth Service in Britain
R5675 Family and Community Services in Britain

Stated baldly, the social services are designed to meet various kinds of human need, of the individual and of society as a whole, that cannot be met without some form of outside assistance. These needs can be categorised in a variety of ways. First, there are those consequent upon the unavoidable dependencies of child-birth, infancy, childhood and adolescence, and whilst preparing for adult status and employment. Secondly, there are the needs of the mature adult, and thirdly there are those of old age if and when it is accompanied by infirmity of mind or body. The first and last categories involve dependencies arising from normal stages of human life common to everyone; other than those whose life comes to an untimely end. The second category involves dependencies which arise from misfortune which may include poverty, unemployment, sickness, disability, homelessness or poor housing, unmarried parenthood, widowhood, or marriage breakdown.

There is another category of a particular nature. This comprises the need of the offender, whether inside or outside the prison or other detentional institution, together with that of his or her family. Such a person may be regarded by some as having brought misfortune upon himself and thus not a proper recipient of the benefits of the social services. The history of penal reform and treatment of the offender, however, shows a steady and constant departure from such a view. To meet the needs of the offender and the misfortune of his family is, therefore, looked upon here as a proper function of the social services.

The extent or degree of need or needs in a man's life may vary in the different circumstances of his life, as also in different income groups, different periods of time under differing conditions of living, but the basic nature of the needs remain the same. Whilst they can be aggravated by economic, environmental or social stress it makes no difference whether a man is born into a developed or an under-developed country, into a rural or an urban community, into an extended or a nuclear family. His needs as a human being are the same. It is misleading when reference is made, as it often is, to the changing nature of human need or to the rise of new needs. For example: 'Demographic, economic, political and administrative factors are particularly important in helping to generate needs. . . .'[1] These factors do not generate, if by this is meant bring needs into existence. They may produce new problems of living which identify, emphasise or extend existing needs. They do not cause the needs themselves.

Or again: 'Human needs arise by virtue of the kind of society to which individuals belong.'[2] They do not. They arise from the nature of man himself. He has a need for food, clothing and shelter, for contact with other social beings, for occupation and education (in its widest sense), for rest and play, for care in illness, disability or infirmity. These do not change. What does change is the way in which, or the extent to which, needs are satisfied, and the understanding of what they are, how they arise and whether or not they can be met.

If human needs are not met men die, or live short, stunted or impoverished lives, in ignorance, ill health or unhappiness. This they have frequently done in the past, still do in many parts of the world today and would do to a greater extent in this, if the social services no longer existed. The incidence, extent, or severity of need can change. They themselves remain the same. What may appear to be a new need is simply an old one writ large, or one which once was but is no longer met. Thus the contemporary problem of loneliness amongst old people arises, not from any new need, but from the fact that more of the old are living alone, are without families, or suffer greater physical or mental infirmities by reason of the fact that many of them live longer. It is the change in their circumstances, not of their need, that gives rise to the necessity for some social service to mitigate or resolve the problems which arise from the lack of human contacts which all human beings require.

The fact that more disabled people live today than once was the case, because of improved medical treatment, does not give rise to a new need. The disabled have always had need of care and attention which they cannot give to themselves. But in the past they have often gone without it and more would do so today, or to a greater extent than they do, if social services did not make some provision, even if not enough, for them. It is the extent of need and the recognition of its nature, and the means to satisfy it, that have changed and not the need itself.

This view of needs is supported in the report of the Committee on Local Authority and Allied Personal Social Services (the

D

Seebohm Committee), which observed: 'We do not suggest that all countries will find similar solutions to (such) problems. But the fact that (these) problems have been so widely recognised at much the same time by countries at similar stages of social and economic development suggests the emergence of new and changing *conceptions** of the nature of human need and the manner in which it can best be met.' The Committee, it is true, referred later in the report to voluntary organisations playing a major role in revealing new needs. Unmet need is what the Committee in fact meant in this instance.[3]

The same view of needs was born out, unexpectedly enough, in a booklet published in 1963 entitled *New Thinking for Changing Needs*.[4] Whilst this title in itself suggests the above argument is wrong, the content of the booklet supports it as right. This comprised considerations of marital problems, unmarried parenthood, deprived or disturbed children, mental illness and teaching in social work. None of these, except the last, which is not of itself a human need, is in any way new. Each situation or condition is found throughout the history of man. What may be new or changing is the incidence or degree of need, the attitudes of society towards it or the recognition that it has yet to be met. Fresh thinking on unmet need, or new provision for continuing need, would thus have been a more appropriate description of the subject-matter.

Some individual needs may on occasion be so gross and so obvious that to overlook them becomes increasingly impossible, as when the physical needs of the barefoot, ragged, undernourished children shocked the conscience of Octavia Hill and others as they moved about the streets of Victorian London. Other needs may lie hidden or half hidden behind general prosperity, as today when an infirm and aged person lives alone and lonely in the dirt and discomfort of a slum dwelling which long since should have been demolished. Other needs may be generally recognised only when studies confirm that what is suspected is correct; that the emotional need of a deprived child, for example, calls most often for the love of a substitute mother rather than the impersonal care of a large orphanage. In other instances need is revealed or heightened by the changing conditions of life of minority groups;

* Author's italics.

of immigrants or gypsies, for example, faced with new ways of life in an unfamiliar environment.

In some instances the nature or extent of individual need is revealed only if and when a service is actually made available or, put another way, when the supply begins to meet the demand. As Davies pointed out: 'The extent to which people know about what services are available is clearly an important factor influencing the amount of need revealed.'[5]

One example of this is to be found in the response of young people to the first centre opened to offer them help and advice in confidence in any kind of personal trouble or anxiety. This was the Young People's Consultation Centre in Hampstead which was established in June 1961 by the Youth Studies and Research Foundation which was used by nearly 550 young people in that and the following three years. Since then a number of other centres of the same nature have been opened, both by voluntary bodies and local authorities, to be concerned with domestic, parental, or sexual difficulties of young people, or alcoholism or drug addiction amongst them. The provision and knowledge of such facilities both generate 'demand'; that is to say, increase the use or wish to use a service. This in fact is one of the major problems of planning to meet or assessing need. It may grow on what it feeds on.

Provision of an improved service can also encourage an increased demand for satisfaction of a need previously only partly met, as when the Assistance Board (the successor to the Unemployment Assistance Board and predecessor to the National Assistance Board) took over from the Poor Law in 1940 the function of paying supplementary pensions to old people, who at once applied for grants in substantially increased numbers.

Recognition or revelation of individual need can be hindered by a variety of factors—lack of sympathy or concern on the part of those in a position to introduce measures to meet it—genuine ignorance about personal suffering or social conditions—misunderstanding of causes—fear, guilt, pride or shame on the part of those in need and their consequent hesitation or refusal to ask for help or to make known their misfortunes. All these discourage or delay the introduction or extension of social services, just as may such practical problems as lack of trained personnel, economic setback,* or the pursuit of goals other than human welfare. But whenever or wherever a social service is introduced it is to meet a need that has, whether soon or late, been recognised as real and unmet. Associated with the categories of individual need are the needs of a society to maintain and protect itself, to develop its resources, raise its standard of living, and compete or co-operate in the international market and affairs of the world. These require that its members are educated, trained, physically and mentally fit, and generally able to contend with the challenge of modern life.

Social services to meet human need can be regarded today as having four objectives—to prevent or reduce suffering, premature death, or social ill when and where this is possible—to protect the weak or vulnerable from dangers or pressures which they cannot stand up against alone—to redress the balance whereby some people are deprived of opportunities available to others—and to promote in a positive way the good of each and of society as a whole. Examples of these four objectives are to be found respectively in the health services, the child care service, the concept of positive discrimination and the education service. It is clear, of course, that successful promotion often involves protection and always requires prevention. The objectives go hand in hand. But they can and should be distinguished the one from the other, for the importance of one may take precedence in particular situations or times. Or the pursuit of one may be neglected in the pursuit of another, as when more is spent on promoting the good of deprived children than in preventing the homelessness of the family from which they came and which caused their deprivation in the first place.

The four objectives—prevention of suffering—protection of the weak—redress of balance—promotion of individual and social good—are never ending and so therefore are the social services, and this is no cause for concern unless one shares Seldon's view that: 'The notion that the social services are here to stay for all time is not ennobling but degrading. . . . We must see [them] as dispensable. Their only place in a free society is to help make

---

* For an examination of the problems of meeting needs in conditions of scarce resources see: R. A. Parker 'Social Administration and Scarcity', *Social Work*. Vol. 24, No. 2. April 1967.

themselves superfluous.'[6] This view emerged as part of an argument that State assistance is fully justified in some cases and could be more generous if it were not uniform but adapted to the circumstances of the individual, but the permanence and universality of all services is to be criticised. One would not willingly accept the social services as never ending either if one agreed with the speaker in the House of Lords debate who said that the welfare services 'represent failures' and the view that everyone will use them sometime 'is awful . . . a shocking attitude' to take, because 'the things we have to deal with in the welfare services are loathsome and should be got rid of'.[7]

But is there evidence that any of the social services can be dispensed with or made superfluous?* Do the welfare services necessarily represent failure and are the things they deal with always loathsome? Before attempting an answer to these questions one last point is made about human need. To need and to want are not identical although they may be simultaneous. There are three possible combinations: 'I want and I need'; 'I want although I do not need'; 'I need but I do not want'.

Thus: 'I want and I need a home help' may mean, 'I live in my own home but am physically disabled and cannot clean my house myself'; 'I want but I do not need a home help' may mean, 'I live in may own home, am quite capable physically and mentally but I do not like housework'; 'I need but I do not want a home help' may mean, 'I live in my own home and am physically disabled, but I would rather live in dirt and disorder than have someone else busybodying about my house.'

These differences between needs and wants are obviously important when it comes to attempting any assessment of the nature and extent of need. If the satisfaction of all human wants, as well as all human needs, were to come within the purview of the social services the mind would indeed reel. But they do not and one can, therefore, return realistically to attempt to answer the questions posed above.

The first dependency need of human life is that of the newborn infant who has a physical need to be fed, clothed, and sheltered, and an emotional need to be loved. He is wholly dependent on

* For an examination of the future of the social services see: *The Political Quarterly* (Special Issue), Volume 40 No. 1. January–March, 1969.

others for the satisfaction of these needs and they are closely linked with those of his mother for medical care and attention before, in, and after childbirth. Satisfaction is fundamental, not only to individual physical and mental health, but to the preservation of life itself and consequently to the maintenance of society. There is evidence to show, however, that for many the needs were long unmet, with consequent personal suffering and wastage of human life.

It was the high maternal and infant mortality rates of the nineteenth century that led to the introduction of maternity and child welfare services designed to meet the primary needs of the mother and her baby. The first health visiting service was begun by a voluntary committee in Manchester and Salford in 1862 to help and advise mothers in child care, clothing and feeding and the first infant welfare centre was opened in St Helens, Lancashire, in 1899. These proved to be the advance guards of a service which gradually extended its scope to include not only advice about infant feeding and clothing, but the supply of cheap milk and foodstuffs for nursing mothers and children of pre-school age, medical care, and finally ante- as well as post-natal care in hospital clinics as well as welfare centres.

Maternal and infant mortality fell in England and Wales from 5·31 and 149 respectively per 1,000 live births in 1890–92, but in 1919 the first was still 4·87 and the second 109 per 1,000 live births. After the First World War the maternity and child welfare services were, therefore, developed further. The Maternity and Child Welfare Act, 1918, empowered local authorities, with the aid of exchequer grants, to make arrangements for safeguarding the health of expectant mothers and children under five and required them if they did so to appoint special maternity and child welfare committees to be responsible for the service. This could include health visiting, midwifery, home helps, day nurseries, ante- and post-natal clinics, dental treatment, maternity hospitals, and the supply of free or cheap milk and foods for mothers and young children.

The services provided still failed, however, even in the 1930s and the 1940s, to meet need fully. Evidence of this failure is to be found in the Final Report of the Ministry of Health Departmental Committee on Maternal Mortality and Morbidity, 1932; of the

Ministry of Health Report on an Investigation into Maternal Mortality, 1937, and a Report of the Royal College of Obstetricians and Gynaecologists on a National Maternity Service, 1944. The first of these concluded on its investigations that had there been forethought on the part of the expectant mother and her attendant, with a reasonable degree of skill in the care of each one, together with the provision and use of adequate facilities for treatment, then at least one half of the maternal deaths occurring in the country would have been preventable.[8] The maternal mortality rate had in fact actually risen and in 1929 was 5·82, although infant mortality had fallen dramatically to 74.

The second report was of an investigation directed to the discovery of why, despite extension of services, and improvement in the general health of the community, the maternal mortality rate still had not fallen and was persistently high in certain areas. Its conclusion was that the rate in the country as a whole was capable of reduction.[3] The Ministry of Health drew the attention of local authorities to these facts, and urged improvements in services upon them. Maternal mortality fell to 2·5 in 1942, but the third report mentioned above regarded this as by no means commensurate with the great improvement in medical science and said that the rate could be forced considerably lower. Of neonatal mortality (in the first month of life), although this had fallen consistently, it said the figures did not bear comparison with what had been achieved in other countries.[10]

It was on this background that the National Health Service Act, 1946, imposed a *duty* on local health authorities:

'to make arrangements for the care, including in particular dental care, of expectant and nursing mothers and of children who have not attained the age of five years and are not attending primary schools maintained by a local education authority'.

Before the Act came into effect a further report was published in 1948, of 'the first large scale attempt to collect basic information with which to measure how fully [the maternity and child welfare services] are used and how far they fulfil the purposes for which they are designed'.[11] This report criticised the services on several counts and observed that child-bearing was a cause of much avoidable ill health. It hoped that the free provisions of the

National Health Service would improve the situation. But ten years after its inception a report of the Committee on Maternity Services to the Ministry of Health, 1959, concluded both that the hospital maternity service needed to be expanded and that a more uniformly high standard of ante-natal care was essential.[12]

By 1963 maternal mortality had fallen to 0·30 and infant mortality to 21·7. Deaths from infectious diseases to which children are particularly prone had been largely overcome. Nevertheless a report on perinatal mortality (still births and deaths in the first week of life) published in 1963 observed that whilst it might be concluded from the reduction in maternal mortality and still births that there was not much room for improvement, nothing could be further from the truth. Still births and deaths during the first month of life totalled 666 in the survey week and it was believed that many of the perinatal deaths could have been prevented had proper care been given during confinement and after. Amongst poorer mother who received the worst ante-natal care perinatal mortality actually increased between 1950–58.[13]

By 1966 the maternal mortality rate had fallen to 0·26 and the infant mortality rate to 19·6 but there still remained clear evidence that if the first dependency needs of life are to be met maternal and child welfare services are a continuing necessity. No doubt the increase in national prosperity has been an important contributory factor in the fall of the maternal and infant mortality rates but of itself it is not enough to maintain health and save life to the highest extent possible.

If the problem of illegitimacy is considered the continuing need is even clearer. Fluctuations in the percentage of illegitimate births is not relevant to the present discussion. It is enough to say that in 1966 it was 7·6 per cent of all live births. Although small proportionately this represented 74,000 children, and illegitimacy inevitably involves great difficulties not only for them but for their parents, more especially their mothers. Infant mortality has always been higher amongst illegitimate babies, although less so now than in the nineteenth and early twentieth centuries. Even so, in 1964 the number of deaths of infants under one year of age per 1,000 illegitimately born was 26 compared with 19 per 1,000 legitimately born. Post-natal mortality rates due to diseases of the respiratory system, enteritis, diarrhoea, congenital malformation and accidents have been particularly high amongst the illegitimate.

The social services have always been available for everyone alike—the married or unmarried, legitimate or illegitimate—whether harshly under the Poor Law, without prejudice in the maternity and child welfare services, or in the cash payments of family allowances, social security grants and maternity benefits. The essential fact, however, is that the illegitimate child:

'is different not because he is illegitimate but because he is fatherless and he is going to miss a father in the same way that any child who loses his father early, through death or separation, misses him', and because 'a single mother is having to go alone through the experience of becoming a parent, an experience which was intended to be shared and in which the deepest emotional demands cry out for the missing partner'.[14]*

It is these two fundamental facts that call, where there is unmarried parenthood, for services additional to those available for the mother and child born in normal circumstances. The old reformatory and orphanage were the forerunners of the more enlightened mother and baby homes begun before the First World War by voluntary societies and church organisations. These provide a place where the mother may stay, before and after the birth of her baby, help her to get work if necessary and find accommodation where she may have her baby with her if she is able and wishes to keep him. But this is not easy and local authorities have always varied considerably in the extent of provision they must make under Section 22 of the National Health Service Act in respect of expectant and nursing mothers and children under the age of five. The large majority rely, so far as the unmarried mother is concerned, upon denominational voluntary bodies whom they grant aid but who often nevertheless struggle with acute shortages of money and staff.

In 1918 the National Council for the Unmarried Mother and her Child was formed to act as a central organisation for the relief, protection and welfare of unmarried mothers and their children, to consider questions and promote legislation affecting their welfare, and to give monetary and other assistance for their

* See also Virginia Wimperis, *The Unmarried Mother and her Child*, Allen and Unwin, 1960.

D*

benefit. Its Annual Report for the year ended March 1963, referred to the fact that often a mother parts with her child, which she would not do if there were more adequate long term supporting services and a more tolerant public opinion. Other mothers seek foster homes or residential nurseries because they find financial pressure and the difficulty of finding accommodation too much for them. There is an obvious need for hostel accommodation before the mother and baby home stage and for lodgings, hostels and local authority housing afterwards, and for an extension of day nurseries.

In a policy memorandum of February 1964, the Council compared the position of unmarried mothers in this country, where approximately 60 per cent keep their children, to Denmark where more extensive social and financial provisions are available and 93 per cent of the mothers keep their children. The general position was summed up by the Council as follows:

'Evidence from all over the country indicates that accommodation for the mother keeping her child is an urgent need and only a few small pioneer efforts have been started. A distressing number of unmarried mothers and their babies end up in Part III accommodation.'*

At a conference on fatherless families organised in 1964 by the National Council for the Unmarried Mother and her Child and the Council for Children's Welfare a plea was made for pressure to be brought to bear upon the Government to set up an inter-departmental committee to review the needs of such children and other incomplete families. A question incorporating a request to the Prime Minister to set up a royal commission to review the position of fatherless families was made in the House of Commons on April 27, 1965, but the Prime Minister replied that in view of the survey of social security provisions then under way he did not consider that any committee of inquiry was necessary. The provisions of the Ministry of Social Security Act, 1966, made little difference, however, to the position of fatherless families and the view expressed by the National Council for the Unmarried Mother and her Child in its 46th Annual Report 1965–66 that the time had come for re-thinking national policy towards the illegit-

* Temporary accommodation for the homeless provided by local authorities under Part III, Section 21, of the National Assistance Act, 1948.

imate, including realistic financial provision for fatherless children, with social services to compensate them for their emotional and social disabilities is still relevant. The only criticism that could perhaps be made of that observation is that it is questionable whether there is in this country, or ever has been, a 'national policy towards the illegitimate', and all that the N.C.U.M.C. has pointed out over recent years still stands.

Whereas the maternity and child welfare services are designed to meet the needs of mother, infant and pre-school child, dependencies continue without a break into middle and later years of childhood. They are different partly in degree and partly in kind but they still demand services for their satisfaction. The growing child has need of more food and exercise for his physical development. His mind develops and his interests widen. He has potential abilities and skills that should be developed both for his own benefit and, in due course, for that of others. In a primitive community these needs can be met in the circle of the family or kin, within the narrow confines of a self-supporting community. In a commercial and industrial society increasing demands are made upon the individual for a high degree of knowledge, technical skill, or professional qualification, and for a high standard of health for the sake of the community as a whole. Finally, the parent cannot meet unaided either his child's physical or his educational needs. He has not himself the knowledge or the means to do so.

Health, welfare and education services are required, therefore, for the growing child. Apart from elementary education itself, however, such services were not provided until after gross deficiencies in adults were revealed by a report in 1904 of an interdepartmental committee on physical deterioration, which had been appointed to consider the large number of rejects for the army because of physical causes at the time of the Boer War. With this report came the realisation that health in manhood requires care in childhood and there followed the first school welfare and health services, apart from medical inspection which had been permitted under the Elementary Education Act of 1870.

The school welfare and health services were provided under the Education (Provision of Meals) Act, 1906, and the Education (Administrative Provisions) Act, 1907. The first empowered local education authorities to provide meals and milk to children in elementary schools if they were unable by reason of lack of food to take full advantage of the education provided for them. The second introduced the school health service under which authorities were required to arrange medical examination at certain intervals in the child's school life and were empowered to provide facilities for medical treatment. After a slow beginning this led to the setting up of school clinics throughout the country and the appointment of school doctors and nurses to staff them. Not until 1944, however, spurred on by the demands of the war years, was the provision of school meals as well as medical treatment laid as a duty upon local education authorities.

The original intention had been that school meals should be provided free of charge in all primary and secondary schools but in the event the provision was subsidised in part only. A charge of 1s. a meal was instituted. This was raised to 1s. 6d. in 1968, remitted, as before, in necessitous cases. Free milk was removed at the same time in secondary schools, the payment of full cost being required of parents of secondary school children.

These changes constitute one example of a universalist social policy giving way to a selective one, the provision of benefit or full benefit being made available only for those regarded as in need or greatest need. How far the change was due entirely or mainly to a genuine change in policy and how far to the economic stringency of the time it is however difficult to say. But whatever the case, and whatever the outcome the days when children attended school with gross evidence of illness, disability, fatigue, malnutrition and dirt are now long since past. And also those when:

'Many of the doctors were indifferent while others ridiculed the findings of the school medical officers and informed the parents that there was nothing wrong with the child or that treatment was unnecessary even when the defect was unhealthy tonsils as large as plums or a squint that could be recognised at a distance.'[15]

That improved health of school children is due entirely to services in the school is not of course the case. Many social and economic factors enter in. But without the school services it is improbable there would have been so substantial an improvement. Even so the position is not as good as it should be.

The report of the Chief Medical Officer of the Department of

Education and Science on 'The Health of the School Child, 1964 and 1965',[16] showed that only a minority of local education authorities undertook annual or biennial vision testing of school children; that 'too many' children still did not benefit from the school dental service; and that the number of school doctors was not keeping pace with the rising school population with the consequence that some school health commitments were not, or were only partially being met.

To discard the school health and welfare services would not yet appear to be justified, even if it ever is. This view had the support of the Medical Services Review Committee (the Porritt Committee) which is referred to in more detail in Chapter Nine, which regarded the school health service as performing a special and valuable function which must be continued.[17]

Clearly it is not only in relation to his physical and mental health that the school child is dependent upon others. He has need for education itself; a service which crept forward but slowly for the best part of 100 years. From the 1830s to the 1930s Lowndes described the situation as successive British Governments endeavouring 'to purchase an educated democracy on the instalment plan'.[18] The first instalment was a State grant of £20,000 made in 1833 for the erection of voluntary schools. The second was the Elementary Education Act, 1870, which set up School Boards to provide rate and tax aided elementary schools where voluntary provision was inadequate. The third was the Elementary Education Act, 1876, which laid upon parents the duty of seeing their children received efficient elementary education and prohibited employment during school hours of children under ten years of age who lived within ten miles of a school. This Act set up School Attendance Committees for areas where there were no elected School Boards. The fourth instalment came in 1880 when school attendance was made obligatory for all children between the ages of five and ten. The fifth was the abolition of payment of fees in elementary schools in 1891 and the sixth was the Elementary Education (School Attendance) Act, 1893, fixing at eleven the age at which a child could be exempted from attending school. This was raised to twelve in 1899.

Thus in the last thirty years of the nineteenth century the provision of education came to be accepted as a State responsibility;

attendance for a short period of a child's life was made compulsory; and free provision became the rule rather than the exception. In quantity and quality the service remained defective, however, at least according to present-day standards, and the twentieth century has seen a slow and continuous battle to raise the school leaving age and provide secondary, technical and further education for all who can benefit from them.

The first milestone of this century was the establishment of the Board of Education in 1900 under the Board of Education Act, 1899. The second was the replacement of the old School Boards by local education authorities, under the Education Act of 1902. This establishment of both central and local authorities was a necessary step towards a comprehensive national policy in education. Technical and higher education was encouraged and secondary education could be provided out of public funds. No other major developments took place before the First World War. The Education Act, 1918, raised the school leaving age from twelve to fourteen, gave local authorities powers to provide nursery schools, opened private schools to voluntary inspection, and finally abolished all fees in public elementary schools. But its professed intention of providing for 'the progressive development and comprehensive organisation of education available for all persons capable of profiting thereby' failed as a result of the post-war economic situation and financial stringency.

The period between the wars is noted less for educational progress than for the educational reports which set the policy for development after 1944; the report of the Committee on the Education of the Adolescent, 1926 (the Hadow Committee)[19]; the report of the Committee on Secondary Education, 1938 (the Spens Committee)[20]; the report of the Committee on Secondary School Curriculum and School Examinations, 1942 (the Norwood Committee)[21]. The Education Act, 1944, was a second attempt to introduce a planned comprehensive educational system but again post-war problems blocked progress. The Ministry of Education, as it then was, in its report for the year 1950 itself admitted that the goal was unattained.

Four reports of the Central Advisory Council for Education (England)—'Early Leaving',[22] '15 to 18',[23] 'Half our Future',[24] 'Children and their Primary Schools'[25]—which appeared between 1954 and 1967, together with the report of the Committee on Higher Education (the Robbins Committee),[26] all provided evidence that this was still the case two decades later, with a consequent lack of educational opportunity and wastage of ability amongst young people. The Central Advisory Council repeatedly urged that the school leaving age should be raised to sixteen without delay, but not until January 1964 did the Government announce a decision to do this in 1970, a date which was further postponed in the financial stringency of 1968.

No reference, however, was made by the Government to County Colleges for part-time education up to the age of eighteen; a provision which was to have been a duty of local education authorities under the Education Act, 1944. The urgent necessity to expand provision for those finishing grammar school education was generally recognised before the publication of the Robbins Committee report with its recommendations for the expansion of places for full-time students in higher education and a substantial increase in public expenditure, both of which were accepted in principle by the Government, but have still to be fully achieved in practice.*

In conclusion, what Lowndes said about the education service in 1937 can be repeated today:

'The millennium is still a long way off. So long as there is one child who has failed to obtain the precise educational treatment his individuality requires . . . so long as the nation fails to train and provide scope for every atom of understanding ability it can find; so long . . . the system will remain incomplete.'[27]†

Before leaving the education service reference must be made to the provisions for children with special needs that arise from the misfortunes of defect or disability, whether of mind or body. No provision was made for the education of such children, other than by voluntary bodies, until 1893 when the Elementary Education

* For a survey of the action taken on the major educational reports up to 1968 see: Anne Corbett, *Much to do about Education*. Council for Educational Advance, 1968.

† For a fuller account of English education up to the 1940s see: H. C. Barnard, *A Short History of English Education from 1760*, London University Press, 2nd ed. 1961, and for the period 1918–1944 see: Gerald Birnbaum, *Social Change and the Schools 1918–1944*, Routledge and Kegan Paul, 1967.

(Blind and Deaf Children) Act made it a duty of every school authority to provide education for blind and deaf children up to the age of sixteen. The Elementary Education (Defective and Epileptic Children) Act, 1899, empowered authorities to provide training for physically and mentally defective, and epileptic children. These powers became a duty so far as mentally defective children were concerned in 1914 and for physically defective and epileptic children in 1918. In 1902 the newly formed local education authorities were given power to provide higher education for blind, deaf, defective and epileptic children.

As with the education service for the normal child so with that for the disabled child the inter-war period is noted for reports rather than progress. Three departmental or interdepartmental reports in the years 1929, 1934 and 1938 influenced the special education provisions of the Education Act, 1944. Local education authorities were then required to ascertain what children in their areas were handicapped and make provision for those who suffered from any disability of mind or body, either in special schools or by means of special educational treatment appropriate to each one. Eleven categories of children were distinguished, the blind, partially sighted, deaf, partially deaf, diabetic, educationally subnormal, epileptic, maladjusted, physically handicapped, delicate and those suffering from speech defects.

Despite great improvements deficiencies remained to be made good as shown in the report of the Chief Medical Officer of the Department of Education and Science for 1964 and 1965, already referred to. This showed, for example, that in January 1966 as many as 13,069 children, of whom 9,143 were educationally subnormal, were requiring places in special schools; that the average waiting period for interview or treatment in child guidance clinics was six months; that there was a continuing shortage of trained staff in these clinics and of speech therapists. In a written reply to a Parliamentary Question on July 25, 1966, the Minister of Health said it was estimated that, excluding hospitals for the subnormal, about 5,800 of the 13,000 children in hospitals in England and Wales were receiving education there. Put the other way about 7,200 children in hospital were not receiving education. Clearly these deficiencies have to be made good before the education service for the handicapped child can be regarded as satisfactory.

In 1968 it was announced that provision for mentally handicapped children in junior training centres was to be transferred from the Department of Health and Social Security to the Department of Education and Science as part of the education system.

Even as or when the education service may be regarded as complete, both for the normal and the handicapped child, he would not lose overnight the dependency of his school years. At some point before he reaches physical or social maturity particular needs arise from his adolescent stage of growth. That it is impossible to assign adolescence to a specific and unvarying age span, or that what are generally accepted as characteristics of adolescence may result not only from his own natural development but from the structure and demands of the society in which a young person lives, are beside the point in the context of the social services. For social services are necessary in large part by reason of the fact that people do live in and are affected by the industrialisation of society and the demands that that makes upon them. The needs of young people are certainly heightened by these demands, and they need professional or vocational guidance, training, and advice about obtaining employment, by very reason of the fact that they are living in a complex, demanding, competitive and a highly developed industrial society. From this there arises the necessity for a youth employment service.

A wise choice of career or satisfying work is one which young people in a modern society cannot normally be expected to make successfully without guidance, information and advice about training requirements, conditions and prospects in different fields of employment. The nature and demands of the commercial and industrial world of today with its constant scientific and technological developments present young people with employment problems which are not found in a less developed community. Neither from the point of view of the young person himself nor of society as a whole can the choice be left to chance, without danger of serious personal frustration and wastage of skill and ability.

This was first recognised by the State in 1909 when the Board of Trade provided special juvenile departments in a number of adult labour exchanges set up under the Labour Exchanges Act, 1909. In 1910 the Education (Choice of Employment) Act empowered local education authorities to provide a similar service for young people under seventeen years of age, with supervision and grant aid from the Board of Education. Thus began a dual service to assist the adolescent in his transfer from school to work.

Despite four formal examinations of the administrative position in 1920, 1926, 1933 and 1945, when the report of the Committee on the Juvenile Employment Service (the Ince Committee)[28] was made, this dual service still persists. It is now provided under the Employment and Training Act, 1948, Part II of which was designed to facilitate the establishment of a comprehensive youth employment service for those under eighteen years of age and those over eighteen still attending school. Under this Act a Central Youth Employment Executive, staffed jointly by the Ministries of Labour and National Service,* and of Education, was set up and also a National Youth Employment Council under the Ministry of Labour and National Service* with local youth employment committees for advisory purposes. But the power of local education authorities to provide a service in their area, with the approval of the then Minister of Labour, was continued. At the end of 1965 144 education authorities in Great Britain were running the service in their areas and the Ministry of Labour and National Service* was providing the service elsewhere through local employment exchanges. These parallel provisions indicate the dual nature of the needs of young people—for an education and for an employment service—and of the difficulty of the policy makers in deciding which should be given precedence. In the greater part of the country today the youth employment service, as shown, is operated by local education authorities through the schools.

The weakness of the service lies in the difficulty of recruiting and training sufficient and suitable staff, and in the fact that there is no way of ensuring that it is used by either employers or young people who, with their lack of knowledge, may still find and take dead-end jobs; those with high wages but no prospects, or in undesirable conditions of work without training or apprentice schemes. The service has to rely on successfully selling its wares to parents, teachers, employers, and school leavers alike, and encouraging their voluntary use of what it has to offer.

The report of the National Youth Employment Council on 'The Work of the Youth Employment Service, 1962–65',[29] stated

* Now the Department of Employment and Productivity.

that a number of weaknesses in the service had been revealed by
the increase in the number of young people reaching fifteen in
the peak year 1962–63 and the recession in employment of that
time, which showed a need to augment the service. It was recognised that much still remained to be done if the service was to be
able to meet the increasing demands being made on it. The report
of the Newsom Committee also expressed the view that a good
deal remained to be done in the youth employment service and
referred in particular to the restriction of information given by
headmasters about school leavers to youth employment officers
which hampered them in their interviewing of young people. It
was pointed out also that many secondary modern schools had no
teachers acting as careers advisers.[30]

In 1963 the then Ministry of Labour appointed a working party
(Albemarle Working Party) to define the main issues facing the
youth employment service in the light of recent developments in
education and the changing needs of industry. This working party
did not view with favour any change in the administration of the
service which they did not regard as detrimental to its development
but they pointed out that the service was still placing only about
40 per cent of the youngest school leavers and a yet lower proportion of those leaving above the age of sixteen. They took the
view that developments in education and industry strengthened
the need for a comprehensive and effective service particularly for
those to whom increasingly exacting and competitive conditions
presented especial difficulties in the transition from school to
work.[31] In 1967 some youth employment bureaux began for the
first time to name their officers careers officers rather than youth
employment officers, as a reflection of the increasing role played
by the service in informing young people about careers and
necessary qualifications as well as in helping them to find work.*

Clearly the needs of the adolescent in his transfer from school
to work are not yet fully met and too many young people are left
to sink or swim in their choice or first years of work. It is as well,
therefore, that the Social Survey began a survey in 1968 of the
work of the youth employment service and the part played in it
by teachers, parents, employers and youth employment officers.
It is a matter of particular importance since many of the same

* For further reading see A. F. Young, *op. cit.* (19 Chap. 1), Chapter 2.

young people have need also of opportunities for the use and enjoyment of leisure, which often they cannot provide for themselves. Provisions to meet this need still fall, therefore, into the social service category known as the youth service.

Broadly speaking the youth service comprises the activities of all national and local voluntary youth organisations and local education authority youth groups for those between fifteen and twenty years of age. These include uniformed and non-uniformed organisations, lay and religious groups, those with paid and with voluntary leadership, and activities provided in the club open only once a week to the youth centre open each day in its own purpose-built premises.

The service is one which has repeatedly attracted surveys and reports over the past twenty-five years. The first was undertaken in 1938 on behalf of King George's Jubilee Trust which included the observation: 'The neglect of adolescent youth has been woeful.'[32] The following year the Board of Education issued Circular No. 1486—'In the Service of Youth'. In this it stated that provision for young people had always fallen short of need; that the needs of those between fourteen and twenty who had finished full-time education had long been neglected; that less than half of them belonged to any organisation; and lastly that war emphasised these defects in the social services. Grant aid was then made available. Local youth committees were set up, together with a National Youth Committee which was replaced by a National Youth Advisory Council in 1942. Reporting in 1943 on the youth service after the war, this Council concluded that the contribution of the voluntary organisations needed to be strengthened and should receive increased aid from public funds. The Education Act, 1944, then laid upon local education authorities the duty to secure provision of adequate facilities for leisure time occupation, including recreation and social and physical training, for any person over compulsory school age able to profit by them, and to have regard to co-operating to this end with voluntary bodies having the same objective.

In 1945 the National Youth Advisory Council issued a second report on the purpose and content of the youth service. In this it asserted that the service was still preoccupied with filling the gaps left by an inadequate national system of education. The same year a second report prepared for King George's Jubilee Trust[33] took the view that regarded as a public service the youth service was still in its first infancy. Forty per cent of the adolescent age group was still unattached to any organisation.

In 1948 a third report for the same Trust observed: 'At present youth welfare agencies waste much of their time attempting to patch up in their young charges the damage caused by the blundering of earlier educational forces.'[34] In 1951 the Trust called a national conference of all organisations concerned with the youth service. The findings of this conference were published in 1955 in *Citizens of Tomorrow*.[35] Shortcomings in the education system, the youth employment service and the youth service were all noted.

In 1957 the Seventh Report from the Select Committee for Estimates, Session 1956–57, 'The Youth Employment Service and Youth Service Grants',[36] noted a decline in grant aid from the Ministry of Education and stated that it gained the impression from its enquiry that the Ministry was little interested in the state of the youth service and was apathetic about its future. This was having a deeply discouraging effect on the work done. The Ministry should have a policy, state it publicly, and not let the service drift into a state where grants would be wasted.

No doubt these criticisms encouraged the Ministry to set up, as it did in 1958, a Committee on 'The Youth Service in England and Wales' (the Albemarle Committee), to review in the light of changing social and industrial conditions and current trends in other branches of the education service the contribution the service could make in assisting young people to play their part in the life of the community. The Committee reported in February 1960.[37] Its recommendations included a ten-year development programme; the setting up of a Youth Service Development Council; the development of the voluntary principle at every level; a generous and well-designed building programme; improvement in indoor and outdoor facilities for physical recreation; emergency and long-term training arrangements for full-time leaders; and improvement in capital and maintenance grants. The Government expressed general acceptance of these recommendations and in November, 1963, the Ministry of Education reported that it had authorised 1,200 capital projects, 540 being local education authority projects, for the years 1960–64 at a value of £11½ million. Increased grants up to £1·3 million in 1963–64 were estimated including the training of youth leaders. Local education authority spending on the youth service doubled in four years and most areas reported an increase in the number of young people using facilities available to them. It would seem that the position of the service was stronger than at any time since the war but it can still safely be said that few youth workers, if any, regarded it as fully meeting the leisure-time needs of young people. In a House of Commons debate on December 3, 1964, it was announced that a committee of the Youth Service Development Council had been set up to assess progress made since the Albemarle Committee Report and to consider future developments.

Another committee (the Milson Committee) was set up in 1967 to study the relationship of the youth service and the adult community and to assess its effectiveness, its appeal, and the success of different youth organisations. Certain confusion arose in 1968 when the Minister of State, who had been appointed to carry particular responsibility for the youth service, announced the setting up of a new and separate organisation, the Young Volunteer Force Foundation, to encourage the development of voluntary service to the community by young people in England and Wales.

This body, if invited by local authorities, was to visit areas and advise about local arrangements to stimulate and co-ordinate voluntary service by young people. It was not to interfere with any existing service by youth organisations. Not a few people, however, doubted its ability to carry out the functions allotted to it and waited with some scepticism the final outcome of its efforts. In all, the youth service and the service of youth has never long been out of the news and never, as yet, free from criticism.

Amongst all children and adolescents there is a minority who have special need either because they are deprived by the death, illness or desertion of parents of a home of their own, or because they are neglected or cruelly treated, are in moral danger, beyond parental control, or have broken the law. The distinction between deprived and delinquent children, or those in need of care, protection or control, is in reality artificial, for all these children have need of understanding, sympathy, help and support. They fall into categories so far as the social services are concerned only by reason of the fact that the necessity for special care of the delinquent was recognised first. This recognition goes back in the nineteenth century to the first Reformatory Schools Act, 1854, and in this century to the Children Act, 1908, and the Children and Young Persons Act, 1933. The child deprived of a home of his own, on the other hand, was cared for under the Poor Law until 1948. The Children Act of that year concerned itself with such children only, leaving others—the delinquent, those in need of care, protection or beyond control—still to be provided for under the Children and Young Persons Act, 1933.

Thus there is a dual service of care for deprived and delinquent children and it is often a matter of chance into which category any child finally falls. The point so far as the present discussion is concerned, however, is that since the human needs of the dependency years of childhood can be affected both by external misfortune and by some inner inability to contend with stress or strain, a social service of some kind has to be provided. It is only to maintain terminology in general use that distinction between deprived and delinquent is kept here. It is not to suggest that the needs of the children concerned are different either in kind or degree.

Shortly after the formation of the National Society for the Prevention of Cruelty to Children in 1889 an Act for the Prevention of Cruelty to and Better Protection of Children marked the first occasion of State intervention to make wilful cruelty to a child a punishable offence. The Children Act, 1908, extended this to include wilful neglect. It also set up juvenile courts and provided alternatives to imprisonment for young offenders. This was a step towards their training and treatment rather than punishment. The Act also empowered magistrates to remove children held to be in need of care or protection from their parents and to make arrangements for their care elsewhere. It protected children in various other ways, for example against being used for purposes of begging.

The Act, in short, represented the more enlightened attitude of the twentieth century towards children and their rights. It remained in force until the Children and Young Persons Act, 1933, which was based on the recommendations of a Departmental Committee on the Treatment of Young Offenders, was passed.

This Act consolidated all earlier legislation, extended powers of the juvenile courts to concern themselves with children and young people from the age of eight to seventeen, and specifically charged the court to have regard to the welfare of the child. Local authorities were required to provide remand homes and approved schools took the place of industrial schools and reformatories.

With its many improvements the Act was not the end of progress in the care of neglected or delinquent children, and it could not have been expected to be. The war, the rise in juvenile delinquency, research into its causes, increased understanding of the importance to a child of a home of his own, and the Children Act, 1948, all led to further concern with the needs of the delinquent child. This resulted in the setting up of the Committee on Children and Young Persons, 1956 (the Ingleby Committee), part of whose brief was to enquire and make recommendations on the constitution, proceedings and powers of juvenile courts, remand homes, approved schools, the probation home system, and the prevention of cruelty to and exposure of children to moral and physical danger. The Committee reported in 1960,[38] and in 1963 the second Children and Young Persons Act was passed. The counterpart in Scotland to the Ingleby Committee was the Kilbrandon Committee which published its report in April 1964.[39]

The Act raised the age of criminal responsibility to ten. It removed parents' powers to bring their own children before the courts as beyond control and substituted the local authority for this purpose in their stead. Powers of the juvenile courts were extended to deal not only with those in need of care or protection, but those in need of care, protection or control, and they were empowered to insist on both parents attending if necessary. It extended restrictions on publicity for juvenile court cases and imposed higher penalties for cruelty to children. It empowered money to be spent on research into child welfare as well as on the causes of delinquency and treatment of delinquents. It did not go as far as many would have wished, for instance in raising the age of criminal responsibility to twelve or older, but it represented a further step in the gradual improvement and extension of services to meet the special needs of particular children.*

* For a review of the development of services to deal positively with the problems of juvenile delinquency see Howard Jones, *Crime and the Penal System* (2nd Part), University Tutorial Press, 2nd ed., 1962.

So far as social services for deprived children* are concerned, these stem from the particular anxiety about the care of children aroused during the evacuation of the war years and its aftermath. This concern coincided with the Government's own intention to repeal the Poor Law which in itself required that homeless children should be looked after by some other means. This intention was furthered by a letter to *The Times* in July 1944, from Lady Allen of Hurtwood who drew attention to the fact that children deprived of a normal home life were at that time too often brought up repressively, without affection or reasonable comfort or security. Early the following year a boy, Dennis O'Neal, died as a result of ill treatment by his foster parents; an event which profoundly shocked the conscience of the nation. All these circumstances led to the setting up of the Care of Children Committee in March 1945 (the Curtis Committee),[40] to enquire into existing methods of providing for children deprived of a normal home life and to consider further measures necessary to ensure that their conditions were such as best to compensate them for the lack of parents. The report of this Committee, and that of its opposite number in Scotland on 'Homeless Children' (the Clyde Committee),[41] was based on a new and more sympathetic approach to human need. Emphasis was laid upon the differences of each child and his value as an individual and there was recognition of emotional and social as well as physical needs. The necessity of furthering the happiness of children as well as their education and training was accepted and the goal of giving deprived children as equal an opportunity as possible as those in their own homes. Although legislation cannot guarantee the achievement of such an ideal the Children Act, 1948, was designed with that end in view.

The Act required local authorities to receive into their care, when necessary in the interests of the child, anyone under the age of seventeen who was abandoned or lost, without parents or guardian, or whose parents or guardian were prevented temporarily or permanently from looking after him properly. Power was given to them also to assume parental rights over a child received into care if there were no parents or guardian or they had aban-

---

* For an account of the general development of services for deprived children see Jean S. Heywood, *Children in Care*, Routledge and Kegan Paul, 1959.

doned him, or were permanently incapable of caring for him or
were of such habit or mode of life as to be unfit to have the care
of the child. The local authority had to appoint a children committee and a children officer and it could make provision for children by adoption or in foster homes, residential homes, hostels or
boarding schools. Voluntary homes were required to register with
the Home Office and comply with regulations made to secure the
welfare of the child. It is important to note that the Children Act
did not empower local authorities to 'take' children into care, that
is remove them from their own homes against a parent's wishes.
Only a court can order this if a child is found to be in need of care,
protection or control. Despite frequent misquotations on this point
a local authority does not take children into care; it receives them.
Even the Seebohm Committee, mentioned below, who should
have known better, refer in one instance to a member of a family
being 'taken into care'.

The humane and enlightened provisions of the Children Act
led to substantial improvements in the care of the children whom
it covered. It was not, however, concerned with preventing
deprivation in the first instance and although local authorities
frequently went further in this direction than they had power,
strictly speaking, to go, this limitation was increasingly criticised.
Consequently the Ingleby Committee on Children and Young
Persons was required to consider whether local authorities should
be given new powers and duties to prevent or forestall the suffering
of children through neglect in their own homes. The Committee
concluded this should be so and their recommendation was
incorporated in Section I of the Children and Young Persons Act,
1963. This required local authorities to make available such advice,
guidance and assistance as may promote the welfare of children
by diminishing the need to receive them into care. Assistance under
this section may include services in kind or in exceptional circumstances cash. The section has been interpreted and used in various
ways by different authorities, one example being the employment
of housemothers to live with a family during an emergency, as for
instance when a mother is in hospital, as an alternative to receiving
the children into care. A second example is agreement by a
children committee to the payment of rent for a limited period to
avoid eviction, in instances where a combination of cash assistance

and casework appears to have a fair chance of preventing the break up of a family.

The intention is family centred rather than child centred and it draws together the categories of the deprived, the delinquent and the neglected child; for effectively to promote welfare to avoid receiving a child into care is a step in preventing any of these conditions. The primary consideration is the need of a child, simply as a child within a family, not because he falls into a particular legislative category.

It is doubtful to say the least whether it has ever been the case as Silberman claimed that 'in discussion between a social worker and the mother of a poverty-stricken family, the social worker will often be heard to say, "Your Johnny must be taken away and properly looked after; he's starved and lousy".'[42] But it is true that too little emphasis has in the past been laid upon prevention and it is a sign of the times that social services for the welfare of deprived and delinquent children can now redress the balance. They have reached a preventive stage new in the history of social provision, and further developments were foreshadowed in a Home Office White Paper in 1965—'The Child, the Family and the Young Offender'.[43] This followed the reports of the Ingleby and Kilbrandon Committees on Children and Young Persons, the Morison Committee on the Probation Service referred to in Chapter Nine, and of a specialist group under the chairmanship of Lord Longford which published a report—'Crime, a Challenge to us all'—in 1964.[44]

The proposals made in the Home Office White Paper included one to abolish the juvenile courts, other than in exceptional cases, and likewise 'approved schools', and to transfer the treatment of young offenders to a family service staffed by trained social workers. Another of its recommendations led in 1966 to the setting up by the Home Secretary, the Secretary of State for Education and Science, the Minister of Health and the Minister of Housing and Local Government, of an independent committee 'to review the organisation and responsibilities of the local authority personal social services in England and Wales and to consider what changes are desirable to secure an effective family service' (the Seebohm Committee).*

* For a critical evaluation of the report of the Seebohm Committee see *Social Work*, Vol. 25, No. 4, October 1968.

Before the committee completed its task, however, its report was preceded by one from the Scottish Education Department and Scottish Home and Health Department in 1966—'Social Work and the Community'.[45] The proposals here were presented as 'a basis for discussion with interested persons and organisations, with a view to comprehensive legislation when opportunity occurred'. The conclusion reached was that in Scotland there should be a social work department of the local authority to provide a wide range of social services, including the child care functions of existing children departments with the addition of compulsory powers where voluntary co-operation from families was not forthcoming or could not be expected, vested in children panels who would decide upon the appropriate treatment or training of the child.

Also to be included in the proposed social work departments were school attendance and welfare, probation, community care, after-care of the ill, welfare of the handicapped, welfare of old people, domestic help, temporary accommodation for those needing such provision. This conclusion clearly rejected the concept of the family or child centred service in favour of inclusive provision for all persons in need.

It was clear that the social service wind was blowing in the same way in England and Wales as in Scotland even before the report of the Seebohm Committee was published. A joint circular of the Ministry of Health (20/66), the Home Office (178/66) and the Ministry of Housing and local Government (58/66) on homeless families, addressed to local authorities in 1966, was evidence of this. In it the health, welfare and children departments were referred to collectively as social service departments, to mark the view of the Ministers concerned that the departments should act as one together with housing departments, 'to provide from the recipient's point of view a unified service'.

The Home Office then published a second White Paper in 1968, 'Children in Trouble'.[46] This modified the proposals made in the first White Paper, 'The Child, the Family and the Young Offender', in the light of discussions which had taken place following its publication. 'Children in Trouble' included the proposals that juvenile courts should be retained but the prosecution of children between ten and fourteen years of age should cease.

Action to help them and their parents should be on a voluntary basis. Only if a child committed an offence and his parents failed to provide adequate care, protection and guidance, or he appeared to be beyond control would it be possible to take him before a juvenile court as in need of care, protection and control.

The varied range of residential institutions for children in care of local authorities, including children's homes and hostels, remand homes, reception centres, remand centres and approved schools, should all become 'community homes' as part of a comprehensive, integrated system planned by joint committees of authorities in consultation with voluntary bodies.*

This concludes what has inevitably been a brief review of needs arising from the dependencies of birth, infancy, childhood and adolescence, in normal and abnormal circumstances, from which has arisen the necessity for provision of social services. How far can these now be regarded as dispensable or superfluous? How far can their continuance be seen as degrading? To what extent can the needs concerned be looked upon as representing failures and the object of the services as loathsome?

Maternal and infant mortality are certainly failures but it is clear the failure would be far greater if maternity and child welfare services were dispensed with. To look upon these as unnecessary or superfluous hardly appears possible in the light of the evidence available. Illegitimacy, delinquency and deprivation of children by reason of cruelty, neglect or desertion, also represent failure and in extreme cases might be regarded as loathsome. If services to meet the needs arising from these circumstances could be dispensed with everyone would rejoice. But each failure is the outcome of a complex of causative factors and to expect their total disappearance would be unrealistic. The services cannot be looked upon as dispensable though their necessity may be regrettable.

The deprivation of children because of the death, illness or disability of parents is regrettable also but it can scarcely be regarded as failure, unless it is failure on the part of some person who caused death or disability or failed to cure sickness. This does not appear to be the sort of failure the critics have in mind, however. Services for the child deprived by misfortune of a home

---

* These proposals were incorporated in a Children and Young Persons Bill which had its first reading in February 1969.

of his own would appear to be here to stay and there is nothing degrading about them. Indeed it would be degrading if society were so callous as to allow them to go.

It is true that the number of children in care of local authorities in March 1967 and 1968 were the highest on record which might at first sight suggest an increasing irresponsibility on the part of parents, but per thousand of the population under eighteen years of age the proportions were little higher than in 1959; 5·3 and 5·2 compared with 5·0. It was also the case that the highest proportion of children received into care in both years were so received on account of the mother's confinement or the illness of a parent and in addition the rise in the number of children in the care of local authorities was largely offset by falls in the number in the care of voluntary bodies.[47]

The education, school health, youth employment and youth services are all designed to meet the needs of normal children, except in the special case of the handicapped child. They are concerned to prevent failure. They do not arise from it. The needs they meet are natural and healthy and can by no stretch of the imagination be called degrading or loathsome. In short, it is impossible to make statements about the dispensability or super-fluity of the social or welfare services as a whole, or about their degrading, loathsome, or any other characteristics. Each service, its purposes and achievements, must be considered separately on its merits. The necessity for its continuance or discontinuance must be looked at individually and in its own right, in the light of the circumstances and conditions of each case.

CHAPTER SEVEN

Misfortune and the Social Services

Whereas human needs before and at birth, in infancy, childhood and adolescence, follow one another in chronological order, giving rise to social services to meet those needs, the needs of the mature adult do not proceed in so regular or characteristic a way. Under normal circumstances, once the dependencies of youth have passed—dependencies which will include those arising from any period of further education or training—every adult person does not necessarily require the same services as each of his fellows. To a large extent his dependency needs arise from misfortune and not from normal stages of human growth or development. Thus social services for the adult are designed, first, to prevent or protect him from misfortune and second, to mitigate or overcome the effects of misfortune should it nevertheless occur.

The misfortunes which can affect people in their adult years, and through them their dependent children, are, as was said in the last chapter, poverty, unemployment, sickness, disability, widowhood, marriage breakdown, homelessness or poor housing, and unmarried parenthood, to which consideration has already been given. The misfortune of the offender and his family has also been included as a separate category of need.

As and where poverty is an outcome of unemployment, sickness, disability, widowhood or the limitations of old age, it is those conditions in themselves that require to be prevented, in so far as they can, or whose effects must be mitigated if they cannot be avoided altogether and attention will be turned to each shortly, but first, poverty arising from other causes is considered.

Poverty is regarded here as the inability of an individual or a family to maintain a standard of living at or above a point which the community accepts as a permissible or reasonable minimum.* Such a minimum may be at or above mere subsistence level

---

* For a general consideration of provision of income in times of adversity see: (i) Karl de Schweinitz, *England's Road to Social Security*, a Perpetua Book, A. S. Barnes & Co. Inc., New York, 1961. (ii) Brian Rodgers, *The Battle against Poverty*, Routledge and Kegan Paul, 1968.

according to the social expectations, standards, or economic circumstances of the time. Poverty, in other words, is relative as well as absolute. It does not follow from this that anyone who is less well off than someone else is therefore and necessarily poor. To argue thus, as some do, is to lose all meaning to the word poverty. Seldon was right when he argued that because a man only had an Austin 7, whereas someone else had a Rover 16, he was not therefore poor.[1] He is less well off, which is quite a different matter. Where being less well off merges into being poor, on the destitution-affluence continuum, may be impossible to plot precisely, but to maintain that there is no difference between the two is to confuse rather than to clarify the issue.*

The number of dependent children in a family has been shown many times to be one of the primary causes of poverty, although the measurement of poverty in the surveys concerned has differed. Rowntree, in his first study of York at the turn of the century, found that the majority of children in working class families were born into and remained in poverty throughout their school life, rose above it during their first years of earning but fell again into it when they married and had children of their own.[2]

Bowley, in surveys of five provincial towns undertaken before the First World War, confirmed that the greatest incidence of poverty was to be found amongst families with children.[3] In his second study of York in 1936 Rowntree showed that of all working class children under one year of age over 50 per cent lived below what he then termed the 'human needs standard'; 47 per cent of them would remain there to the age of five years at least, and over 31 per cent to the age of ten or more.[4]

The report of the Royal Commission on Population, 1949, pointed out that 'to have a large family (of three or more children) before the war and to be in the lower income range was almost of itself enough to guarantee poverty'.[5] When Beveridge examined the findings of all the investigations of conditions of life undertaken before the Second World War he drew attention to the fact that they produced evidence to show that one-quarter to one-sixth of all

* For a study of inequalities in a society and of attitudes towards them see W. G. Runciman, *Relative Deprivation and Social Justice*, Routledge and Kegan Paul, 1966, See also *Research on Poverty*. A Social Science Research Council Review, Heinemann Educational Books Ltd., 1968.

want, that is having means below the standard assumed to be
necessary for subsistence, was due to failure to relate income
whilst earning to the size of the family. Consequently he concluded
that the abolition of want required a double redistribution of
income, through social insurance and by family needs.[6]

Before the implementation of the National Insurance and
National Health Service Acts, 1946, the costs of child-bearing,
that is of medical fees, confinement, maternity wear, layette and
equipment, were many times greater than the maternity benefit
then payable. The average working class family, for example,
spent £28 on these items, whereas maternity benefit was a flat
amount of £2 or £4 according to whether husband, wife, or
husband and wife were insured. Although increased for servicemen's wives the average received was only £6.[7] There was,
therefore, a strong case for the new and improved provisions made
under the National Insurance Act which introduced maternity
grants, payable on each confinement; attendance allowances
payable for four weeks after confinement; and maternity allowances payable over a period of weeks, part before and part after
confinement, for mothers who gave up paid work during this time.
In 1953 the attendance allowance was abolished but a home confinement grant was added for women who were confined at home.
Figures so frequently become outdated as and when insurance
benefits and contributions, for any reason, are changed that they
are not included here and the student should inform himself
what the current rates are.*

The maternity grants and allowances payable under the
National Insurance Act were never intended to cover the whole
cost of maternity but to be a reasonable contribution, in addition
to free medical services, towards the unavoidable expenditure
arising out of childbirth. From a continuing and long term point
of view, therefore, family allowances are of greater importance in
the prevention of poverty. These were first paid in 1946, under
the Family Allowances Act, 1945. At that time the rate was fixed
at 5s. a week for every child other than the first, payable so long
as the child was of statutory school age, or up to the age of sixteen
if he were still in full-time education or apprenticeship. This rate

* See *Everybody's Guide to National Insurance*, Ministry of Social Security,
H.M.S.O.

E

was 3s. less than that recommended by Beveridge. The lower amount was decided by the Government at the time on the ground that school meals were to be provided free of charge which would supplement family income in another way. In fact free school meals for all never materialised owing to initial shortages in school facilities and consequently financial assistance to the family has never been at the rate originally anticipated.

In 1951 Rowntree and Lavers, in a third social survey of York, calculated that 'without [family] allowances 6·46 per cent of working class families would be in poverty instead of 4·64 per cent'.[8] As York was not one of the poorest areas it is probable this figure was an underestimate so far as the country as a whole was concerned. The following year, 1952, the rate of family allowances was raised to 8s. a week, and in 1956 to 8s. for the second child and 10s. a week for the third and subsequent children, each payable up to the age of eighteen for those remaining in full time attendance at school or apprenticeship. In 1963 the age limit was raised again, to nineteen years.

A general study of poverty by Townsend showed that the poorest persons in the United Kingdom in the mid-1960s consisted chiefly of old persons and members of large families.[9] A further and more detailed study published in 1965 by Abel-Smith and Townsend finally dispelled any idea that family poverty was a thing of the past.[10] In this survey it was estimated that about $2\frac{1}{4}$ million or 17 per cent of children in the United Kingdom in 1960 were living in low income households; low income households being those with an income of under 140 per cent of the basic national assistance scale (at that time) plus rent/housing. Amongst these children it was estimated there were some two-thirds of a million or about 5 per cent of all children in the United Kingdom who were living in households with an income actually below the basic national assistance scale.

In 1967 the Ministry of Social Security also published a report of an enquiry made in June and July 1966 into the circumstances of families to ascertain the number whose resources were less than their requirements, as measured by the basic national assistance standards.[11] Estimates were also made in relation to the supplementary benefits which had replaced national assistance under the Ministry of Social Security Act, 1966, to which reference has

has already been made. The report revealed that nearly half a million families, containing up to 1¼ million children had incomes amounting to less than would have been paid in 1967 to a family which qualified for supplementary benefit. Of these families 145,000 were fatherless, 160,000 were of men who were either sick or unemployed and 140,000 were of men in full-time employment.

Some improvement was achieved in October 1968, when family allowances for second and subsequent children were increased to 18s. and 20s. respectively, but at the same time the price of school meals and welfare milk was increased and family allowances continue to be one of the cash paying social services most frequently criticised. The criticism is based on the fact that they are paid out of exchequer funds, not out of contributions as are insurance benefits, and that all parents of two or more children are eligible to receive them despite the fact that the majority, it is said, could afford to make adequate provision for their children without State help; real wages being so much higher than when the scheme was first introduced. In other words, the contention is that family allowances are being paid out of public money to a majority who are not in need as well as to a minority who are or may be. In short, the principle of universality in social service provision is questioned in particular in the case of family allowances.

The criticism overlooks the fact, however, that family allowances are subject to income tax and the higher the income the less the net benefit. It also overlooks the fact that some rebate on income tax is still allowed in respect of dependent children. This is one of the fiscal welfare provisions to which Titmuss drew attention that should never be overlooked in any consideration of the social services.[12] To examine the family allowances scheme without the tax rebate scheme is to exclude a whole means whereby family need, as part of social policy, is met. The principles behind the payment of family allowances stand or fall with those behind tax rebates in respect of dependent children, as indeed do other aspects of social security provision. The likelihood of social security and income tax being merged into one scheme is accepted by many today as both feasible and desirable. The issue so far as family allowances are concerned, however, is complicated by the fact that the provisions are not merely one means of preventing poverty, they are also a means of enabling families to maintain a standard of living comparable to that of childless persons; to prevent parents being in a position of less eligibility. They are a measure of economic justice as well as economic security. But to what extent parents should bear the cost of bringing up their children is a matter of opinion. Any decision on this point involves a value judgement and no final answer can therefore be given. It is certain that whatever the policy of the Government may be it will not please everyone.

However, in 1965 a new voluntary body, the Child Poverty Action Group, was formed to publicise the problem of low income families and to demand Government action to improve their situation.* They have pointed out that the economic position of the families concerned is linked with poor nutrition, low educational levels and high infant mortality. The problem of poverty is part of a whole complex of problems.

Although children can be a cause of poverty, if steps are not taken to prevent this, they are not normally regarded in themselves as one of the misfortunes of adult life. All the other causes of poverty are, however, misfortunes in themselves. They bring with them not only limitations or cessation of income, but social and psychological unhappiness or misery as well. They are frequently wasteful also from the nation's point of view as well as that of the individual and to prevent them is, therefore, doubly justified. The first of these misfortunes is unemployment.

To be unemployed is to be capable of and available for work, that is to say, to be fit for and genuinely seeking work but unable to find any suitable work to do. This state should not be confused with that of being incapable of work; of unemployability resulting from temporary or chronic illness, infimity of disability. Nor should it be confused with electing not to work, either because unearned income is sufficient or because a life of vagrancy or dependency on others has been chosen or imposed by force of circumstances upon a person. This has been called 'voluntary unemployment',[13] but this is not so. To be unemployed a man must want paid work, be capable of it, but fail to find it. In this failure and its economic and social consequences lies both his personal misfortune and the national loss of his unused productive powers.

* For continuing information about and prepared by the Child Poverty Action Group see the Journal *Poverty*.

The stark tale of long term mass unemployment of the pre-war years, blighting the lives of over 2 million people in the 1930s, is too well known or fully described elsewhere to need repetition here. It has now long been accepted by all political parties that the Government should accept responsibility for preventing its recurrence through the maintenance of a high and steady level of employment. Means to this end depend upon the varying nature and causes of unemployment, an examination of which are beyond the scope of this book. It is only the social services which are designed to prevent or reduce unemployment, or to mitigate its consequences, that are relevant here. These services are of two sorts; those provided in kind by the Department of Employment and Productivity and those provided in cash under the National Insurance scheme.

The social services now provided by the Department date back to the Labour Exchange Act, 1909, which authorised the Board of Trade to maintain, or assist others to maintain, labour exchanges in such places as was thought fit. These were renamed employment exchanges in 1916. Their purpose was to collect information from any part of the country about employers seeking workers and workers seeking employment, and to put the two in touch with one another. The success of the exchanges is shown in part by their growth in number from 250 in 1909 to 1,482 in 1947. In 1948 the Employment and Training Act consolidated the work of the then Minister of Labour and through him of the employment exchanges. The Act laid upon the Minister the duty:

'to provide such facilities and services as he considers expedient for the purpose of assisting persons to select, fit themselves for, obtain and retain employment suitable to their age and capacity, of assisting employers to obtain suitable employees, and generally for the purpose of promoting employment in accordance with the requirements of the community'.

The furtherance of employment does not, however, stop with these functions. In order to promote mobility of labour and assist those unable to obtain employment in their own area the Act empowered provision by way of grant, loan or otherwise, to assist any person, with his dependants, with the cost of removal from one part of the country to another for purposes of obtaining employment; with their maintenance and welfare in the course of removal; and their resettlement after removal. It is clear that housing shortages must militate against the success of this provision which is but one illustration of the fact that the successful pursuit of the objects of one service may well be dependent on the adequacy of another. In addition to the provision of information, and encouragement of mobility, the Employment and Training Act allows for training courses to be provided for the benefit of any person above school leaving age, and for the payment, accommodation, recreation and welfare of those undertaking such courses; which may be to assist professional, clerical and administrative, as well as manual workers to obtain the necessary skills or qualifications needed to enable them to obtain employment.

In 1964 a further step was taken in the Industrial Training Act which aims, by setting up industrial training boards, to ensure that enough workers with the requisite skills are available in the right places at the right time and to provide better opportunities to individuals to develop their skills and use their abilities to the full.

In all, the functions of the Department of Employment and Productivity are concerned with the dual nature of need that the social services are designed to meet—of the individual and of society. Without them the individual would, as he once did, waste much time and energy seeking work, or be faced with insuperable obstacles in getting to it, or lack the training and skills enabling him to undertake it. Society would suffer from the waste of the unused talents and abilities of its members. Not even the severest critics of the Welfare State have questioned the value of these particular services, though their criticisms have often overlooked their existence.*

It is not only assistance in obtaining work, however, that an unemployed person requires, but income for himself and his family. Without this he would, and frequently has, suffered not only enforced idleness but poverty. In the nineteenth century, three-quarters of the poverty found by Rowntree and Booth was due to low wages. In the 1920s and 1930s a substantial proportion —35 per cent in 1924 in Bowley's second five towns survey,[14] and

* For further examination of the employment services for the adult see A. F. Young, op. cit. (19 Chap. 1), Chapter 1.

63·2 per cent in 1934 in the Merseyside area[15]—was due to unemployment or irregular work.

The need for some income maintenance in time of unemployment was recognised in practice in 1911 when the payment of unemployment insurance benefit, including dependants' benefits, was first introduced. But the scheme was limited to a specific group of industries only. It was not generally applied until 1920. Then it excluded higher income groups and benefits were still only payable for a period of fifteen weeks, although the unemployment was frequently of a longer duration. Above all the benefit was not, and was never intended to be adequate. As Rackham said: 'It was to be a help to men who needed "tiding over" until they found work again.'[16] By the 1930s this was quite unrealistic. But those people who were not or were no longer eligible for unemployment benefit had to look to the Poor Law for financial help, until the Unemployment Assistance Board was established in 1934 to take over the payment of transitional payments available on a means test for those suffering from long-term unemployment.

The urgent necessity for change and improvement was recognised during the war in the recommendations of the Beveridge Report and the subsequent National Insurance Act, 1946. This introduced unified comprehensive provisions with unemployment benefit payable up to a minimum of 180 or a maximum of 492 days, changed to 312 days in 1966, according to the number of contributions paid. The rate of benefit was intended to be adequate but the intention was thwarted by post-war rises in the cost of living which necessitated continuous upward amendments of contributions and benefits payable under Acts amending the 1946 Act.

Although unemployment as a cause of poverty was wholly absent in the third survey of York, Rowntree and Lavers observed:

'The rates of that benefit payable under the National Insurance Act are not alone sufficient to maintain a family above the poverty line even if other welfare measures are taken into account. . . . A recurrence of large scale unemployment could result in widespread poverty.'[17]

It is the maintenance of full or near full employment since the war that has prevented poverty resulting from the misfortune of unemployment, not the specific cash paying social service designed to this end.

A brief reference may be made at this point to one group who, although they are not seeking work, clearly have unmet needs. These are the erstwhile vagrants or tramps, now termed officially those without a settled way of living. The more obvious needs of these men and women are a home, a job, and an income, all of which require a lesser or a greater degree of rehabilitation. Their less obvious needs may be for medical or psychiatric treatment or continuous care in a residential setting. Their number relatively is small but it appears unfortunately to be increasing.[18] Their problems are many. Voluntary agencies have long made some provision in hostels, Homes, or church crypts. In 1948 the then National Assistance Board was given the duty of providing reception and re-establishment centres for the provision of temporary board and lodging and to make provisions attempting to influence those concerned to lead a more settled way of life. This duty became the responsibility of the Supplementary Benefits Commission when it replaced the Board in 1966 under the Ministry of Social Security Act. Twenty Reception Centres were available throughout the country in 1967 providing 2,000 beds, of which 1,200–1,300 were occupied each night.

The Board never made any exaggerated claims to success but in 1952 it concluded: 'In spite of disappointments the attempt to persuade and help casuals to settle down and play a normal part in the community is worth pursuing.'[19] Those who believe that the welfare of the individual in need is always worth pursuing will agree, but that the pursuit through reception and re-establishment centres will ever be successful is far from certain. One user of a centre said:

'From six weeks' experience of one (as a resident) I should say that, while they are pleasant places with little oppressive authority, they are nevertheless totally inadequate because of the point of view of the authorities which is benevolent but based—inevitably—upon the general mores of society outside.'[20]

The writer offered no practical alternative, however.

Sickness or disability constitutes a second misfortune which can affect anyone; giving rise not only to medical, but frequently to economic and social problems as well. The first are, or are intended to be met by the national health service, introduced in

1948 under the National Health Service Act, 1946. The maternity and child welfare services, now part of the national health service, were discussed in the last chapter. All that is added here is that in view of the liability to accidents and greater susceptibility to infectious diseases in childhood (which do not appear to be affected by housing standards or maternal care), that call for early preventive measures and for the services of the general practitioner and specialist, it is surprising that wives and children were excluded from the provisions of the national health insurance scheme of 1911, right up to 1948. Only insured persons, not their dependants, were entitled to the services of the doctor and the supply of medicines. Even they were not all assured of specialist, ophthalmic, dental, hospital or convalescent treatment, medical or surgical appliances. Not until the introduction of the national health service in 1948 was a full range of services made available to the whole population regardless of age, occupation, sex or income.

The national health service now includes provision of hospital and specialist services, general medical and dental services, pharmaceutical and ophthalmic services, and local health authority services. In addition to maternity and child welfare the last must include midwifery, health visiting, home nursing, domestic help, arrangements for vaccination and immunisation, and ambulance services. They may include other measures to prevent illness or to promote the care and after care of the sick, and since 1959 they may include a chiropody service. Under the Health Services and Public Health Act, 1968, a local authority may provide or arrange for the provision of laundry facilities for households for which home help is being or can be provided.

The value of the national health service, as such, is not now questioned but there are still controversies about its cost and its charges; its effectiveness in promoting health rather than treating disease; the status of the general practitioner; and its administrative structure, to which reference is made in Chapter Eleven. The necessity for a service to meet need in time of sickness or disablement, whether physical or mental, is, however, no longer seriously challenged. The medical profession itself had 'no difficulty in reaching the conclusion that basically the concept of a comprehensive national health service is sound'.[21] It is clear that many deficiencies have to be made good, including grave shortages

E*

of staff, outdated hospital buildings, limited provisions for the old, and inadequate in-patient and after-care services for the mentally ill and handicapped. But there is nothing to suggest that the services could contract other than at the expense of the health of the individual and of the nation.*

The economic as distinct from the medical needs of the sick or disabled person are met by the National Insurance and National Insurance (Industrial Injuries) Acts, 1946, and subsequent amending Acts. The first made the same provision for the sick person as for the unemployed; that is to say, it assured an insured person of a weekly cash payment as long as sickness continued. Whilst open to criticism the scheme was an improvement on that which preceded it. It included for the first time dependants' benefits. It is not reduced or stopped after a period of illness as it was after 104 weeks under the old scheme, and the benefits are payable at the same rate, not a lower rate than those in respect of unemployment.

The provisions of the National Insurance (Industrial Injuries) Act, for those who suffer personal injury caused by accident arising out of and in the course of employment, or those who suffer from a prescribed disease or injury due to the nature of employment, are more generous than those of the National Insurance Act. The differences have been justified on the grounds that many industries vital to the community are particularly dangerous and special provision against risk should, therefore, be made; that a person disabled during the course of his employment is not a free agent but is disabled whilst working under orders; and that only if special provision is made for the results of industrial accident or disease, irrespective of negligence, would it appear possible to limit employers' liability at Common Law to the results of actions from which he is morally and in fact responsible.[22]

Whatever force these arguments may have, serious anomalies inevitably arise. Thus the weekly rate of injury benefit, payable for a maximum of 26 weeks, is higher than sickness benefit to which it then gives place. Further, a disablement benefit for any continued disability is payable after injury benefit stops, according to the degree of disablement. This can be increased by a special

---

* For a general account of its origin, structure and achievements, see Harry Eckstein, *The English Health Service*, Oxford University Press, 1959.

hardship allowance, an unemployability supplement, a constant attendance allowance, or a hospital treatment allowance. Consequently the person suffering injury, disablement or disease arising out of and in the course of employment is better off financially than the person whose illness, injury or disablement results from other causes, whether or not the economic situation of the first is more serious than the second. Changes in rates introduced in 1965 further emphasised the discrepancies between the two schemes which became increasingly difficult to justify.

Sickness and disability do not give rise to medical and financial needs only. Both, as in unemployment if it is of long duration, may result in a need for physical rehabilitation, training or retraining, to enable the person concerned to return to, or obtain new employment on recovery, or to lead an independent life domestically at home or socially in the community. There are also sick or disabled people who require continuing domiciliary services, sheltered employment, or residential care other than in hospital, by reason of the serious nature or permanency of their illness or disablement. Income of itself, however ample, is not enough in such cases to satisfy need. A sick or disabled person of assured means can be overwhelmed by loneliness, idleness, isolation, frustration, dependency, feelings of uselessness, or family tensions, unless he or she is given such training, help, care and support as may be needed in each case.

So far as rehabilitation is concerned, the first industrial rehabilitation units were set up under the Disabled Persons (Employment) Act, 1944. It is clear that this Act—the first of its kind—was furthered as much by the exigencies and experiences of the war and the demand for all available manpower, as by a recognition of the needs of the disabled themselves. The dual motive behind the Act is clearly illustrated in the report of an Inter-departmental Committee on the Rehabilitation and Resettlement of Disabled Persons (the Tomlinson Committee) which preceded it. This Committee recommended the provision of post-war schemes on two grounds:

'that there is a national duty to see that persons who have suffered disablement are given an opportunity of leading as full and as useful a life as their disablement permits; and that as disablement represents a double loss to the community, viz., a reduction of the total productive capacity and an increase in the cost of maintenance and remedial services, the restoration of the disabled person to productive employment will be an economic advantage'.[23]

The Ministry of Labour and National Service as it then was was required to set up a register of disabled persons and was empowered to provide or financially assist others to provide, vocational training courses, industrial rehabilitation courses and, for the more seriously disabled, sheltered employment. Employers of not less than twenty persons were required to fill a given percentage, fixed subsequently at 3 per cent, of vacancies from those on the disabled persons register.

A Committee of Inquiry on the Rehabilitation, Training and Resettlement of Disabled Persons (the Piercy Committee), which was set up in 1953 to review the provisions for the disabled, reported well on them in 1956.[24] Criticisms have been made, nevertheless, on the grounds that disablement resettlement officers are insufficiently aware of and not trained to deal with the social problems of disabled persons; that some employers manage to evade their statutory duty under the Act; that the cost of Remploy factories providing sheltered employment has been excessive; and that registration as a disabled person stigmatises the person concerned. No one, however, has suggested that the services should be curtailed although, like those which assist the unemployed to find and keep work, their existence has escaped mention by the critics of the Welfare State.*

Promotion of the general welfare of all disabled persons, as distinct from meeting their medical or employment needs, became part of the statutory social services only on the implementation of Section 29 of the National Assistance Act, 1948. The blind were provided for under the Blind Persons Act, 1920, but other categories of disabled persons prior to 1948 had either to depend on their families, the services of voluntary bodies, or on the Poor Law. Even after 1948 many were still at a disadvantage because some local authorities were slow to use the powers then accorded to them. They were not required to do so by the Minister of Health until 1960 and even then some were very slow in making a

---

* For further examination of services for the disabled in employment, see A. F. Young, op. cit. (19 Chap. 1), Chapter 3.

start. The disabled can in fact be regarded as late entrants into the benefits of the Welfare State.

Up to the presentation by local authorities in April 1963, of plans for the development of community care* 'a number of authorities had not even made schemes for the deaf or dumb or for the general classes [of disabled persons]. . . . The numbers of handicapped people registered with local authorities covered only a small proportion of the total handicapped population.'[25] In fact no one really knows even yet how many disabled people there are in the community, apart from the blind, nor the nature and extent of particular disabilities.

One step towards overcoming this ignorance was an announcement in October 1967 that the Government Social Survey was to undertake a study, expected to be available in 1970, of adults living at home who were substantially and permanently handicapped by limitations in their movements and the extent to which they received and needed help from local authority services. It was announced at the same time that a survey of younger chronic sick patients in hospital was in progress and that the possibility of a similar survey in local authority Homes was in mind.

Such ignorance as there still is need not have lasted so long, for the powers of local authorities given to them under the National Assistance Act are wide. They are able to compile and maintain classified registers of handicapped persons; assist the disabled in methods of overcoming the effects of disability; provide guidance and advice on personal problems; provide or assist in the provision of recreational, social and holiday facilities and transport in their use; make domiciliary provision for assistance and recreation at home; appoint welfare officers; provide home work schemes and assist in the marketing of work; and provide sheltered workshops and hostels to accommodate those employed there. It has been a manifest disadvantage for a disabled person to live in an area in which the local authority did not choose to or is only slowly providing any one or more of these facilities, for unless the work

---

* These plans were revised in 1964 and 1965. See Ministry of Health. *Health and Welfare; The Development of Community Care.* Revision to 1973–1974 and revision to 1975–1976 of Plans for the Health and Welfare Services of Local Authorities in England and Wales. H.M.S.O., 1964, and Cmnd. 3022. H.M.S.O., 1966.

of voluntary bodies is well established, adequately supported and widespread, his needs have been and may still be unmet.

The third and too common misfortune of adult years, which gives rise to economic, social and emotional needs, is widowhood. Whilst it may just be possible on occasion to regard some unemployment, sickness or disability as self-caused, that is to say, as the result of not acting in an ideally responsible way, *vide* 'The Welfare Society'; it is scarcely possible so to regard widowhood, unless of course it is the result of homicide, or the grossest of domestic carelessness that causes the death of a husband. Widowhood is a misfortune with which any married woman may be faced and which leaves her at one blow bereft of marriage partner, life companion, father and wage earner. It is not possible for the social services to meet all the resulting needs but they can attempt to soften the blow and they should assure the widow with her dependent children of an adequate income and such support in her social problems as can be given. It is clear, however, that they have not yet done this, although widows number some 2,500,000 in England and Wales alone.

The pension under the first Widows, Orphans and Old Age Contributory Pensions Act, 1925, was 10s. a week plus small allowances for dependent children. This constituted no more than pocket money. Under the National Insurance Act, 1946, and its subsequent amendments, more generous provisions were made but payment of widows' pensions was subject to an earnings rule up to 1965. The earnings rule is an arrangement (still applicable to retirement pensions) whereby pension is reduced in respect of every complete shilling earned above a stipulated figure each week. In other words an increase in earnings, after a certain point, is matched by some decrease in pension. This is not to be confused with the 'wage stop' referred to shortly.

In 1957 Marris's study of widows and their families concluded:

'National Insurance seemed to the widows . . . neither just nor adequate. It did not meet even their subsistence needs, nor did it seem to them a fair return for the contributions their husbands had paid. They felt victimised by the earnings rule, and humiliated if they had to appeal to the National Assistance Board. National Insurance, therefore, fell far short of protecting them against hardship, and the sense of being degraded by their misfortune.'[26]

The Annual Reports of the National Assistance Board and the Ministry of Social Security have shown a continuing need to supplement widows' pensions. The earnings rule was relaxed in 1964 but not repealed until 1965, despite the fact that there was never any such rule for widows of servicemen nor those covered by the National Insurance (Industrial Injuries) Act, and no regard was ever taken of unearned income of widows, however substantial.

That financial need is not the only problem faced by widows is shown by the response to the establishment of Cruse Clubs, a voluntary body incorporated in 1959, with a general counselling service for widows and their children. This organisation sends out monthly letters dealing with individual problems and references and in one town alone 150 widows responded immediately to an advertisement relating to the opening there of a Cruse Club.

Perhaps this is the point at which a further brief reference can be made to the National Assistance Act, 1948; Part II of which was intended to provide financially for those not covered, or insufficiently covered, by the National Insurance Acts. These were expected to be but a residual minority. In the event, however, this expectation was proved wrong by the continuous post-war rises in the cost of living which outran upward amendments in insurance contributions and benefits. This was illustrated in the Annual Reports of the National Assistance Board, before it was replaced by the Ministry of Social Security in 1966, which each year gave the number of persons grant aided and the cause of their need. At the end of 1965, for example, weekly allowances numbered 1,997,000 relating to the needs of approximately 2,841,000 persons including dependants.[27] This compared with 1,612,000 weekly allowances paid in December 1955, relating to approximately 2,250,000 persons,[28] a rise of 591,000 persons in receipt of grants. National Assistance, in short, played an increasingly important, although unintended, part in the prevention of poverty after it was introduced in 1948.

In November 1966, the cash paying services of the National Assistance Board were transferred to the new Ministry of Social Security established under the Ministry of Social Security Act, 1966. National Assistance grants were then replaced by non-contributory benefits as of right and of two kinds; supplementary pensions for those over pensionable age, and supplementary allowances for those under, in both cases where resources were otherwise insufficient to meet requirements; such pensions or allowances being added to any pension or benefit payable under the National Insurance Acts. These non-contributory benefits are determined on application to the Supplementary Benefits Commission set up under the Act.

In heralding the changes the then Minister of Pensions and National Insurance said that the proposals were intended to preserve what was good in existing social security schemes whilst getting rid of the features which had created dislike or misconception. What these were was not identified. It was the view of the Government, however, that the proposed alterations would ensure that the elderly would have no hesitation in claiming the new supplementary benefits. Over 600,000 new applications were in fact made in the first three months after the new scheme came into force but this still left a substantial number who could have applied but did not do so.

It remains to be seen whether over the years all who can apply will do so and whether the new arrangements will continue to be acceptable or will come once again to be regarded as poor relief under another name. Supplementary benefits are still subject to a test of means and the 'wage stop', required under the provisions of the National Assistance Act, has been continued.

The 'wage stop' is the statutory provision which requires that any supplementary allowance payable to a person in receipt of sickness or unemployment benefit shall not be such that his income exceeds what his net weekly earnings would be if he were in full time work in his normal occupation. Such cases inevitably result in a man and his family having to live on an income less than that which the Supplementary Benefits Commission, in recommending rates of supplementary allowances, regard as a reasonable minimum. The provision is intended to discourage recipients of supplementary allowances from relying upon them rather than seeking full time employment, but it inevitably results in many families with children living below bare supplementary allowance level. The Supplementary Benefits Commission reviewed the situation in 1967 with a view to easing the position as far as this could be done.*

* See Ministry of Social Security, *Administration of the Wage Stop*, H.M.S.O., 1967.

In addition to the non-contributory benefits payable under the Ministry of Social Security Act a person who is in receipt of a supplementary pension, or has been in receipt of a supplementary allowance for a continuous period of not less than two years (other than the unemployed), may receive an additional 9s. a week. This is intended to make provision for long-term cases such as the chronic sick living at home, widows or other women with dependent children, or others who may have special needs arising from the long term or permanent adverse circumstances of their lives. The Supplementary Benefits Commission also have discretionary power, as did the National Assistance Board, further to increase supplementary benefits in exceptional circumstances or cases of exceptional needs.

The fourth misfortune of adult life to which attention is drawn is marriage breakdown, whether through desertion, separation or divorce. With the causes and the extent of this problem this book is not concerned. It is concerned only with the needs to which marriage breakdown gives rise and the social services designed to assist those who are affected. Beveridge recognised that for a woman, divorce, legal separation, desertion or voluntary separation may cause needs similar to those resulting from widowhood and he recommended that she should, therefore, be insured against the risk, unless the breakdown was her fault or with her consent.[29] This recommendation was not, however, accepted and thus where there is no mutual and satisfactory agreement between the partners in the event of marriage breakdown, a woman is entitled only to what a court may allow and her husband is required to and actually does pay towards her maintenance and that of the children.

That there are unmet financial needs under these arrangements has been shown in the Annual Reports of the erstwhile National Assistance Board and now in those of the Ministry of Social Security. Wynn also showed that the risk of requiring to apply for financial assistance is much greater amongst the unmarried, the divorced and the separated wife, than amongst the widowed mother.[30] On the other hand, those who suffer from a broken or a breaking marriage can at least receive some personal help and advice if they seek it from probation officers attached to the courts. These officers are concerned with some 76,000 such cases a year.

There is also a power of the divorce court to appoint probation officers to act as welfare officers where it is thought desirable that any child involved in a divorce case should be under the supervision of an independent person. Lastly, there are the advisory services of the voluntary bodies; the National Marriage Guidance Council, the Catholic Marriage Advisory Council and, in London, the Family Discussion Bureau.

None of these services can wholly compensate for the suffering of anyone involved in the unhappiness of a broken marriage, whether he or she be child or parent. The need goes beyond that which the social services, however humane or extensive, can meet to the full, and to expect that they could do so would be unrealistic. All that can be hoped for is that they may relieve some of the suffering and assist towards the solution of the personal problems involved.

Homelessness and poor housing conditions are misfortunes about which there has been re-awakened public concern in recent years. They are not new problems but the continuance or re-emergence of old ones. With the rapid growth of urbanisation in the nineteenth century and the lack of planning and sanitary provision, gross overcrowding and unhealthy conditions affected a large part of the working class population. The report of the Royal Commission on the Sanitary Conditions of the Labouring Population in Great Britain, 1842, and two reports of the Royal Commission on the State of Large Towns and Populous Districts, 1844 and 1845, described conditions of squalor, overcrowding and lack of sanitation, which in themselves were enough to account for the rise in the death rate that occurred between 1820 and 1850. The report of the Royal Commission on the Housing of the Working Classes, 1885, revealed continuing and serious inadequacies and led to the first housing legislation, the Housing of the Working Classes Act, 1890, which gave powers to local authorities not only to abolish undesirable dwellings but to provide new dwellings for the working classes.

In the present century and particularly since the First World War, there have been successive Housing Acts attempting either to increase the supply of houses and overcome shortages, demolish the slums, abolish overcrowding, improve standards, or prevent undue rise in rents. It is impossible in the short space available here even to outline the provisions of each Act. Between the wars alone there were six major Housing Acts. Reference, however, can usefully be made to the evidence showing the relationship between overcrowding, homelessness, and the size of family. First, the Housing Survey of 1936 showed, according to the over-crowding standards as laid down in the Housing Act, 1935, that small families of up to four units accounted for 30·4 per cent of all overcrowded families, and families of four and a half units and more for 69·6 per cent, the largest extent being amongst families of six units.[31] (Each person over ten years of age counted as one unit; each child between the ages of one and ten years as half a unit; and a child under one year was not counted at all.) As the overcrowding standard was a very low one the figures under-estimated the problem. If measured on a standard that required separate self-contained accommodation for each family, separate living and sleeping accommodation, and for the space allowed in local authority building today the extent of overcrowding would have been substantially higher.

After the Second World War in a time of acute shortage of housing, a survey undertaken in 1946 provided further information about the size of family and overcrowding. Nine per cent of families lived more than two persons to a room in the case of first, second, and third birth orders and this increased to 31 per cent with higher birth orders. It was also found that many confinements took place 'in what were regarded as appalling conditions of over-crowding'.[32] By 1950, with post-war increases in housing provision, the proportion of overcrowded families was shown to have fallen.[33] But the problems of housing were not solved. There was concern in particular about the situation in the larger towns and about the number of parents with children in accommodation provided by local authorities for the homeless under Part III of the National Assistance Act, or whose children had to be received into care by reason of their homelessness.

Towards the end of 1966 concern was evident in the issue of a joint circular by the Ministry of Health (20/66), the Home Office (178/66), and the Ministry of Housing and Local Government (58/66), asking local authorities to review their arrangements for the homeless in various types of temporary accommodation and to report to the Minister of Health, by March 31, 1967.

The urgency of the need was emphasised by a survey published in November 1966,[34] undertaken by the National Assistance Board shortly before it was absorbed by the Ministry of Social Security. The number of homeless persons, mainly men, was there estimated as 13,000–14,000. A new voluntary organisation was set up to raise £1,000,000 to ease the plight of those living in hostels or elsewhere in intolerable conditions. Five bodies showed their common concern in sponsoring this organisation—'Shelter'. These were the Housing Societies Charitable Trust, Christian Action, Housing the Homeless Central Fund, the British Churches Housing Trust and the Catholic Housing Aid Society.

It would seem clear that housing must remain a social service in the sense that State intervention—necessary in the first instance to overcome the grossly low standards of living and overcrowding of the last century—must continue if slum clearance is to proceed and additional housing be provided at a rate necessary to meet the urgent needs of the growing population. To say this is not to argue that all housing should be provided and managed by local authorities at subsidised rents. It is but to recognise that public as well as private enterprise is necessary to meet immediate and future need. Market mechanisms will not of themselves solve shortages at prices all can pay, in particular families with dependent children. With a population expected to rise to over 70,000,000 by 2002, and a child population under the age of fifteen likely to rise from 12,296,000 in 1962 to 18,776,000 the problem is likely to remain such, throughout the present century at least, that State intervention will be essential. In 1961 Greve estimated that in the next twenty years about two million more houses would be required just to keep pace with the growing number of households.[35] That figure took no account of slum clearance needs or improvement in quality generally.

Thus the Government's one-time target to build 500,000 homes a year by 1970, even if reached, would not have solved the overall shortage of accommodation resulting from the growth of population, the increase in the number of households, the replacement of a million houses condemned as slums and another two million in so called twilight areas. In short, as Donnison said: '. . . the pressures compelling government to assume responsibility for the solution of housing problems are likely to increase rather than diminish', and, 'the replacement and modernisation of (old) houses . . . will prove an expensive and laborious process that can only be carried through effectively at the instigation of government.'[36]*

To turn now, so far as the social services are concerned, to the needs and misfortunes of the offender and his or her family: It is appropriate to begin this brief outline with reference to the Probation of Offenders Act, 1907, which provided for the first time under statute a personal service as an alternative to imprisonment of the offender. This statutory service, provided through the probation officer, was the successor of the voluntary work of the Church of England Temperance Society which appointed its first Police Court Missionary in 1876. Probation Officers are the servants of the court to which they are attached and their duty is to advise, assist and befriend the offender placed under their supervision.

In 1964 the probation service was expanded to include the after care of those released from detention, taking over this work from the voluntary Discharged Prisoners' Aid Societies and the Central After-Care Association. The Home Office accordingly now has a Probation and After-Care Department and an Advisory Council for Probation and After-Care.

In 1966 social work with the offender whilst in prison also became a responsibility of the probation officer. This had previously been undertaken by the National Association of Discharged Prisoners' Aid Society by means of public funds made available for the appointment of prison welfare officers. This National Association ceased to function when the change took place. But another voluntary body was formed, the National Association for the Care and Resettlement of Offenders, whose function is not to work with offenders as such, but to involve and inform the citizen in and about preventive work and the after-care of offenders; to maintain a liaison between voluntary workers and the Probation and After Care Department of the Home Office; and encourage by research the development of after-care and prevention.

In the various ways outlined the probation officer now provides what has come to be called the social service of the courts. This

* For further reading see Stanley Alderson, *Housing*, Penguin Books, 1962.

includes enquiries for and reports to the courts, supervision of those on probation, advice and assistance of those in prison and planning for their after-care. The intention is to protect society at the same time as the offender is enabled either to live and work in the community under supervision, or to return to it with help and advice designed to further rehabilitation. Clearly where it is successful the service is of benefit not only to the offender concerned and his or her family but the community as a whole.

Old age constitutes the last of the dependency periods of life that call for services to prevent suffering, protect weakness, redress the balance and promote the good of the individual and society. The needs of the old are in many ways no different in kind from those of the young but they are often different in degree. All people have need of a home, income, sustenance, occupation, affection, companionship and social contacts. But old people when they are failing in body or mind may need sheltered housing or employment, special nourishment, greater warmth, physical protection, domestic aids, personal and supportive attention, and more medical care. A small minority require permanent nursing or residential accommodation.

The point at which the heightened needs of the old become apparent is not decided by chronological age, nor by retirement from work, but by the onset of some degree of physical or mental infirmity which clearly varies from one person to another. Some may never reach this point, but those who live into their late seventies, eighties or over are likely to need at least some special provision or attention if their growing dependency is not to be the cause of sickness or disability, the onset of loneliness, idleness, or of anxiety, confusion or depression.

The needs of the old in the nineteenth century who could not be cared for by their families went unmet other than under the limited provisions of the Poor Law or through the charity of voluntary bodies. Although outdoor relief was countenanced more willingly by Boards of Guardians in the case of the aged and infirm, even as late as 1885 47 per cent of all those over seventy years of age spent their last years and died in the workhouse. More than a third of the 'pauper population' between 1848 and 1910 were aged and infirm persons or their dependants. The report of the Royal Commission on the Aged Poor, 1895, confirmed the suspicion that the circumstances and conditions of many old people were mean and miserable. As a result less harsh discipline gradually appeared in the workhouse and the first non-contributory old age pensions were introduced in 1909 for hitherto respectable old people of seventy years of age or over. This was but a bare minimum, however, and the development of better provision both in respect of pensions under the Widows, Orphans and Old Age Contributory Pensions Act, 1925, and the National Insurance Act, 1946, and in respect of welfare under the National Assistance Act, 1948, waited until the passing of the two world wars. Even in the 1960s however, although the lot of the old had substantially improved in comparison to pre-war days, it was still true to say that in no respect had their needs been fully met.

In 1961 Political and Economic Planning went so far as to conclude: 'The needs of old people in retirement both social and economic are perhaps the most neglected in contemporary society.'[37] So far as housing was concerned Greve observed at the end of 1961: 'It is a bitter commentary on our society that the old are the worst housed of its people . . . Failing a programme of two or three times its present size, the special housing problems of the aged will be prolonged for decades, possibly into the next century.[38] Of residential homes Townsend's study of 1962 concluded: 'Communal Homes of the kind which exist in England and Wales today do not adequately meet the physical, psychological and social needs of the elderly people living in them'.[39]

In 1966 Townsend and Wedderburn in a study of community care and income of old people reached the conclusion that both national assistance (as it then was) and other social services failed to reach significant numbers of old people who qualified for and needed to receive them.[40] Tunstall's study of old people living alone, also published in 1966, found continuing deficiencies in the extent of services provided for the care of the aged living in their own homes.[41]

In short it is possible that the old person, particularly the unmarried, widowed or childless, frail in body or confused in mind, with diminishing faculties of hearing, sight or movement, anxious or confused, housebound or bedbound, constitutes the final answer to those who criticise the provision of social services and the Welfare State on the ground that they are necessary only because people are poor, irresponsible or ignorant. Neither past health nor present wealth, wisdom nor learning, the skills of youth nor the independence of adult years, are guarantees against the limitations, fears, frustrations and dependencies that advanced age too often brings and which frequently call for services of the highest skill and the greatest variety.

From all that has now been said it can be concluded that the case for providing social services rests on four basic assumptions. First, that every man has an intrinsic value or moral worth which is not lessened by infirmity, disability, defect, or any other physical or mental condition, whether or not this limits or prohibits his usefulness to society. Second, that where human suffering can be prevented or alleviated it should be, whether that suffering springs from physical or mental pain, bodily, intellectual or emotional frustration, family or social tensions, isolation or breakdown. Third, that the society in which a man lives has a need, within limits, to make certain claims upon him for the good of all and to promote his wellbeing for its sake as well as his own. Fourth, that men have a capacity to respond positively to efforts made to promote their good, only a small minority in adverse circumstances passively accepting what is offered, taking everything but giving nothing in return.

The present and the last chapter have served also to show that in every stage of development or harsh circumstance of life which are touched by the social services, there is some degree of need (as distinguished from want), not yet fully met. This may well always be so if knowledge continues to increase and higher standards of care are made possible. The view that social services will prove to be a permanent feature of modern life, is supported by Lafitte who said: '. . . social services are not mere devices to equip citizens for intelligent competition as workers and consumers. Nor are they temporary crutches to help the working man in his upward climb from dependence to autonomy, to be thrown away at the door of the Affluent Society. On the contrary, a large section of communal services, growing at least as fast as the economy itself, is an indispensable instrument for a society which wants to make its industrialism serve democratic ends.'[42]

But is such permanence of the social services a matter for concern as some critics suggest? Ever to relieve suffering, protect the weak, redress the balance and promote the good, are surely neither dishonourable nor undesirable goals. It is the means to reach them, rather than the goals themselves, that require constant examination in order that services do not become burdensome, out-dated or unrealistic.

CHAPTER EIGHT

The Machinery of Administration

It requires little imagination to appreciate that the successful introduction, organisation and maintenance of all the social services now outlined have called and still call for administrative arrangements of a highly developed, complex and efficient nature. Speaking of five social services, which are in fact typical of all, Mackenzie observed:

'The administrative organisation of these five services is so complex that one feels a sense of oppression as one studies it: and that feeling weighs particularly on those of us whose job it is to teach about it. It takes a term's lectures to go through the main outlines of the system in a way intelligible to students who come fresh to it.'[1]

If this be so what can be done in one chapter? No more than promote insight into and appreciation of some of the reasons for and the merits of the different organs of social service administration, without attempting an examination of any one in detail.

Before looking at the administration of the social services it is wise, however, to enjoin the student always to remember that men stand behind and work the machine at all points. No social service is self-starting, self-generating or self-perpetuating. These things are and must be done by people, sometimes acting individually but more often as members of organised groups. Since this is so and since the services touch the citizen at all points of his life, for better or worse, for richer or poorer, in sickness or in health, their administration must be as sensitive and sympathetic, and as flexible and free as imagination, reason and justice can expect. So it is as the Working Party on Social Workers in the Local Authority Health and Welfare Services (Younghusband Working Party) said: 'Services which meet human needs cannot be considered apart from the officers who staff them',[2] for it is the officers who personalise the services. 'The problem is not *what* is the administration of the social services, but *who* is it.'[3] Or perhaps one should say the problem is both 'what' and 'who'. 'What' is considered here. 'Who' is considered in Chapter Ten.

The existing organs of social service administration and those who man them have not sprung like Aphrodite, the Greek Goddess of beauty, love and fruitful increase, fully fashioned from the sea. They have grown over the years by processes of practice, precedent, occasional planning and much tinkering. Both voluntary and statutory organisation go back to early days in British social history and can be traced through the centuries to the present day. It may not be possible to see the beauty of Aphodite in the men and machinery that have finally emerged but the discerning eye may perceive behind outward appearances the intention and the means of promoting love and fruitful increase. The way a service is staffed and administered is in fact part of the answer to the question 'How?', posed in Chapter One. How is a social service to be made available to the would-be user once some person, whether an individual philanthropist, a self-appointed body of citizens, or Parliament, has decided it should be provided? How is the day-to-day organisation of the service to be carried out? The answer to these questions lies to a large extent in having efficient organs of administration and enough staff of all kinds, as will be seen later.

There are three traditional forms of administrative organisation in the social services. The first is through the creation of a self-selected, self-perpetuating or terminating, in part or in whole self-supporting body of people; in other words a voluntary organisation. Long before the State assumed responsibility for the welfare of the citizen voluntary organisations did so; at least in respect of the more important categories of need. The sick; the crippled; the old; the ignorant; the poor and the hungry; the delinquent; deranged or defective; the widow; the orphan; the homeless—all these were provided for first by voluntary organisations in so far as they were provided for at all other than by themselves or their families. The private benefaction—the charitable institution—the hospital—the hospice—the asylum—the orphanage—the school—the reformatory—each was the creation in the first instance of one or more persons acting alone or in concert outside the aegis of State provision; always excepting the primitive provisions of the early Poor Laws, which did not claim to promote welfare; only to prevent idleness, relieve destitution or discourage dependency.

The coming of statutory social services, to a minor extent in the nineteenth and prolifically in the twentieth century, changed the field of work of the voluntary bodies, but neither reduced their number nor their importance as a means of social service provision and administration. Voluntary effort as a whole was described in 1959 in the report of the Younghusband Working Party as having become 'an integral part of the health and welfare services'.[4] It became an integral part by virtue, on the one hand, of being first in the field, thereby gaining public acclaim, financial support, specialist knowledge and organisational experience and sometimes, it must be added, vested interest and unwillingness to give up what statutory bodies in due course became better equipped to do. In addition voluntary organisations have been given, over recent years, increasing support, both moral and financial, by government departments and local authorities in respect of the statutory social services. That is to say, they have frequently become agents for central or local authorities.

In many ministerial circulars and all major post-war social legislation sections have been included encouraging or empowering local authorities either to grant aid, or to use as their agents, or both, voluntary bodies providing particular services. For example, since the Board of Education Circular, Number 1486 (referred to in Chapter Six), and the Education Act, 1944, the work of voluntary youth organisations has been inextricably interwined with that of local education authorities and the Ministry of Education [now the Department of Education and Science], so far as leisure time provision for young people is concerned. It is impossible to appreciate the strength of the one without understanding the powers of the other. Each supplements and complements the other, together forming the various parts of the youth service.

The National Health Service Act, 1946, empowers local health authorities, if they so wish and with the approval of the Minister, to contribute to any voluntary organisation formed for any purpose relating to the care of expectant and nursing mothers and of children under the age of five; to make arrangements with voluntary organisations for the employment of midwives whose services it is the duty of the authority to secure; to discharge their duty to provide health visitors, home nurses and ambulance services by making arrangements with voluntary organisations; to contribute to the funds of any voluntary organisation formed for the prevention of illness, the care of those suffering from illness, or for their after-care.

Section 20 of the National Assistance Act, 1948, empowered the National Assistance Board to make contributions to the funds of any voluntary organisation maintaining centres for purposes similar to the purpose of re-establishment or reception centres then maintained by the Board. On the dissolution of the Board under the Ministry of Social Security Act, 1966, the Supplementary Benefits Commission, established under that Act, were given the same functions as the Board in relation to re-establishment and reception centres which presumably included the power, as before, of making contributions to the funds of voluntary organisations.

Section 26 of the National Assistance Act empowers local authorities to make arrangements with a voluntary organisation in lieu or in supplementation of the provision of accommodation it has a duty to provide under Section 21 of the Act for those who by reason of age, infirmity or any other circumstances, are in need of care and attention not otherwise available to them, and also to make contributions to the funds of any voluntary organisation providing such accommodation. Section 30 empowers them to employ as their agent, or make contributions to the funds of any registered voluntary organisation having as its sole or principal object or objects the promotion of the welfare of those handicapped by illness, injury, deformity or other disability. Section 31 of the Act, as amended by the National Assistance Act, 1948, (Amendment) Act, 1962, empowers authorities to employ as their agent any voluntary organisation whose activities consist in or include the provision of meals or recreation for old people, or to assist them by financial contribution or by permitting the use of authority premises or providing, by gift or loan, furniture, vehicles or equipment, and making available the services of staff connected with such premises or vehicles.

Under Section 46 of the Children Act, 1948, the Home Office can, with the consent of the Treasury, make grants to voluntary organisations in respect of the improvements of premises or equipment of voluntary homes or for securing their better provision of qualified staff. Local authorities may, with the consent of the Secretary of State, make contributions to any voluntary organisation whose object or primary object is to promote the welfare of children. Under Section 1 (2) of the Children and Young Persons Act, 1963, a local authority in carrying out its duty to make available such advice, guidance and assistance as may promote the welfare of children by diminishing the need to receive them into or keep them in care or bring them before a juvenile court, may make arrangements with voluntary organisations to this end.

Under Section 46 (3) of the London Government Act, 1963, the Greater London Council has like powers to contribute to the funds of voluntary organisations as the National Assistance Act, 1948, conferred on the London Metropolitan Boroughs. The Greater London Council is also empowered under Section 47 (4) to make contributions to any voluntary organisation whose subject or primary object is to promote the welfare of children or who are providing advice, guidance and assistance such as to promote the welfare of children by diminishing the need to receive them into or keep them in care or bring them before a juvenile court. It has like powers also of contributing to voluntary organisations as are conferred on the London Boroughs as local health authorities under the National Health Service Act, 1946.

Section 45 (5) of the Health Services and Public Health Act, 1968, empowers a local authority to employ as its agent any voluntary organisation having for its sole or principal object, or among its principal objects, the promotion of the welfare of old people. Sections 64, and 65 (1) and (2), empower the Minister of Health, a local authority and the Greater London Council to give assistance by way of grant or loan to a voluntary organisation whose activities consist in or include the provision, promotion, publicising or giving of advice on the best way to provide a service relevant or similar to one which must or may be provided under the National Health Service Act, 1946; Part III of the National Assistance Act, 1948; and the National Health Service (Family Planning) Act, 1967. Local authorities and the Greater London Council have power also to provide the use of premises for such services or make available furniture, vehicles and equipment by gift or loan.

Finally, there is an umbrella clause in the Local Goverment Act, 1948, which virtually allows a local authority, provided it has the consent of the Minister of Housing and Local Government, to give grant to any voluntary body. A local authority, Section 136 of the Act states, may, with the consent of the Minister, contribute towards the expenses of any body carrying on activities within its area for the purpose, amongst other things, of giving advice, information or other assistance to residents in the area or otherwise for the benefit of the area and the residents.

It is under these various Acts that voluntary youth organisations, community centres, old people's welfare associations, citizens' advice bureaux, councils of social service, children's societies, marriage guidance councils, family welfare agencies, family service units, residential schools, homes and hostels for the old, physically disabled or mentally ill, and many others, receive grant or other help from government departments, or local authorities, or are used by them as part of the administrative machinery of the statutory social services.

In view of this it is difficult to understand the observation in a report on community care for the mentally subnormal in London, published in 1966,[5] that co-operation between statutory and voluntary agencies in the provision of premises by the one for the use of the other is against their traditionally separate roles and that the barriers between them may become increasingly obstructive to the development of welfare services. This is contrary to what is happening in many places and areas of work. The barriers between statutory and voluntary agencies are so collapsing that it is at times difficult to separate the one from the other, and the provision of premises is a common form of help offered to the voluntary body.

All this does not mean, however, that every voluntary organisation receives what or as much as it wants. Far from it. It only means that local and central authorities are empowered to give grant or other assistance and that the work of voluntary bodies is approved in principle and may be supported in practice if the authority concerned wishes to use its powers in this way. This, of course, it may not always have a mind to do.

Rodger's and Dixon's study of social work in a northern town reported, following the commendable concern of an authority about the eviction of council house tenants for rent arrears and the separation of families as a result, that 'it had been suggested that a neighbouring family service unit should be asked to extend its activities to the town, but the majority of councillors felt that since they would be paying for the service they could not relinquish control to an independent organisation. Thus it was decided that the family caseworker should be a council employee.'[6] In other words, the council did not use its powers to grant aid the voluntary body concerned. In view of the ineffectiveness of the untrained, inexperienced person who was in due course appointed by the council and the fact that doubts about the value of her work made any new appointment after she left unlikely, this was an instance in which it might have been better had the authority made use of the voluntary body already working with the families concerned instead of attempting to provide a similar service itself. But it was acting entirely within its rights in not doing so.

In 1962, at the time it was concerned with the first ten-year hospital plans and the development of local authority health and welfare services, the Ministry of Health issued Circular Number 2/62 to all county and county borough councils, in which reference was made to the *necessity** of their consulting voluntary organisations providing health and welfare services in *all** aspects of plans for the future development of local authority services. This admonition may well be honoured more in the breach than in the observance, but it is worth noting that the Committee on the Management of Local Government (the Maud Committee), found that the great majority of councillors saw advantages in helping and using voluntary organisations to meet some needs though very few thought they should attempt to provide all new or extended services. The Committee recommended that closer relationships should be developed by local authorities with voluntary organisations both to supplement the work of the authority and to further association of the community with their work.[7]

It seems safe to conclude that although the nature or field of their work may change, the voluntary bodies will remain as important in providing or sharing in the provision and administration of some social services in the future as they have been in the past. Whether or not this is always desirable is a question that should, however, be asked.

* Author's italics.

The frequent claim that the voluntary organisation is more personal, more adventurous and more flexible, and that it appeals to the user more than the statutory organisation does not stand up to careful examination. And in any event, as Marshall said:

'It would be a grave mistake if, by stressing virtues of voluntary action, we were led to neglect the possibilities of developing those same qualities in the statutory services. It is all very well to exalt the one; there is no need to malign the other.'[8]

That the voluntary organisations are free from parliamentary control and political controversy; that they can more easily experiment and pioneer; can pick and choose and concentrate their efforts; can act quickly and offer variety; that they provide opportunities for self-help and are channels for the expression of religious conviction, citizen good will and generosity; have to be weighed against the often thinly spread, uneven nature and uncertainty of their work; the danger of duplication of effort; the frequent meagreness of their resources; and their response at times to sentimentality rather than to reason. At worst a voluntary body can be out-dated, ill-financed, under-staffed and inefficient. At best it can be generously supported, well informed, professionally staffed, energetic and pioneering; making a unique contribution in the field of social administration. Taking the situation all in all, Marshall's view that 'the achievements of the system prove that its merits outweigh its defects',[9] is probably correct.

It must, however, be pointed out that the voluntary organisations are not all as free as they once were, to do what, as, and how they will. Both the concern of the State and its provisions for the welfare of the citizen, and the powers to receive grant, brought with them some control of voluntary organisations which was intended to promote at least a minimum standard of service. The National Assistance Act, for example, requires that Homes managed by voluntary organisations for disabled people, or for the old, must be registered with the local authority, be open for inspection, and satisfy the authority about the fitness of staff, premises and equipment and the general conduct of the Home. Voluntary Children's Homes must be registered and inspected under the Children Act and the Secretary of State can control by regulation the making of arrangements by voluntary organisations

F

for the emigration and boarding out of children deprived of homes of their own. Adoption societies, under the Adoption Act, 1950, must be registered with a local authority who can satisfy itself about the charitable nature, control and staff of the society.

A local authority or government department can withhold or withdraw grant from any local or national voluntary body at any time if not satisfied about the nature or standard of its work. And to satisfy itself it may require to be furnished with a copy of the constitution, accounts and annual reports, approve staff appointments, or be represented on an executive or management committee. To this extent a voluntary body is not entirely free and where the care of dependent people and the expenditure of public money is concerned it is right it should not be. Freedom should not be absolute in administering a social service. That the safeguards there are may not always be adequate may be true but it is much less likely (although unfortunately not impossible) that there would today be a Children's Home, for example, which could be described as some were by the Curtis Committee:

'In these Homes the children may be shut away from any outside contact or advice for the whole of their childhood; they may be in the hands of untrained and narrow-minded staff . . . alike in their disregard of new ideas and new methods in child care, in their misunderstanding of the needs of present-day children, and in their failure to make any provision for the individual such as individual dress, possessions and liberty.'[10]

Whatever the merits of the voluntary organisation, the aid they receive or the standard of their provision, it is clear, however, that the administration of the growing number and variety of comprehensive, nation-wide social services—of the post-war years in particular—could not be carried entirely or even in major part by them alone. The task is too important and complex and involves too large an expenditure of public money. Once the role of government has departed from its ancient functions of the maintenance of law and order, defence and the management of external affairs, and come to include provisions for the welfare of the citizen, so must the State become involved, in one way or another, in the administration of those provisions. Direct responsibility for the citizen means direct participation by government in their social affairs. The second and third traditional forms of administrative organisation become necessary, therefore, as new services are introduced or old ones are expanded.

The second form is through the creation and use of local authorities, or local government departments, for the purpose of administering in each locality services which they are required or empowered to provide under different Acts of Parliament. This is not the place for a detailed examination of the development of contemporary local government. It must suffice to say that it stems from the Municipal Corporation Act of 1835 and 1882, the Local Government Act of 1888 and 1894, and the London Government Act, 1899 and 1963.

Today in the social service field there are local authorities for education, health, welfare, children and housing. The first four consist of the elected councils of counties and county boroughs and in London, from April 1, 1965, under the London Government Act, 1963, the councils of the Greater London boroughs with the exception of education which is administered by what is designated the Inner London Education Authority as a special committee of the Greater London Council. The Inner London Education Authority consists of the twenty-eight metropolitan boroughs, as they were before being combined under the London Government Act into twelve of the thirty-two new Greater London boroughs. This arrangement was to have been reviewed in 1970 but the necessity for such a review was cancelled in the Local Government (Termination of Reviews) Act, 1967, which terminated the Local Government Commissions for England and Wales which are referred to shortly.

The education service can be delegated by county to non-county borough and urban district councils with a population of not less than 60,000 which can have the status of excepted districts under the Education Act, 1944. Delegated powers can also be given to non-county borough and urban district councils with a population of less than 60,000 if the Minister, now Secretary of State for the Department of Education and Science, agrees.

It is possible also under the Local Government Act, 1958, for health and welfare services, excluding the ambulance service, to be delegated by county councils to county district councils. Only in exceptional cases is it likely, however, that such delegation be applied to residential accommodation for the old, disabled or mentally ill.

The local authorities for housing are the councils of non-county boroughs and the urban and rural district councils and in London, from April 1, 1965, the councils of both the Greater London boroughs and the Greater London Council. The councils of county boroughs are the local authorities for all services.

These administrative differences cause considerable confusion, for the ordinary citizen as well as for the student, but to seek a logical reason for them is to set out on a wild goose chase, doomed to failure from the start. The position must be accepted as having come about without reference to any consistent guiding principles. The student of social administration, although he may find *a* reason for what is if he searches hard enough, will not and must not expect necessarily to find *good* reason for everything he discovers. Indeed the Local Government Commission for England, set up in 1958, observed of one area:

'No one in his senses, if he was setting up a system of local government from the beginning, would do it like this.'[11]

Another similar observation was made in 1966: 'Viewed without its historical background the present administration of health and welfare services might well appear to be part of some overworked administrator's nightmare.'[12] Movements towards the reform of local government are instanced shortly.

To appreciate what a local authority must or may do in respect of the social services it is necessary to examine the relevant Acts and amending Acts of Parliament which together state in precise terms what their powers and duties are. To take two examples: Under the National Assistance Act, 1948, the local welfare authorities—that is the councils of all county and county boroughs —have a duty to provide residential accommodation for persons who by reason of age, infirmity or any other circumstances are in need of care and attention which is not otherwise available to them. They must also provide temporary accommodation for persons who are in need arising in circumstances which could not reasonably have been foreseen, or in such other circumstances as an authority may in any particular case determine. In the exercise of these duties authorities are required under the Act to have regard to the welfare of all persons for whom accommodation is provided.

On the other hand, local authorities were only given powers under the Act, as pointed out in Chapter Seven, to make arrangements for promoting the welfare of the blind, deaf or dumb or other persons substantially and permanently handicapped by illness, injury or congenital deformity, but not required to do this unless the Minister of Health directed them to exercise these powers. This he did without delay in 1948 in the case of the blind, who had been provided for since 1920 under the now repealed Blind Persons Act, but in the case of other handicapped persons he did not use his powers of direction until 1960. At the same time as he then directed local authorities to exercise their powers in respect of the handicapped he directed them to provide for the welfare of persons suffering from mental disorder, who had been specifically added to those covered by the welfare provisions of the National Assistance Act by the Mental Health Act, 1959.

To take the second example: Under the Nurseries and Child-Minders Regulation Act, 1948, local health authorities—that is councils of counties and county boroughs—are required to keep registers of premises in their area, other than private dwellings, where children under five are received to be looked after for the day or for any longer period not exceeding six days (longer periods are covered by the Children Act, 1958), and of persons who likewise receive for reward into their homes more than two children under the age of five. The authorities have power to lay down conditions controlling this care and inspect the premises and to refuse registration if not satisfied. Despite these provisions there was growing concern about the number of mothers leaving their babies and children under five in the care of unregistered child-minders, in many cases in unsuitable conditions detrimental to the health of the child, without the local authority having any contact with or knowledge of this practice. A section was there-fore included in the Health Services and Public Health Act, 1968, to amend the Nurseries and Child-Minders Regulation Act. This empowered local authorities to impose stricter conditions on the safety, cleanliness, equipment and maintenance of premises and the provision of food, and to specify the number of children to be looked after in a home or other premises and the number and qualifications of staff required to look after them.*

* For more careful consideration of the care of children under five outside their own homes and related problems see: Simon Yudkin, National Society of Children's Nurseries, *0–5 a report on the care of Pre-School Children*, George Allen and Unwin Ltd., 1968.

Space does not allow for setting out, as with the foregoing examples, every duty and power of local authorities in administering the social services. The student must seek these for himself in the National Health Service Act and the Health Services and Public Health Act, the Education Acts, the Children and the Children and Young Persons Acts, the Mental Health Act, and the Housing Acts.

There was at one time a proposal by the Labour Party to introduce a 'Local Authorities Enabling Bill' to permit local authorities to undertake any enterprise which was not reserved as a function of a central department or a private agency and the Committee on the Management of Local Government (the Maud Committee) which is referred to again shortly, recommended that local authorities should be given a general competence to do whatever in their opinion was in the interests of their areas or their inhabitants, subject to any necessary protection of public or private interests and provided they did not encroach on the duties of other governmental bodies. Neither of these have yet meterialised, however, and the practice of permitting local authorities only to perform those duties and exercise those powers specifically conferred by Act of Parliament remains.

Despite this braver and more enterprising authorities have at times gone beyond the strict letter of the law. Many children authorities, for example, went beyond the duties and powers conferred upon them by the Children Act, 1948, to receive children into care, and undertook preventive work in order to avoid family break up even before the passing of the Children and Young Persons Act, 1963. No exception to this was taken by the Home Office and the position was ultimately regularised by the second Act. Other authorities provided domiciliary care for the old in their own homes in ways not specifically covered by the National Assistance or any other Act prior to the passing of the Health Services and Public Health Act, 1968, which did empower them to do so. This kind of action on the part of local authorities is both an indication that dependence on voluntary bodies is no longer adequate to meet need and that social legislation is lagging behind the recognition of a problem. It is evidence that the time has come for new or amending legislation either to legitimise what is in fact being done in some areas or to require or encourage it being done elsewhere also.

Local authorities carry out their duties and exercise their powers through the medium of appropriate committees—the health committee—education committee—welfare committee—children committee—housing committee—each of which is under a chief officer; a medical officer of health, a director of education, a chief welfare officer, a housing officer and a children officer. The councils are, however, ultimately responsible for what is done in their name. More attention is given to the committees of local authorities in the next chapter.

Administration of social services by local authorities has the merit of independence, within certain limits, for they are free of central control except where this is laid down by statute. It encourages local citizens to concern and interest themselves in services which have a particular local colour or characteristic. It reduces the power of a central bureaucracy. It makes possible the democratic participation of people in services provided for their own as well as the benefit of others. It furthers direct face to face question by those who may be dissatisfied by the quality or quantity of the service they are receiving.

It has the disadvantages, since it is subject to law, of limiting although not excluding experiment; of control by laymen of services which have become highly specialised; of conflict between expenditure on those in need and local demands for economy; and of lacking uniformity, as many a student knows from personal experience when he learns that he is receiving from his authority a smaller further education grant than a fellow student from another authority although he has the same means and the same qualifications, is pursuing the same course of study at the same institution, and with the same goal in view. Because of these disadvantages and also by reason of the many and great social and economic changes which have taken place over the last hundred years the system and structure of local government established in the nineteenth century have been repeatedly under fire. Increase in population, movements in population, shifts of industry, technological development, urbanisation and conurbanisation, new and speedier forms of transport, extension of public services, have all made their impact on local government. And they have raised questions about the suitability of local administration of the social services. Donnison, for example, said:

'After 1945 we attempted to rationalise and standardise our pre-war social services and extend them to all parts of the country. Few of the administrative devices in this system were new, and the needs it was designed to meet were the needs of the thirties. The system was obsolescent from the start.'[13]

It was because of this obsolescence that the local authorities lost in 1946 the administration of their hospitals to the regional hospital boards under the Ministry of Health; that the education and personal health services passed out of the hands of the district councils in 1944 and 1946 to the county councils. It was also why, under the Local Government Act, 1958, a Local Government Commission for England and one for Wales was set up, although this was not for the first time. There had been a Royal Commission on London Government in 1921; a Royal Commission on Local Government in 1923; and a Local Government Boundary Commission in 1945 which was dissolved after presenting a report that was unacceptable to the Government.

The functions of the 1958 Commissions were to review the organisation of local government outside the metropolitan area and to make proposals for such changes as appeared desirable in the interest of 'effective and convenient local government'. By 1966 the Commission for England had produced reports on nine areas. It was then discontinued, together with the Commission for Wales (whose report had already proved unacceptable to the Government) in view of the setting up the same year of another Royal Commission on Local Government (the Maud Commission), which was to make a more radical review of local government as a whole.

In London the position was reviewed by the Royal Commission on Local Government in Greater London (the Herbert Commission),[14] and was changed on April 1, 1965, by the London Government Act, 1963. Thirty-two Greater London Boroughs took over administration of the social services from the London County Council, following general acceptance by the Government of the recommendations of the Commission. The London County Council was abolished, together with the Middlesex County Council and the Metropolitan Boroughs, and the Greater London Boroughs became local health, welfare, housing and children authorities. This was one of the reforms which the Commission regarded as necessary to achieve 'secure and effective local government' in the Greater London area. It referred to its attempt to keep in mind 'administrative efficiency and the health of representative government, as well as the organic relationship of both'.[15] Donnison, however, suggested that boroughs of the size recommended by the Commission could not be administratively effective and therefore either the Greater London Council would become more powerful, or there would be informal integration of the boroughs into larger groups, or there would be increasing intervention by central government.[16] Development in London is an aspect of social administration that it will be particularly important to watch during the next few years both from the point of view of administration as such, and of the standards of the social services provided.

Whatever may happen to local government in London or the rest of the country in the future, it is clear that central government, which is the third traditional form of administration in the social services, cannot now opt out. It has become too entrenched and too important, both as a means of administering some services from the centre, and as a controller and regulator, or sometimes stimulating or setting standards of those administered locally. The central authorities or central government departments concerned with the social services today are the Home Office, the Department of Education and Science, the Department of Health and Social Security, the Ministry of Housing and Local Government and the Department of Employment and Productivity. These are frequently called the social service ministries or departments, whether in respect of all or part of their work.

There may also be public corporations specially created as *ad hoc* bodies to administer a particular service. These are not identical although they have a close relationship with a government department. Central government or central organs of administration have been defined by Willson as 'the government departments whose spiritual if not physical headquarters are to be found in Whitehall: for whose every action Ministers are directly and completely responsible to Parliament: and whose officers are in all but a few exceptional cases, civil servants'.[17]

A public corporation, on the other hand, is an autonomous or semi-autonomous body created to provide a particular service,

F*

which although financed out of public funds and ultimately responsible to Parliament has its own Board, chairman and full-time staff, and is free from day to day ministerial control. In the past the Poor Law Board, 1847–71, the General Board of Health, 1848–71, the Board of Control, 1913–59, the Unemployment Assistance Board, 1934–40 and the National Assistance Board, 1948–68, were five such corporations.

Today the regional hospital boards are the only such bodies in the social service field. But in July 1968 the Minister of Health issued a Green Paper on the administrative structure of medical and related services in England and Wales 'as a basis for public discussion and consultation'.[18] In this Paper it was proposed that Area Health Boards should be appointed throughout the country to replace and take over the functions of the present executive councils, regional hospital boards, boards of governors of teaching hospitals and hospital management committees, all appointed under the National Health Service Act, together with the present functions of the public health departments of local authorities; health centres, home nursing, health visiting, prevention of illness, care and after care of the sick, maternity and child health, medical and nursing care of the long-term sick, disabled, elderly and mentally disabled, vaccination and immunisation, family planning clinics, and ambulance services.

The intention of this proposal was to bring together under a unified administration all medical and related services in order to further co-ordination of policy and administration, plan efficient use of resources and strike what was called 'the right balance between care in the community and hospital care'. The Green Paper made passing references to the Committee on Local Authority Personal and Allied Services (the Seebohm Committee) and the Royal Commission on Local Government in England and Wales (the Maud Commission), and paid lip service to the necessity of having regard in due course to the recommendations of both these bodies. But as a later reference to the report of the Seebohm Committee will show, it would have been impossible to implement all the recommendations of the Green Paper without affecting some of the recommendations of the Seebohm Committee. The two did not march together all the way. This is an obvious illustration of the fact of having two bodies considering administrative changes in related services without the closest consultation with each other throughout is liable to lead to contradiction or confusion of some sort. The proposals made in the Green Paper were, however, dropped.

Broadly speaking, social services which can best be provided according to rule and regulation applicable to everyone everywhere —for example, national insurance and family allowances—and those which require a nation-wide catchment area to be effective —as do the employment services—can best be administered by a central department, with regional or area offices for direct contact with the user of the services as necessary. There is no advantage and may well be positive disadvantage, economic or administrative, in splitting between different local authorities responsibility for services which do not attach to themselves any peculiar local differences, colour or interest. The part of central government departments in the administration of the social services does not, however, end with those services which lie entirely within their jurisdiction. It extends, as already pointed out, to control, supervision, advice and assistance of local authorities in the fulfilment of their duties and exercise of their powers.

As with all government departments the social service ministries have been created and given their functions by Act of Parliament. The first was the Home Office under the Home Secretary. The Home Office was created in 1782 but its responsibilities for social welfare are more recent. They began with the supervision of reformatories which in due course became industrial and then approved schools; with the probation service and somewhat oddly, from 1897 until 1946, with the oversight of the workmen's compensation scheme. Later it became responsible for supervision of infant life protection provisions, the treatment of young offenders and the care of the deprived child. A special Children Branch of the Home Office was established in 1920, subsequently the Children Department, which in 1948 was given responsibility for the guidance of local authorities under the Children Act; for appointing an Advisory Council on Child Care; and for grant aid to persons training for child care. There was some feeling at the time that the Ministry of Health or the Ministry of Education would have been a more appropriate department to undertake these duties but they were laid on the Home Office.

The Board of Education was established in 1899. It remained such under a President until 1944 when it was reconstituted a Ministry under the Education Act, with the increased powers and responsibilities outlined in Chapter Six. In 1963 it became the Department of Education and Science. Over the years it gradually shed functions other than those relating to education proper. For example, powers relating to expectant and nursing mothers and children under five, and the medical inspection and treatment of young children, passed to the newly formed Ministry of Health in 1919, and likewise in 1925 the administration of grants for the training of midwives and health visitors. The oversight of grant and classes and centres for unemployed young people passed to the Ministry of Labour in 1922 and similarly in 1929 the supervision and grant aid of local education authorities' youth employment services. Responsibility for the vocational training of blind and physically handicapped persons over sixteen years of age followed in 1945. These changes are interesting examples of how the functions of a government department can change over time or be transferred with alteration of circumstance. They reflect in themselves the particular needs of a period or the passing of new legislation calling for administrative change at the top, although administrative changes at government level are not necessarily made on rational grounds. This is suggested in Willson's remark about the housing situation in 1945, when it was not 'easy to imagine that so prominent a Minister of Health as Mr. Bevan would willingly have relinquished his interest in housing'.[19]

The Department of Education and Science finally emerged as a central department of great importance and with developments in the education service, including that of the universities, over the next three or four decades it is likely to become increasingly so. The Robbins Committee went so far as to recommend that there should be a separate Ministry of Arts and Science.[20] This, however, was one of the few recommendations not accepted by the Government. It decided instead that a Secretary of State for Education and Science would be put at the head of a single, federal type Ministry with total responsibility over the whole educational field. There are thus now two administrative units, one concerned with schools and the other with civil science and institutes of university status.

The Ministry of Health as it was originally has had a more varied career than the Ministry of Education. Established in 1919 after the First World War, it was 'to promote the health of the people and to take all such steps as may be desirable to secure the preparation, effective carrying out and co-ordination of measures conductive to the health of the people'. But it inherited a wide variety of functions from its predecessors and was by no means concerned only with health. In the social service field it inherited all the responsibilities of the Local Government Board in respect of the Poor Law, of public health matters, and the general supervision of local authorities. It took over administration of the health insurance scheme from the Insurance Commissioners for England and Wales; powers of the Privy Council respecting midwives; those of the Home Office relating to infant life protection (returned later to the Home Office); and the treatment of lunacy and mental deficiency. It became responsible also for the medical examination and treatment of young people in the place of the Board of Education and for the maternity and child welfare services. In 1932 it acquired central responsibility for housing, sewage, water supply, and for town and country planning, and in 1938 it became responsible for the Emergency Hospital Service. It was, therefore, something of a hotch-potch of a Ministry. At the end of the Second World War some rational changes were made. The Ministry of Health then gradually shed most of its other responsibilities to become, in the main, responsible for the new national health service. But it retained oversight of local authorities in respect of welfare services provided under Part III of the National Assistance Act, and certain health functions are still outside its jurisdiction.

The Department of Education and Science retains responsibility for the administration of the school health service; and the Department of Employment and Productivity for the collection of statistics relating to notified industrial accidents and diseases and investigation of their causes, and of the enforcement of the Factories Acts which cover medical examination and certification of fitness for employment in factories of young persons under sixteen years of age, and general health and welfare provisions relating to conditions of work, safety and general amenities. The Ministry of Housing and Local Government is concerned with environmental health in its supervision of local authority housing, slum clearance, water supply and drainage and the Ministry of Agriculture, Fisheries, and Food is responsible for policy on food standards and public hygiene. The Home Office is responsible for the administration of the Shops Acts which cover provision for the health and welfare of shop workers and sanitary arrangements, ventilation, temperature and lighting of shop premises. Thus health matters as a whole are part within and part without the purview of the Minister of Health and a case for some transfer of functions can easily be made.

Under the Mental Health Act, 1959, which repealed and replaced the various Lunacy, Mental Deficiency and Mental Treatment Acts from 1890 to 1938, the Board of Control which had been created in 1913 and reconstituted in 1930 was dissolved. Its responsibilities were taken over by the Ministry of Health. These included the supervision of the administration of local authority mental health services, the inspection and approval of premises, and the provision and maintenance of State institutions. This transfer reflected the breakdown of the unfortunate separation between treatment of those suffering from mental and physical ill health, which the divided statutory responsibility had hitherto encouraged.

In November 1968 the Ministry of Health was merged with the Ministry of Social Security to become one Department of Health and Social Security in charge of one Secretary of State for the Social Services and two Ministers of State, one for health and one for social security.*

In 1942 town and country planning passed from the then Ministry of Health to the oversight of the newly established Ministry of Works and Planning, and subsequently to the new Ministry of Town and Country Planning set up in 1943, which became the Ministry of Local Government and Planning in January 1951, to be renamed the Ministry of Housing and Local Government in November of the same year. These quick changes were made possible under the Ministers of the Crown (Transfer of Functions) Act, 1946, which was passed to facilitate alteration and adjustment without resort to cumbersome machinery and

---

* For the role of the Ministry of Health in supervising the pattern of standards in local authority provision of services see: Bleddyn Davies, *Social Needs and Resources in Local Services*, Chapter 5. Michael Joseph, 1968.

long delays. As well as town and country planning the new Ministry took over oversight of local government, housing and environmental health services from the Ministry of Health.

In this way the Ministry of Housing and Local Government emerged by stages until now it exercises control over local authority house building, approval of borrowing money for purchase of land, road works, and erection of houses, the payment of subsidy, guidance on lay-out of housing estates, ensuring standards of housing design and equipment, and confirmation of proposals for compulsory acquisition of land. The Minister also assumed responsibility for the direction of housing as a national campaign, fixing a level for the national housing programme, controlling the volume of local authority and private enterprise house building, reviewing building costs, collecting housing statistics and concerning himself with such matters as maintenance, conversion, and improvement of older houses, rent controls, housing for special purposes and so forth. The Ministry represents the continuing concern about post-war housing problems and it seems likely to remain of considerable importance in the foreseeable future. The first regional office of the Ministry was set up at the end of 1963 to strengthen the position in the north-east and to advise and help local authorities about an increase in their output of houses both for slum clearance and to meet general housing needs. A regional office for the north-west followed in 1964.

A Ministry of Labour was first established in 1916, taking over administration of the labour exchanges hitherto carried by the Board of Trade. It consolidated and extended its services, assuming responsibility at the end of the war for the training and employment of disabled servicemen and of the dependents of deceased servicemen. It became responsible also for administering the 1911 unemployment insurance scheme and took on from the Board of Education in 1927 the vocational guidance of young people. In 1939 it became the Ministry of Labour and National Service, dropping 'National Service' in due course and becoming the Department of Employment and Productivity in May 1968.

In his report on Social Insurance Beveridge recommended that there should be one Ministry of Social Security to undertake the administration of social insurance, national assistance, voluntary insurance and family allowances.[21] Such an arrangement would have included unemployment insurance then carried by the Ministry of Labour and National Service, health insurance carried by the Ministry of Health, workmen's compensation carried by the Home Office, supplementary pensions carried by the Assistance Board, non-contributory pensions carried by the Board of Customs and Excise, and public assistance carried by the local authorities, but no such Ministry was then established. The Ministry of National Insurance Act, 1944, allocated to a new Ministry of that name, the unemployment insurance functions of the Ministries of Labour and National Service and of Health, the workmen's compensation of the Home Office and the payment of family allowances, but not voluntary insurance or the administration of the new national assistance scheme. In 1953 this Ministry of National Insurance was amalgamated with the Ministry of Pensions which had been created in 1916 to administer pensions for servicemen and their dependants. The joint Ministry was named the Ministry of Pensions and National Insurance and became concerned with both service and non-service men and women. It continued as such until it was replaced by the Ministry of Social Security in 1966. This was merged with the Ministry of Health in November 1968 to become in due course the Department of Health and Social Security, as already explained.

The Ministry of Pensions and National Insurance, as also the Ministry of Labour and National Service, established and appointed regional and local offices and officers in direct touch with the user of the services. This signifies the need for close and continuous contact between the public and the staff of a central department providing a service for the immediate benefit of the individual. It is one sign of the closer relationship between government and governed which is characteristic of the twentieth-century social scene.

The administration of financial assistance to those not covered, or not adequately covered by the national insurance scheme, which was not put under a Ministry of Social Security in 1944 as recommended by Beveridge, was placed instead under the National Assistance Board in 1948 at which date the Poor Law was finally abolished. The Board inherited the work of the Assistance Board set up in 1940 to take over from local authority public assistance committees supplementation of incomes of old age pensioners. The Assistance Board had in its turn taken the place of the Unemployment Assistance Board, established in 1934 to take on responsibility from local authority public assistance committees for the able-bodied unemployed who had exhausted their unemployment benefit. The separation of insurance and assistance in 1948 and the establishment of a public corporation to administer the latter was due to the desire of the Government to maintain a clear distinction between the two. Insurance benefit was of right and assistance only on proof of need. Assistance was intended to be at a lower rate and thus less desirable than insurance—an intention thwarted by the rising cost of living and necessity to raise national assistance rates accordingly. The political controversies of the 1930s about the means test and memories of the Poor Law caused fear that anything which might connect insurance and assistance could tar both with the same brush. And the machinery of the Board was already in being and working well.

By the middle of the 1950s, however, the usefulness of continuing to separate the insurance and assistance schemes was questioned. The growing inadequacy of insurance benefits, the increase in the number of recipients of national assistance grants, together with evidence of refusal on the part of some, particularly the old, to make application for such grants (with the result that substantial numbers went without help they could have received) all supported a case for change. This came with the Ministry of Social Security Act, 1966, which set up the new Ministry to take the place of the Ministry of Pensions and National Insurance and the National Assistance Board. This Ministry was given overall responsibility for the administration of all social security benefits including national insurance, war pensions, family allowances and the supplementary benefits which replaced national assistance grants.

A Supplementary Benefits Commission within the Ministry of Social Security was set up under the Act to administer the new scheme of supplementary benefits. This was charged to have regard to the welfare of the beneficiary and the members were to be chosen for their interest in and knowledge of social problems. The duties of the officers of the Commission were to be very similar to those of the National Assistance Board and they were to endeavour to ascertain social as well as financial needs of those applying for supplementary benefit and refer them as appropriate to a local health or welfare authority or voluntary body.

A return is made briefly at this point to the Regional Hospital Boards. The constitution of these Boards, of which there are fifteen in England and Wales, is laid down in the National Health Service Act. They must consist of a chairman appointed by the Minister of Health and such other members as the Minister thinks fit who must include persons appointed after consultation with the University with which the hospital and specialist services is associated; persons appointed after consultation with such organisation as the Minister may recognise as representative of the medical profession in the area or generally; persons appointed after consultation with the local health authorities in the area; and persons appointed after consultation with such other organisations as appear to the Minister to be concerned.

It is important to note here that the Minister of Health makes all these appointments. The Boards are not composed, like county and district councils, of elected representatives of local people. The constitutional procedure is not a democratic one and the Boards are answerable to the Minister not to the people for whom they provide a service. The same is true of the Boards of Governors of teaching hospitals all of whom are appointed by the Minister from those nominated by the University, the Regional Hospital Board, the medical and dental teaching staff of the hospital, local health authorities and other organisations that appear to the Minister to be concerned. Similarly all hospital management committees consist of appointed not elected persons although in this case the appointments are made by the regional hospital board not the Minister.

In view of the fact that the boards and management committees of hospitals must carry out their duties subject to and in accordance with such regulations and directions as may be given by the Minister, and administer the hospitals on his behalf as part of the national health service it can be argued that membership by appointment is more appropriate than by election, and that the setting up of these *ad hoc* bodies is merely a convenient administrative device relieving the Minister of certain specific day-to-day responsibilities. Those who are concerned for strong local government, however, regret the diminution of local responsibility and regard the procedure as a rejection of democratic principles.

This outline of central government departments concerned with the social services may be completed by a reference to the General Register Office which was founded in 1837. This Office is under the control of the Registrar-General who is answerable today to the Minister of Health, and is responsible for the census of population, the registration of births, marriages and deaths, and the collection and analysis of national statistics relating to such matters as health, fertility, age structure, social class, and causes of death. Clearly the reports and records of this department are of considerable importance on many aspects of health, welfare, and social conditions. The statistics it prepares, the most important of which appear in the Annual Abstract of Statistics of the Central Statistical Office, are a mine of information for the student of social administration. He should, however, never lose sight of the fact that the figures relate to the conditions or affairs of men, women and children all of whom love and hate, sorrow and rejoice, work and worry, are at peace or war, and the further-ance of whose welfare, wellbeing, and opportunity comprises the sole purpose of the collection of factual data. Statistics are a means to an end, not an end in themselves.

The conclusion from this broad outline of the part of voluntary bodies, local authorities and central departments in the admin-istration of the social services can perhaps best be summed up in the words of the Committee on the Law and Practice relating to Charitable Trusts (the Nathan Committee):

'The greatly extended mandatory and permissive powers of central and local authorities in the field of social services make it virtually impossible to find any activity which could not be undertaken by the state or local authority. In spite of this, voluntary societies have an important part to play; indeed many public services could not be carried without their help or the help of voluntary workers.'[22]

Before turning from the organs of administration to the staff who man them, one particular piece of machinery is further examined. This comprises committees and bodies of similar purposes but other names, the importance of which have been steadily growing over recent years.

CHAPTER NINE

Royal Commissions, Councils and Committees

The use, and what may sometimes be regarded as the misuse, of commissions, committees, councils and similar bodies has now become a familiar part of social administration; whether in the examination of social problems, the formulation of social policy or the administration of the social services. They are likely to have a permanent and possibly a growing part and consequently merit careful consideration. Precise distinctions in use or purpose between the different types of bodies cannot always be discerned, and indeed may not be there, but it can be said that a royal commission, partly by reason of its comparative rarity, generally carries the highest status. It is a government or government department that decides one should be set up but it is composed of members appointed by the Sovereign under Royal Warrant. The resounding phrases of the Warrant, issuing from the Court at St James's, signify the serious intention of the exercise:

'ELIZABETH THE SECOND [runs the Warrant today] by the Grace of God of the United Kingdom of Great Britain and Northern Ireland and of Our other Realms and Territories QUEEN, Head of the Commonwealth, Defender of the Faith, To our Trusty and Well-beloved [naming the appointed members with their honours and titles] Greeting!

'Whereas We have deemed it expedient that a Commission should forthwith issue to examine [whatever the matter is]: Now know ye that We, reposing great trust and confidence in your knowledge and ability, have authorised and appointed, and do by these Present authorise and appoint you the said [repeating the names] to be Our Commissioners for the purposes of the said inquiry: . . . And Our further Will and Pleasure is that you do, with as little delay as possible, report to Us your opinion upon the matters herein submitted for your consideration.'

It may not always be appreciated that these solemn words lie behind enquiries into such mundane matters as the system of local government or population trends. The student of social administration who may for a time be finding his work less exciting than he might wish would do well to read them aloud to himself as a stimulant to his imagination. The pomp and majesty of British Sovereignty creeps through them into the study of the ordinary affairs of daily life and encourages a nice balance between the poetic and the prosaic.

Apart from the regal phraseology framing its appointment a royal commission, which is generally known by its chairman's name, is set up to investigate or enquire into a matter or problem which is looked upon as being of some substance and importance, possibly one of a controversial nature, and to make a report and recommendations. Its manifest purpose is to prepare the ground and provide material to assist in the solution of social or economic problems, the fashioning of social policy or the settlement of disputatious issues. Its latent purpose may be to shift the burden of responsibility from the Government, to prepare the way publicly for action already decided upon in private, to shelve or postpone action on unpopular matters, or to divert or silence criticism of Ministers of the Crown.

Royal commissions are not of course confined to enquiring into matters relevant to social administration but these have frequently been the subject of such investigation. Thus since the last war there has been a Royal Commission on Population (the Simon Commission),[1] a Royal Commission on Capital Punishment (the Gowers Commission),[2] a Royal Commission on Marriage and Divorce (the Morton Commission),[3] a Royal Commission on the Law relating to Mental Illness and Mental Deficiency (the Percy Commission),[4] a Royal Commission on Local Government in Greater London (the Herbert Commission),[5] a Royal Commission on the Public Schools (the Newsom Commission),[6] a Royal Commission on Medical Education (the Todd Commission), and a Royal Commission on Local Government in England (the Maud Commission).[8]

The subject of enquiry of each of these commissions may be said to involve important matters of social policy but it does not follow that their recommendations have been or necessarily will be accepted. The recommendations of any royal commission will certainly not be accepted if or as long as they run wholly contrary to the views of the government of the day. 'The influence of

Commission inquiries upon legislation is generally too elusive for accurate determination',[9] said Clokie and Robinson. But in some instances it is clear. Thus the recommendations of the Herbert Commission above were, in the main, accepted and implemented in the London Government Act, 1963, and those of the Percy Commission were accepted and implemented in the Mental Health Act, 1959. The recommendations of the Simon Commission, on the other hand, were not reflected in later legislation. Their report illustrates also that a royal commission is not and should not be expected to be infallible. Thankfulness was expressed, although the Commission was very cautious in its observations, that no further increases in population were probable. Today there is the expectation that the population will rise by approximately twenty million by the turn of the present century.

There is no exact ruling on procedure of a royal commission. This can vary according to the nature of the subject of the enquiry and the wishes of the commissioners. A Departmental Committee on Procedure of Royal Commissions concluded in 1910 that precise instructions would not be fitting and only a general guide was thought suitable and necessary. In addition to individual study of the subject under consideration, a royal commission is free, therefore, to call for written evidence, hear witnesses (including it is to be hoped, though not always so, those who are at the receiving end of a service or whose problems constitute the subject of enquiry), examine reports, consult experts, undertake visits or carry out research with the use of special investigators. These methods are no different from those open to any other body of enquiry.

A model of method of procedure, suited to the subject of the enquiry, is to be found in the introduction to the report of the Committee on Administrative Tribunals and Enquiries (the Franks Committee).[10] Eight stages of its work are there outlined: the addressing of a questionnaire to government departments to obtain comprehensive factual data; the issuing of special invitations to a number of persons and organisations to submit memoranda; the announcement in Parliament of a general invitation to submit evidence and a notice of this in the press; the public hearing of evidence on twenty-seven occasions and the holding of private meetings on thirty-four occasions; the consideration of memoranda and other written material; the hearing of witnesses from government departments, local authorities, academic authorities, organisations representative of interested parties and professions; the publishing of answers to the question-naire and of memoranda submitted and the minutes of evidence.

A royal commission can, although it very rarely does, hold all its sessions in secret. Or it can open all its hearings to the public and make available the full text of its interrogations of witnesses and of the written documents it has received. It can prepare a selective or a full report for submission to the government depart-ment concerned, for presentation to the Sovereign to be laid 'by Command' before Parliament.

The setting up of departmental or inter-departmental com-mittees to enquire into, advise about, and make recommendations concerning matters or problems of particular interest to one or more government departments is another and more common procedure than the setting up of a royal commission. These committees differ from commissions in that they are, for their duration, part of and subordinate to the department which set them up. They are not wholly independent bodies as are commissions. They report to their department but the report is not necessarily submitted to the Sovereign for presentation to Parliament 'by Command'. Some departmental committees are of an *ad hoc* temporary nature, that is to say they are required by the Minister or Ministers who appoint them to concern themselves with one particular issue and thereafter, having completed their task, they cease to exist. Others are of a permanent nature.

Examples in the social administration field of the more important war and post-war committees of an *ad hoc* nature, whose reports were published between 1942 and 1968 and which like royal commissions are commonly known by the name of their chairman as below, are:

The Beveridge Committee on Social Insurance and Allied Services, 1942.[11]

The Tomlinson Committee on the Rehabilitation and Resettlement of Disabled Persons, 1943.[12]

The Fleming Committee on the Public Schools and the General Educational System, 1944.[13]

The McNair Committee on Teachers and Youth Leaders, 1945.[14]
The Ince Committee on the Juvenile Employment Service, 1945.[15]
The Curtis Committee on the Care of Children, 1946.[16]
The Cope Committee on Medical Auxiliaries, 1951.[17]
The Macintosh Committee on Social Workers in the Mental
Health Services, 1951.[18]
The Hurst Committee on the Adoption of Children, 1954.[19]
The Phillips Committee on the Economic and Financial Problems
of the Provision for Old Age, 1954.[20]
The Underwood Committee on Maladjusted Children, 1955.[21]
The Guillebaud Committee on the Cost of the National Health
Service, 1956.[22]
The Piercy Committee on the Rehabilitation Training and
Resettlement of Disabled Persons, 1956.[23]
The Franks Committee on Administrative Tribunals and En-
quiries, 1957.[24]
The Wolfenden Committee on Homosexual Offences and Prosti-
tution, 1957.[25]
The Albemarle Committee on the Youth Service in England and
Wales, 1960.[26]
The Ingleby Committee on Children and Young Persons, 1960.[27]
The Morison Committee on the Probation Service, 1962.[28]
The Milner Holland Committee on Housing in Greater London,
1965.[29]
The Bessey Committee on Service by Youth, 1966.[30]
The Mallaby Committee on Staffing of Local Government, 1966.[31]
The Maud Committee on Management of Local Government,
1967.[32]
The Seebohm Committee on Local Authority and Allied Personal
Social Services, 1968.[33]

In addition to the above departmental or inter-departmental
committees there have been at least five bodies designated working
parties:

The Taylor Working Party on the Employment of Blind Persons,
1951.[34]
The Jameson Working Party on Health Visiting, 1956.[35]
The Younghusband Working Party on Social Workers in the
Local Authority Health and Welfare Services, 1959.[36]

The Stewart Working Party on Workshops for the Blind, 1962.[37]
The Albemarle Working Party on the Future of the Youth
    Employment Service, 1963.[38]

There is no particular reason why a committee should be called
a working party but Wheare suggested that because of the increasing number of committees set up: 'It may have been from
feelings of shame that official circles began to speak of committees
as "working parties" . . . [which] had a more businesslike sound
about it.'[39] Shame, businesslike sound or not, it makes no difference to the functions and procedures of the bodies concerned, nor
to the likelihood or otherwise of their recommendations being
accepted.

Another title or description of an advisory body crept into the
Green Paper on the administrative structure of the medical and
related services in England and Wales referred to in Chapter
Eight;[40] viz. 'Long Term Study Group'. The major differences
between this group and the committees of enquiry listed above
are that its members were not named in the published document
that followed its deliberations; the reasons for the advice it
evidently offered the Minister were barely touched on; and little
evidence was produced on which its conclusions were based. In
short the setting up of this long-term study group was a device
to produce ideas for public discussion, not to examine in detail
the existing method or problems of administering the national
health service.

One thing that frequently puzzles students, sometimes teachers,
and no doubt the man in the street if he ever asks himself the
question, is why some of the reports of committees of enquiry,
both inside and outside the field of social administration, are
published as Command Papers whereas others are not. The reports of the Curtis and Ingleby Committees were both Command
Papers. The report of the Underwood Committee was not. The
reports of the Piercy and Tomlinson Committees were Command
Papers. The report of the Ince Committee was not. The report
of the Albemarle Committee was a Command Paper. The report
of the Hurst Committee was not. And so on. None of the reports
of the Working Parties referred to above was published as a
Command Paper. The nature or importance of the subject of an

enquiry does not decide the issue, nor the length or substance of a report, nor the likelihood of its recommendations being accepted. There is in fact a certain amount of obscurity about the whole thing and a spokesman in the head office of Her Majesty's Stationery Office said on enquiry that no one was really clear about the matter.

To add to the confusion there are also 'House of Commons' papers which are printed by order of the House of Commons. These may be reports presented to Parliament in accordance with sections of particular Acts which require a statutory council or other body to make an annual report to a Minister to be laid before Parliament with any comment he may wish to make. On the other hand there are reports laid before Parliament and published but not by order of the House in which case they are not House of Commons papers. There appears to be no rhyme or reason behind these differences.

As far as can be clarified briefly, Command Papers are those 'Presented to Parliament by (the relevant Minister or Ministers) by Command of Her Majesty', as stated on the title page of the printed report. Such Papers relate to issues first raised or debated in Parliament. All royal commission reports are Command Papers. Reports on matters about which there has been no question or debate in Parliament but which have been enquired into because one or more Ministers thought it a good thing to set up a committee to do so, are not published as Command Papers. They are presented in due course to the Minister or Ministers who was responsible for them and are published by his department. The publishing of Command Papers was begun in the 1830s but no numbers were allotted to them at that time. This practice was begun in 1870 when the number was preceded by the letter 'C'. In 1900 this became 'Cd.' In 1918 it became 'Cmd' which continued until the series reached 'Cmd 9999' when it was concluded, the Hollerith machines used in the numbering process not being able to carry more than four figures. Current Command Papers now carry the reference 'Cmnd.' These last points are not matters of major importance but to understand them is of practical assistance to those searching for a report in a library, or simply, like the Elephant Child, having an insatiable curiosity quite proper to the student.

Lastly there are White Papers and Green Papers (called such because of the colour of their cover), which serve to make known publicly the ideas or intentions of a government or department about policy or legislation. Such Papers may be kite flyers to gauge public opinion, or the presentation of decisions already reached by the government or department concerned and made known in this way before being put into effect.

To return to the consideration of the committee system: In addition to *ad hoc* committees set up for specific purposes there are a large number of standing committees or councils, that is to say permanent or long-term bodies continuously, or for substantial periods of time, observing, commenting, and advising as they are requested or empowered to do. Many of these must now be set up under statute, including several in the social service field. Others can be set up if it is the wish of a Minister so to do. Whether they are called central, national or merely committees or councils makes no difference to their purpose. A rose by any other name smells as sweet. A committee by any other name works as well.

There must under the Education Act, 1944, be a Central Advisory Council for Education for England and one for Wales and Monmouthshire. There must be a National Advisory Council on the Employment of Disabled Persons, together with district advisory committees, under the Disabled Persons (Employment) Act, 1944; a Central Health Services Council (with a number of standing advisory committees) under the National Health Service Act, 1946; a National Insurance Advisory Committee and an Industrial Injuries Advisory Council under the National Insurance and the National Insurance (Industrial Injuries) Acts, 1946. These last two bodies are responsible for considering draft regulations as well as performing general advisory functions, and they can thereby exercise considerable influence. There must be a National Youth Employment Council and Area Advisory Committees on Youth Employment under the Employment and Training Act, 1948; an Advisory Council on Child Care under the Children Act, 1948; an Advisory Committee under the Legal Aid and Advice Act, 1949; a Central Housing Advisory Committee under the Housing Act, 1957; and under the Health Visiting and Social Work (Training) Act, 1962, there must be an Advisory Committee to the Council for Training in Social Work, to advise them on matters relating to the exercise of their functions so far as they concern Scotland.

Advisory Committees had to be set up throughout Great Britain under the National Assistance Act, 1948, to secure that full use was made of advice and assistance both on general questions and on difficult individual cases, of persons having local knowledge and experience in matters affecting the functions of the Board. When the Board was replaced by the Ministry of Social Security in 1966 the Minister made regulations by which the National Assistance Board Advisory Committees became the first Advisory Committees to the new Ministry, on the administration of the system of supplementary benefits which replaced national assistance grants. These Committees and the Local and National Insurance Advisory Committees were replaced by one single set of committees in 1967.

Using permissive powers the Minister of Labour and National Service set up for a time a National Advisory Committee on the Employment of Older Men and Women but laid it down again after only a few years of life. There is now a Central Training Council to co-ordinate and supervise the activities of the training boards established under the Industrial Training Act, 1964, and towards the end of 1963 the intention to set up a Central Advisory Corporation for Workshops for the Blind was announced. A number of other long term or standing committees have been set up by different Ministers. These include a Central Training Council in Child Care which not only advises but promotes training courses and participates in the selection of trainees; an Advisory Council for Probation and After-Care; an Approved Schools Central Advisory Committee; an Advisory Council on the Treatment of Offenders; an Advisory Council on the Penal System, and an Advisory Council on the Employment of Prisoners. All these advise the Home Office.

There is a National Advisory Council on the Training and Supply of Teachers; an Advisory Committee on Handicapped Children; and a National Youth Advisory Council, to advise the Secretary of State for Education; a Health and Welfare of Handicapped Persons Advisory Committee, and a National Consultative Council on the Recruitment of Nurses and Midwives, to advise the Minister of Health. In 1964 the Lord Chancellor set up a

National Advisory Council on the Training of Magistrates. This list is not inclusive and it is not static. Advisory bodies can be set up and, except for those required under statute, disbanded whenever a Minister thinks fit to do the one or the other.

A new kind of advisory service was envisaged in *Social Work and the Community*; the White Paper referred to in Chapter Six. In view of the fact, it was said, that the developing social services had no long tradition of professional work in local authorities it was very important they should have the help and guidance of a professional advisory service. It was stated that the Government intended, therefore, to set up a central service, in advance of new legislation relating to the establishment of social work departments, composed of well-qualified people with collective experience in several branches of social work.

Several of the bodies now referred to have, over the years, published important reports some of which have been specifically designed to influence social policy. The Central Advisory Council for Education (England) has published reports on transition from school to independent life,[41] on out-of-school activities,[42] early leaving[43] and on primary schools.[44] It has been suggested that because there are certain other educational bodies which comment on the education service this particular Advisory Council 'is liable to find itself searching for suitable problems to tackle, in order that its interludes of inactivity may not be unduly prolonged'.[45] Whether or not this be so the problems it has tackled have included ones of some substance.

Other published reports of standing advisory committees include those of sub-committees of the Central Housing Advisory Committee, for example on living in flats,[46] on unsatisfactory tenants,[47] on moving from the slums,[48] and one entitled 'Homes for Today and Tomorrow', better known as the Parker-Morris Report.[49] The Advisory Council on the Treatment of Offenders has published amongst others a report on the after care and supervision of discharged prisoners,[50] and on the treatment of young offenders.[51] Before being laid down the National Advisory Committee on the Employment of Older Men and Women presented two reports.[52] Some standing committees are required to prepare and publish regular reports, for example the Central Health Services Council must do this each year. One of its committees also published an informed and humane report on the welfare of children in hospital,[53] and another one published a report on the pattern of the in-patients day.[54] On some advisory committees there must be at least one woman. This was so for the National Assistance Board and remains so for the Advisory Committees to the Ministry of Social Security. In view of the part which women have for long played in public affairs Wheare held that ' "the statutory woman" is now almost an anachronism'.[55] In other words, there should be no need to require by law that a woman should be on a particular committee. She should be there if she can make a contribution to its work as a matter of course. Indeed, the legal requirement is not 'almost' an anachronism. It is an anachronism.

What may be said now about the significance or importance of advisory committees or councils, which have proliferated with the proliferation of state activities; these deliberately cultivated off-shoots or by-products of extending statutory responsibility? First, they allow for regular consultation by Ministers and civil servants with persons who have specialist knowledge or interests in par-ticular areas, or those with legal, sociological, administrative or practical knowledge in the field, or those who may be regarded as representing the 'common sense' view of the ordinary man whom legislation affects or for whom services are provided. They offer a two-way channel of communication, between the committees and interested parties, the expert, and the general public. They both receive information and give information. They enlighten and are enlightened. They reduce the labour and possibly the influence of civil servants who are caught up in daily administrative routine and are perhaps less able to see the whole of a picture, or be disinclined to propose change or innovation which in some cases would add to their duties or in others reduce their powers. They can undertake detailed examination of technical matters by the use, if desirable, of sub-committees on which specialists and experts can be co-opted.

They can also be a check or a spur on Ministers in making or implementing social policy. They can provide views which may support the introduction of unpopular but necessary measures and they can shield a Minister against ill-informed criticism or untimely pressure. Since no Minister is able to dispense with any committees required to be set up under statute these have a stability and strength enabling them to withstand his displeasure or disagreement, although they cannot force their views upon him. They combine a convenient measure of proper formality with freedom, and a systematic procedure with separation from departmental control.

But it is not necessarily or always the case that committees fulfil only their more manifest or beneficial purposes. 'Governments, like individuals, ask for advice for many reasons besides the want of wise counsel. On occasions they do it in order to flatter, to find support, to seek out opposition, to learn facts and shift responsibility.'[56] Nor is the advisory committee democratic. Members, who serve in an honorary capacity, other than on the National Insurance Advisory Committee and Council, are appointed by a Minister on the advice of his department or after consultation with professional or other interested bodies and he can, if this is his ill intent, ensure that membership is made up of men and women of his own persuasion and point of view. It would, however, be imprudent for him to do this too openly. It would undoubtedly lead to question and criticism and possibly defeat its own ends. Whether or not there is ministerial partiality in the appointment of members there is no guarantee, as has been seen in the case of royal commissions, that the conclusions of a committee will be accepted. A Minister can reject, delay or postpone action indefinitely. Many a report has been published without apparently affecting the views of a Minister or his department. Alternatively, if he is in agreement with it a Minister can use a reactionary report as a bulwark against reform which many consider he ought to institute.

The value of a committee may be circumscribed by its terms of reference which it cannot exceed. The Curtis Committee, the Younghusband Working Party, and the Seebohm Committee for example were all limited in this way, though this is not to suggest that within their briefs their work was not of outstanding importance. The Curtis Committee itself observed:

'The consideration of the welfare of children deprived of a home life has inevitably raised in our minds and in those of many of our witnesses the question whether this deprivation might not have been prevented. This is a question which we regard as of the utmost importance and we hope that serious consideration will be given to it; but it is not the problem with which we have been asked to deal.'[57]

This was in 1946 but not until 1960 were recommendations relating to prevention of deprivation made by the Ingleby Committee and not until 1963 were these implemented under the Children and Young Persons Act of that year.

The Younghusband Working Party also, by its terms of reference, was confined to considering the field of work, recruitment and training of social workers in health and welfare services of local authorities only, although time and again observers had pointed out, and pointed out to the Working Party itself, the need to review the situation in relation to social workers as a whole, whoever their employing body might be. The Working Party observed:

'We were struck, in planning the field enquiries, by the lack of any systematic study of the part played by social workers in meeting needs within the framework of the social services. Such information could have had an important bearing on our own enquiry. We should like to draw attention to the desirability of such study.'[58]

The Seebohm Committee drew attention to the fact that their terms of reference excluded recommendations on the structure of central government although 'We must record', they said, 'that many of those who gave evidence . . . were emphatic that it would be no use altering the organisation of the local authority services unless the organisation of central government was changed to correspond with it. We entirely agreed with this view', they concluded.[59]

From these examples it can be seen that it is not always the case that 'where a Committee particularly wishes to discuss or pronounce upon a subject it usually manages to get around any limitations in its terms of reference'.[60] The limitations for the Curtis Committee, the Younghusband Working Party and the Seebohm Committee were too precise for this, although they all drew attention to the fact that their reports had a significance beyond their terms of reference.

Summing up the merits and demerits of the use of advisory committees and councils, and committees of enquiry, it may be said that they can, on the one hand, be a useful tool in attempting to get at the facts; in obtaining views representative of different interested persons and parties; in removing the examination of controversial issues from the Party political arena; in providing a continuing means of evaluating services and their administration; and in the formation of informed social policy or the review of existing policy.

On the other hand, advisory bodies and committees of enquiry can be intended primarily or merely to delay decisions or to act as smoke screens behind which nothing at all is being done; to pacify or quieten criticism, if possible until public concern has died down; or to produce a bromide or innocuous report that may soothe some and upset none but those who ardently wish to reform. Donnison said, for example, of the Ingleby Committee: 'Their report was respectable and cautious, lacking all sense of urgency, and offering no vision of the future structure of the social services.'[61] If a committee is over-large it may sink in a sea of words. If it is over-small it may have too narrow a horizon. In all probability, however, the merits of advisory and enquiry bodies outweigh their demerits, and since in any event they have clearly come to stay 'the question is not how to do without them but how to make the best of them'.[62]

Before turning to the use of committees in local government it is interesting to note in passing that in 1962 a major voluntary body, the National Council of Social Service, took a leaf out of the government book and set up its own committee of enquiry— the Williams Committee—to proceed along the same lines and by the same methods as a departmental committee of enquiry. Its self-appointed task was to enquire into the staffing of residential homes and institutions other than prisons and hospitals. There was no doubt of this being a very real problem requiring careful investigation and although interested Ministries are even less committed to accepting the recommendations of a committee they do not set up themselves the enquiry was a valuable exercise. The committee had amongst its members consultants from the Home Office and Departments of Health and Education, as well as those experienced in local government affairs, the social sciences and voluntary service. Its report was published in 1967.[63]

Another committee of enquiry set up other than by a government department was one which the National Institute for Social

G

Work Training, acting jointly with the National Council of Social Service, initiated in 1966 to enquire into the role of voluntary workers—the Aves Committee. Such a study emphasised the importance increasingly ascribed, not only to the role but to the selection, training and use of voluntary workers in the social services at a time when professional staff remained in very short supply.

Attention may be drawn once again also to the Porritt Committee appointed in 1958 by nine professional medical organisations 'to review the provision of medical services to the public, and their organisation, in the light of ten years' experience of the National Health Service, and to make recommendations'.[64] The report of this committee was of interest not only because of the importance of its subject but because it revealed what 'a group of doctors representing medicine in all its branches' thought about the place of the profession in and its contribution to a national service. The way in which people see themselves is as revealing and important as the way in which others see them. Self-perception or awareness influence provision and administration of any service and all will not be well if the personnel in a service is not satisfied with its standards or structure, or with conditions of work, or if they either under- or over-estimate their own importance. To leave decisions on policy matters to a committee entirely composed of one profession is, however, another matter, for it is virtually impossible for bias in their own favour not to enter in.

Thus one cannot regard the Porritt Committee as being wholly disinterested when it recommended that there should be set up area health boards which should become responsible, *inter alia*, for all local authority domiciliary health services, including hostels and training centres for the mentally handicapped, and the home help service; that the Central Health Services Council should be replaced by an advisory committee consisting of chosen representatives of the medical profession; that the clinical head of what were called domiciliary teams should be a general practitioner; that responsibility for the school health service should be transferred to the Ministry of Health and the area health boards; that the nervously or mentally sick child should no longer be referred to school child guidance clinics but only through a doctor to the hospital; that admission of old people to hostels and Homes as well as to hospitals should be decided by a doctor, not a welfare officer; that medical advice should always be taken in the housing of elderly people; that what it called the tendency of medical auxiliaries, in particular psychiatric social workers, to develop their own ideas on training and functions, without sufficient control by the medical profession, should be checked. Had all these recommendations been accepted the medical profession would have come to dominate the social services in a way which many people, both lay and professional, would have found unacceptable.

To turn now to the use of committees in local government: This is, in the main, of a different nature from that of the committees discussed so far. Committees in local government are not primarily to enquire into nor to advise, although they can of course do either or both of these things. They are first and foremost part of the actual machinery of administration itself. They are executive bodies. Laski said that the committee system in local government stood, 'with the Cabinet and the modern Civil Service, as one of the fundamental English contributions to the difficult art of self-government'.[65]

None of the services which a local authority provides, including social services, are administered other than by means of a committee. Some must be set up under statute. The Education Act, 1944, requires local education authorities to set up an education committee which must co-opt onto it some members other than councillors. The National Health Service Act, 1946, requires local health authorities to have a health committee which must also have on it some co-opted members from outside the council. The Children Act, 1948, requires children authorities to set up a children committee. Margaret Cole once expressed the hope that this committee would 'eventually find its task diminishing rather than increasing'.[66] But subsequent developments, in particular the additional duty laid upon it by the Children and Young Persons Act, 1963, to undertake preventive work, render this unlikely. Authorities may also have a welfare committee, although some combine this with the health committee, to administer the services laid upon them by Part III of the National Assistance Act, 1948; and a housing committee to carry their housing responsibilities under the Housing Acts. The Committee on the Management of Local Government (the Maud Committee) took the view, as yet not acted upon, that local authorities should be free to determine their own internal organisation and that legislation prescribing the appointment of particular committees should be repealed.[67]

Any of the local authority committees referred to here can and frequently do appoint sub-committees, such as a mental health sub-committee, a schools sub-committee, or a youth service sub-committee, and these can co-opt members with specialised knowledge or experience. *Ad hoc* committees can also be appointed from time to time to concern themselves with particular issues, but it is the standing committees that are of major importance.

The value of the committee in the administration of local authority services is in most ways different from that of a central advisory committee. Local authority committees, for example, break up into manageable parts the overall responsibility of a council which is too large and meets too infrequently for detailed consideration of all plans and procedures of every service that it must or may provide. They serve also to prevent local services being entirely in the hands of a small number of officials, whether they be medical officers of health, directors of education, chief welfare officers, or any others, and they ensure that a group of representative lay men and women jointly bear responsibility for the quality and efficiency of local services. Clearly a good committee can be hampered by a poor official and a good official can be frustrated by a bad committee, for each must work with the other, giving and receiving reports, planning services and deciding policy. Together they are responsible for the administrative process.

The committee system in local government enables the users of services and ratepayers to have a direct approach, not only to officials but to chairmen and other members, if they so wish, thus reducing the dangers of bureaucracy or misuse of power. In short, in theory at least, the committee system furthers the process of democratic self-government. It is scarcely necessary to add, however, that things do not always work in practice as they do in theory. Committees in local government as anywhere else have their weaknesses as well as their strengths. They may meet in public but reach decisions in private. Proposals may be put openly before members as a body but be decided upon behind the scenes by a small influential inner group. Members of the public, using their right to express their opinion may, as Maud and Finer pointed out, 'proceed to lay their advice and use their powers of persuasion, before the appropriate committee, and may even succeed in convincing it; only to find that the final decision is taken elsewhere, by persons who have not had the benefit of their evidence, who meet in secret, and are, for the most part, unapproachable'.[68]

If there are several committees, each concerned with one aspect of a particular issue, action or procedure proposed by one committee or officer may require the concurrence of all the others, and the reports to the council may consequently be numerous and lengthy, resulting in tedious and time-consuming reading and discussion. Reports need not of course be lengthy. One, of a large authority welfare committee on a matter of considerable importance, consisted of the words 'I concur', and the signature of the officer concerned.

Committees can be dominated, even if not actually controlled, by forceful senior officials. Or they can be unduly influenced even if they are not dominated by an official who suggests what should be put on the agenda; speaks to or reports in writing in a particular way about certain items; deals too briefly or prosily for members to be aware of or interested in what is afoot; or brings matters forward for discussion too soon or too late. Any reasonably perceptive person who has sat on any committee, whether it be of a central government department, a local authority, or a voluntary body, knows full well how much it depends for its effectiveness upon its chairman and officers. And honesty should compel every chairman and officer of any standing, particularly if they see eye to eye with one another, to admit that it is not difficult to manipulate a committee to achieve the ends they have in mind, if they are prepared to act in so dubious a way. Their problem is to give a lead, check foolishness, and encourage decisions, without denying a committee the right genuinely to reach its own conclusions.

It is not only that an officer can dominate, unduly influence, or manipulate a committee that has to be recognised, however, but also that he can hide behind a committee, shirking responsibility, or pressing his own ideas in its name. Not only in Old Testament days could a soft-voiced Jacob take on Esau's skin to obtain a paternal blessing. Whatever the balance of merit and demerit, however, local authority committees are probably here to stay. They have a long history and a closer part in the machinery of social administration than any central committee and the question is not how to get rid of or circumvent them, but how to ensure that they are composed of the best personnel possible and used in the right and wisest way.*

Since the voluntary organisation was included in the last chapter as one of the traditional means whereby social services have always been and still are provided or administered, it is only right that the setting up and use by them of committees or councils should also be referred to here. In this instance the term is used primarily to denote a body as a whole, whether national or local, including all its purposes and activities, rather than one part of its *modus operandi* as is the case in central or local government. Thus there is, for example, the National Council for the Unmarried Mother and her Child; the London or Plymouth Council of Social Service; the Exeter, Liverpool or Manchester Old People's Welfare Committee, and many others too numerous to mention. It would be quite as appropriate for these bodies to call themselves, as indeed many do, Associations or Societies, as for example the National Association for Mental Health, or the National Society for Mentally Handicapped Children. The style of address merely indicates a preference on the part of the original or the current governing or executive body for a particular title. In short, the term committee, council, society, or association, as the case may be, with reference to a voluntary organisation, denotes the body *in toto*. This may have a single or a multiple purpose. What that purpose or purposes may be can only be known by an examination of the constitution of the organisation or its published aims and objects. For example, the Invalid Children's Aid Association was set up to supervise, relieve and

* For discussions of the local authority committee and its personnel the student is referred to the essay by Laski in 'A Century of Municipal Progress', *op. cit.*,[65] and to Volume 5 of the report of the Committee on the Management of Local Government, *op. cit.* (7 Chap. 8).

assist invalid and crippled children, and the objects of the National Association of Youth Clubs are to help girls and boys through leisure-time activities so to develop their physical, mental and spiritual capacities that they may grow to full maturity as individuals and members of society.

Voluntary committees or councils may be pressure groups, self-help groups, groups pursuing the welfare of others, the dispensers of alms or charity. They may be educators, reformers or watchdogs. They are composed of a large variety of men and women: clergy and laymen—employed and retired—professional people and housewives—volunteers and salaried staff. The idea that they are still the spiritual home of the paternalistic, authoritarian, philanthropic-minded but not too well-informed middle class personage is today a travesty of the truth. Hobman, for example, in speaking of voluntary work, which could as well apply to voluntary bodies, said:

'Some people think of voluntary work as "do-gooding" in which a privileged minority of well-meaning ladies with secure incomes and time on their hands descend on the needy. This image is altogether wrong. In fact, both men and women are involved; they are of all ages and from every walk of life; there is no place today anywhere, for the patronage of Lady Bountiful.'[69]

Chambers in an earlier sociological study of three voluntary organisations—the Women's Institutes—the Women's Voluntary Services—the British Red Cross Society—concluded:

'The organisations discussed are sometimes criticised by working-class groups on the grounds of the superior social status of their members and particularly their leaders and because of the patronage and condescension which is believed to colour their work. The former assertion was probably true to a great extent ten years ago (1943); it is much less true now, but beliefs of this kind are very difficult to dislodge. . . .'[70]

That some voluntary committees or councils are in the hands of an unimaginative group of ineffective people may be true, but so may some local authority and central department committees. None of the different parts of the machinery of social administration is controlled by paragons. No body of people is the exclusive repository of all wisdom and virtue, nor of all ignorance and vice.

The effectiveness of any committee, whether it is one to enquire, advise, plan or execute, is dependent, within its constitution or terms of reference, upon its personnel, that is to say upon its members. It is important, therefore, to know who the members of a committee are and how and why they became such. So far as royal commissions and departmental committees are concerned the first question—'Who?'—is simple. It waits only upon the public announcement of names by the Minister or Secretary of State concerned. The second question—'How?'—is in one sense simple also. The members of a royal commission are appointed by the Sovereign on the recommendations of advisers, Ministers or Secretaries of State. Ministers receive suggestions or nominations from relevant persons or bodies—from their own advisers or senior civil servants, from trade unions, professional organisations, Party colleagues or personal friends—as to who should or might be appointed as members of departmental or statutory committees. But the third question—'Why?'—is not so easy to answer.

Why a particular name is put to the Sovereign or to a Minister is not necessarily known other than to an inner circle or to a professional body. And why a Minister accepts or rejects a name if he does so, or substitutes another, may be known only to those closest to him or even only to himself. He is not required to give reasons for particular choices, though he may do so if questioned. His choice may depend upon his personal views; the time available for him to consider carefully any suggestions made; the political issues at stake; the fact that someone has caught his ear or his attention at a particular moment; whether or not he is a man of independent judgement; whether he has a secret axe to grind; and on other factors or combinations of factors. The public may be left guessing why certain people with or without particular gifts, knowledge, interests or experience are or are not appointed as members of commissions, committees or councils. And reasons purporting to explain why cannot always be accepted at their face value, as the Webbs pointed out:

'When we are told that a particular person has been appointed on a Royal Commission or Government Committee . . . on the ground that he is or claims to be an "impartial party", we may rest assured that this means merely that the selector and the selected *agree in their bias*.'[71]

Parkinson also issued the warning: 'Solemn conclaves of the wise and good are mere figments of the teacher's mind.'[72] It is possible, however, that he overestimated the innocence of the teacher.

Some of the 'Whys?' of recent years are: Why were there so many lawyers and justices of the peace on the Royal Commission for Marriage and Divorce—eleven out of a total of nineteen members—and why were there no social scientists at all? Why, with the exception of the Chairman, was the Beveridge Committee on Social Insurance and Allied Services composed entirely of civil servants? Why did the Guillebaud Committee of Enquiry on the Cost of the National Health Service consist of five persons only, none of whom were connected with the medical profession? Why did the Seebohm Committee on Local Authority and Allied Personal Social Services have no practising social workers among the members? There may well be reasonable answers to such questions but they are not necessarily or easily available to those interested in the working of the machinery of government, in official procedures or the outcome of a committee's deliberations. The composition of a particular commission or committee may remain a matter of conjecture, but as Clokie and Robinson pointed out: 'If the Government has in mind simply the satisfying of a public demand for investigation of a current problem . . . distinguished nonentities will serve just as well as the . . . most experienced and capable persons. If, on the other hand, the Government . . . is in a dilemma between two lines of conduct it will take care to seat on the Commission men whose practical sagacity in seeking a compromise will carry weight with the interested public.'[73] And the same goes for departmental committees.

Civil servants can and often are appointed to serve as members of departmental committees. This has the advantage of allowing for the expression of a department's point of view and offering advice on problems of administration. But it is a serious disadvantage if those who serve begin with set ideas about the conclusions they wish the committee to reach, or feel it necessary to oppose policy proposals because they are contrary to those followed by their department. For these reasons it is often the case that officials are present only as advisers or assessors and do not sign a final report. Even in this capacity, however, they can exercise

G*

considerable influence even though they may consciously and intentionally play this down.

For any commission or committee to be expected to produce a valuable report and useful recommendations its members must not only be informed and intelligent people but also be able and willing to set about and complete their task in an efficient and effective way. Much depends in particular on the secretary and chairman who, as has already been suggested, can exercise considerable influence on those over whom they preside. The secretary of a royal commission or departmental committee is normally a civil servant, bringing with him the expertise of the administrator and experience of work in a government department. He is an official with skills and facilities to assist in the smooth running of the committee, and possibly with the drafting of memoranda or reports.

The chairman is of the greatest importance not only because of particular knowledge or experience he may have, but because of the need on his part for tact, diplomacy, clarity, impartiality, firmness and patience, as well as the ability to draw out, guide and encourage. A chairman may well write, or take part in writing, reports for discussion or final approval and in this way he can fashion or shape the outcome of a committee's considerations. A bad chairman may well seriously damage, if not actually ruin, the best of committees. A good chairman can at least bring out the limited virtues the poorest may have. His (or her) importance cannot be over-emphasised. Either an official of a government department or an independent person can be the chairman of a departmental committee. Thus Sir Godfrey Ince, Chairman of the Committee on the Juvenile Employment Service, was at the time Permanent Secretary to the Ministry of Labour, whereas Dame Myra Curtis, Chairman of the Care of Children Committee, was then Principal of Newnham College. A Minister may choose whomsoever he thinks is the best person for the position of chairman, or accept suggestions made by his advisers, but why he thinks that a person is the best one for the position, or whether it is his independent choice or that of his advisers, may not be known to those outside his confidence.

The significance of a particular person or persons as chairman or members of a commission or a committee can perhaps be appreciated to the full by the student if he reads what Lord Beveridge had to say in *Power and Influence*[74] about the Interdepartmental Committee on Social Insurance and Allied Services, of which he was Chairman, and that part of the diary of Beatrice Webb in *Our Partnership*[75] which related to the 1904–9 Royal Commission on the Poor Laws, of which she was a member. It may well be that few others, if any, could combine all the advantages she had as a commissioner; great intellect; strength of purpose; many years of work on the subject under consideration; private wealth to carry out personal investigations, to employ staff and to print reports; a husband of prodigious energy and ability to give her support and assistance; the means to mix with and entertain the select and the influential and to carry out propaganda amongst politicians, medical men and churchmen; and freedom from the necessity to earn a living and hold a job at the same time as attending to the business of the Commission. Undoubtedly all these assisted her in her determination to reject the preconceived ideas about methods of procedure and ultimate goals presented to the commissioners; to stand up to opposition; to reject the view of the Majority; and to draft the Minority Report. She may indeed be exceptional as an example of individual influence but she recorded what was in fact done by one person with both means and determination. She also described the chairman, secretary and some of her follow commissioners in a graphic if tart way, incidentally revealing something of her own personality as she did so.

Enough has been said now to show that it is people who determine, in large part, what comes out of a commission's or a committee's deliberations. It is they who are the essence of the process. Likewise it is people who determine ultimately the effectiveness of the social services which are so often the subject of a committee's brief, and it is, therefore, to their staff to whom attention is now turned.

CHAPTER TEN

Staff and the Social Services

As well as those authors quoted in Chapter Eight, who emphasised the importance in any consideration of the administration of the social services of not overlooking those who staffed them, Titmuss pointed out, in discussing the administrative setting of social service, that 'the study of the person and the situation are complementary. The effectiveness of the social worker and the effectiveness of a service cannot in practice be divorced if there is any meaning in the principles of case-work.'[1] This is true not only of social workers and the principles of case-work, although it may be more clearly marked there, but at all levels of staffing and in all areas of work in the social services. It is through staff that the administrative machine works or fails to work smoothly and efficiently. It is by staff that social policy is successfully implemented or marred. It is the clarity or obscurity of expression of staff that decides the intelligibility of the spoken and the written word. It is in staff that the immediate users of a service find the presence or absence of human understanding.

Donnison emphasised that all those who staff the services must be aware of the personal nature of their work, when he expressed more concern about the danger today of loss of touch with individuals and families, than with the adequacy of nationwide specialised social services.[2] This awareness should be found at all points. No administrator can help people, or help them to the best of his ability, without an appreciation of the necessity at times, for instance, of speed as well as accuracy in administrative procedure. It is not enough for a student to be informed that he is to receive a grant, and of what amount, from his local education authority or a central government department. To help him to the full it is necessary for the grant actually to be paid to him before he is required to meet his fees or maintenance expenses and not after he has got into debt.

No worker in an office can help people best without sensitivity in each interview with all those who call there. The adoption society officer who *began* with the question, incredible though it may sound: 'Have you or your husband ever been in prison?', was failing to help the couple anxious to adopt a baby. No person of professional skill can help fully merely by diagnosing and treating the cause or causes of physical ill. The doctor who gives a prescription to cure a disease but fails to sense the anxiety underlying the patient's condition has helped him in one way only. No field worker can help all concerned without having regard to how and when something should be done as well as whether it should be done at all. The welfare officer who waited until an old man's spirit was 'worn down' by his family before attempting to discuss with him the question of his going into a Home, was of little, if any, help either to him or the other strained members of the household.

These are but three examples, all authentic, illustrating that all those who staff the social services are important in the process of helping people, whether the staff be administrators in central or local government offices; social workers in voluntary or statutory agencies; those whose work has some social work content although they are primarily concerned with other duties, for example youth employment officers; or those who are in professions that have increasingly been drawn into the social service field—doctors, nurses, health visitors, teachers. All these and others have a responsibility for bringing to the social services not only comprehension and efficiency, specialisms and skills, but warmth and understanding; each and all directed towards helping the individual and his family in whatever way he needs assistance. That the importance of this is recognised at central departmental level was illustrated by an appointment in 1967 of a social work adviser to the Ministry of Social Security to advise on the performance of, and training for those aspects of the work done under the aegis of the Supplementary Benefits Commission which are analogous to, and have connections with, the functions of social workers. In addition 29 special welfare officers were trained to relieve the staff at local offices of particularly difficult cases.

The Local Government Commission for England was clearly impressed with the need for enough of the right kind of staff in the social services when in their first report they observed:

'The developing of social services such as education, health and welfare depend more and more for their quality, scope and character on the ability of the authority to carry a first class team of professional, supervisory and other staff.'[3]

In their second report they added:

'In education, in the personal health services, in mental health, in all the branches of the welfare service, there is an increasing need for people with special aptitudes, special training and experience of the particular problems.'[4]

But this applies not only to local government, which was the particular concern of the Commission, but to central social service departments, quasi-government departments, and voluntary bodies as well.

It is manifestly impossible to examine here every detail of staffing of all kinds, and at all levels, in the social services. Consideration must be limited to one or two of the more important aspects of the subject as a whole. First, there is a need to appreciate the wide variety and large number of staff that is now required. The variety of staff may be said to be of an eightfold nature. The social services need staff to administer, to organise, to inform and advise, to diagnose and treat, to solve and support, to teach and instruct, to inspect, and personally to care for, whether in a residential setting or in a person's own home. These varieties are not of course mutually exclusive. One person may combine two or more kinds of activities in his particular duties, although one may take precedence over the other. Youth employment officers are primarily concerned with informing and advising school leavers and young workers about employment opportunities but in the course of so doing they may find problems in home backgrounds or personal difficulties which they cannot ignore because their solution is necessary before a boy or girl will settle in a job. Teachers are employed to teach but they may well find particular pupils need advice and support before they can learn. The eightfold variety of staff in the social services can be separated for purposes of analysis but their work inevitably has some overlap.

The work of administrators in the civil service has been briefly but usefully described as comprising six things: advising Ministers on policy; implementing or executing policy by preparing memoranda or other written documents and making decisions on cases which may establish precedents or procedure; drafting bills and preparing speeches or replies to parliamentary questions; dealing with *ad hoc*, departmental or inter-departmental committee work; discussing and negotiating with industry, trade unions or other interested and relevant bodies; and managing matters of staff appointments, salaries, promotion and superannuation.[5] These six aspects of the administrator's job are alike in central and local departments, except that in the latter policy making is subject to overall government control, and advice to ministers becomes advice to chairmen of committees or councillors. Administrators, both centrally and locally, are assisted by executive and clerical officers who are responsible for day-to-day routine work, referring to senior officers any doubtful issues or policy matters that require decision at a higher level.

It is self-evident that the more social legislation there is and the wider the scope of the social services the greater the importance of the administrator, the executive and the clerical officer. The national insurance scheme, for example, called for the establishment of an entirely new Ministry, as was seen in Chapter Seven, and after being merged with the National Assistance Board to become the Ministry of Social Security in 1968 it employed approximately 62,000 non-industrial staff dealing with over 22,000,000 claims for benefits and allowances in a year, and for providing over 1,000 local offices with guidance, information and supervision.[6]

It is clear that delay or confusion in carrying out these tasks would adversely affect, in an immediate and practical way, any one of the host of people claiming or drawing pensions, benefit, or allowances. That this is recognised at the top administrative level was shown by the observation of Sir Geoffrey King, late Permanent Secretary to the then Ministry of Pensions and National Insurance:

'Most of the men and women who claim benefits and pensions . . . rely on the prompt and regular payment of sums due to them and any delay or interruption in the payments can cause serious hardship. Many of them moreover are ill or injured or too old to cope with complicated forms and procedures and must therefore be able to draw their money with the minimum of fuss and have help and advice in case of difficulty.'

Later he said:

'Plenty of people were suspicious of civil service administration and doubtful of the ability of civil servants to handle humanely the large section of the public that would resort to the Ministry', but, he claimed, 'those fears were confounded by experience.'[7]

This may indeed be so but it must never be forgotten that confidence is easily lost. The claimant for a widow's pension under the National Insurance (Industrial Injuries) Act who was duly and correctly informed that she was not eligible as her husband's death could not be regarded as arising out of or in the course of his employment, had no legal ground for complaint. But the fact that the letter of regret reached her on the first Christmas Eve of her widowhood caused distress that could have been avoided by a little more sensitivity on the part of the administrator who signed the letter or the executive officer who sent it for despatch that particular week. Points of this nature are not trivial when dealing with bereaved, disabled, or infirm persons, with whom the social services are frequently concerned.

The establishment of the national health service is another example of a service which called for the appointment of substantial numbers of administrators, executive, and clerical officers whose work has a direct and immediate bearing on the nature and effectiveness of help given to people, whether in hospital or their own homes. The Ministry of Health alone, before being merged into the Ministry of Social Security in 1968, employed some 5,000 non-industrial staff. In local government the position is the same. In certain instances here the appointment of persons of professional standing to administrative posts has become a statutory requirement. Under the Local Government Act, 1933, all county and county districts councils must appoint one or more 'fit persons', who must be qualified medical practitioners, to be medical officer or officers of health. Under the Education Act, 1944, every local education authority must appoint a 'fit person', after consultation with the Minister of Education, to be chief education officer. Under the Children Act, 1948, each local children authority must appoint a 'fit person', after consultation with the Secretary of State, as children's officer, and must secure the provision of adequate staff for assisting him or her.

Although no specific reference was made to staff in Part III of the National Assistance Act, 1948, Circular 32/51 of the Ministry of Health, of August 1951, said that for the discharge of its functions under approved schemes for the welfare of the disabled, a council should employ such number of welfare officers as might be determined from time to time, who should be people holding a diploma or certificate in social science or similar qualification or those whom the council were satisfied enjoyed a special aptitude for the work, a broad knowledge of the social services, and some experience in the field of welfare. No guidance, then or at any other time, was given in respect of the appointment of chief welfare officers, or of housing officers, both of whom local welfare or housing authorities normally appoint.

In view of the powers and duties given to or placed upon local authorities since the war, and the consequent development of services for the old, the disabled and the homeless, it is unfortunate that there are no qualification requirements and no necessity for consultation with the Minister on the appointment of chief welfare officers, as there are for chief officers in health, education and children departments. This suggests that the work of welfare departments has been regarded as less skilled or exacting than that of other departments which is not so. And it may explain what the Committee on the Staffing of Local Government (the Mallaby Committee) pointed out, that the low intake of staff in welfare departments of local authorities from universities and colleges was in marked contrast to the high level of graduate recruitment to children departments.[8]

The proposals contained in *Social Work and the Community* (outlined in Chapter Six) envisaged the appointment of a director of social work as the head of a new social work department. This recommendation was implemented in the Social Work (Scotland) Act, 1968, which required also that the qualifications of the director of social work should be prescribed by the Secretary of State.

The report of the Committee on Local Authority and Allied Personal Social Services (the Seebohm Committee) set out a list of qualities required in their view of the principal officer of their proposed social service department. Anyone possessing all the qualities listed would be little lower than an angel and in the present state of the social service labour market it was not surprising perhaps that the majority of the Committee recommended that there should be ministerial approval for all first appointments of principal officers and for any further appointment during the first twelve months.[9] These recommendations, if accepted, would go further than existing requirements in respect of chief education and children's officers that they be 'fit persons' appointed only after consultation with the Minister or Secretary of State, and are an indication of the importance attached by the Seebohm Committee to the responsibilities of the principal officer to the social service department which they envisaged.

It is only in children departments, although not always there even now, and in the probation service, that those with professional social work qualifications have as yet been appointed to senior administrative posts. In the case of children departments this is clearly the outcome of the recommendation of the Curtis Committee that the children committee should appoint an executive officer of high standing and qualifications who should be a specialist in child care.[10] That similar appointments are not more general may well be the cause of some administrative officers in other departments failing, as Titmuss said, 'to understand what it is the social worker is trying to do', and why she in turn 'is often hostile because she does not see the administrative purpose as a whole.[11] More is said about the need for mutual understanding and co-operation between different workers in the next chapter.*

Contrary to all that has now been said on the appointment of chief officers of local authorities and to existing legislative requirements the Committee on the Management of Local Government (the Maud Committee) took the view that Ministers should in fact play no part, whether by consent, veto or sanction, in the appointment or dismissal by local authorities of their principal officers.[12] It remains to be seen whether or not the Government will accept this view.

Maud and Finer distinguished four reasons why local authority work should be carried by salaried staff. First, because unpaid elected councillors lack sufficient leisure and time to carry on a continuous administrative process; second, because they necessarily lack the knowledge required to administer specialist services; third, because whole-time officers, outside the political

* For an examination of social work and administration see Joyce Warham, *An Introduction to Administration for Social Workers*, Routledge and Kegan Paul, 1967.

arena, are less open to corruption; and fourth, because there could not be enough elected members, even if they served full time, to carry all the responsibilities now placed upon a local authority's shoulders.[13] This brief résumé invites the question: 'What then do elected members do?' This is not the place for a lengthy answer. It must suffice here to say that elected members debate principles, decide policy, consider reports, approve or disapprove specific proposals, appoint senior staff, give moral and general support to staff, and hold final responsibility for the work of the council as a whole. These are no mean tasks but it is safe to assume that the full-time salaried administrator has come to stay and that the social services will increasingly be included in his field of work.*

The organiser in the social services has been found more frequently in the past, and to a large extent still, in the ranks of voluntary bodies, for voluntary bodies are organisers *par excellence*. They organise conferences, courses, and all manner of meetings. They organise clubs, and inter-club activities, holidays, recreation and outings. They organise home visiting and voluntary workers. They organise fund raising and the dispensation of material assistance. There is really no parallel in the statutory services to the organiser or organising secretary employed by the voluntary body, although the staff of the former are not precluded from and indeed undertake more organisational work today than once was the case. With the extension of powers to provide recreation services, domiciliary meals services and domestic help, the organiser is becoming more common in the local authority; the home help organiser, the meals service organiser, the old people's clubs organiser, the youth service organiser.

The place of the organiser in the social services is clearly an important one. Despite views to the contrary, often held by grant-aiding bodies, personal services cannot be made available in practice without someone to organise them in the field; any more than departmental decisions and processes can be made and carried through without administrators, executive, and clerical officers. There are some, however, who appear to believe that the adminis-

* For a detailed examination of the role and functions of councils and councillors in local government see the report of the Committee on the Management of Local Government (Maud Committee), Ministry of Housing and Local Government, H.M.S.O., 1967.

trator and the organiser alike can be dispensed with so that funds can be used, they say, for the direct benefit of those for whom they are intended. Administration and organisation can get out of hand, it is true. Parkinson's 'Law,' that 'work expands so as to fill the time available for its completion',[14] may operate in the social services as elsewhere. But it is not possible to do without administrators or organisers and to claim this is so is mere moonshine, though moonshine with which a speaker can often dazzle his audience, raising applause from the body of the hall because it highlights economy and what are termed the right priorities.

Staff to inform and advise become increasingly important as social services become more varied, extensive, and often more complex. People may need information or advice on education, careers, marriage, child care, welfare of the old, house purchase or tenancy, their statutory rights and obligations, or many matters of law. Some of this information or advice may be provided by the voluntary body, for example the Citizens' Advice Bureau or Marriage Guidance Council. Some may be provided by the local authority in the county or district council information and advice centre. Some may be provided under the Legal Aid and Advice Act. Some may not be provided at all. Discussion of these ways and means of providing information and advice, and the adequacy of the services and their staff, is left until Chapter Twelve.

The last five of the eight categories of staff which it has been suggested are required in the social services are those which call for specialist knowledge of one kind or another. These consist of doctors, dentists, consultants, nurses, and other medical staff, to diagnose, prescribe, operate, nurse or treat within the health service; teachers, instructors, and lecturers, in the school, training centre, college, or university within the education service; social workers and health visitors to assist and support in their respective spheres of work, in the health and welfare services; the staff of residential homes, hostels, special schools and the like, to care for the residents of varying ages and needs; and inspectors of institutions or activities—who may also act as guides, advisers and supporters of those whom they visit—when and where certain standards are required by regulations laid down by statute or in order that the institution may receive grant aid.

It is clear from this brief outline that the field of employment in the social services is an immense one and that the demands made upon their staff are of great variety and importance. These two facts give rise to problems of a personal and a practical nature. These include the expansion and recruitment of a sufficient number of staff; the growth of professionalism; the achievement of mutual respect and understanding; and the need for co-operation amongst and between staff in different areas and in different grades of work.

The shortage of teachers is perhaps the most publicised in the social services. Without allowing for any improvement in existing staffing standards the additional number of teachers needed, merely to keep pace with the increased number of pupils attending school, was estimated as 100,000 by 1976 and 140,000 by 1986.[15] In 1968 a new set or projections given by the Department of Education and Science in a Report on Education (No. 51) on the Supply of Teachers suggested that the existing shortage would drop to 13,000 in 1973, then rapidly to 1,000 in 1977 and by 1978 there should be a surplus of 5,000. Whilst an end to the present shortage is, therefore, in sight it remains until it is achieved one shortage amongst many. It is accompanied by a shortage of doctors and nurses; of medical auxiliaries; of virtually all kinds of social workers and health visitors; and of staff of residential homes and voluntary bodies. Estimates of requirement have been made from one year to another in one field after another and everywhere serious shortages have been found. No one estimate for the social services as a whole has, however, yet been prepared and since recruitment in one field must affect that in another the individual estimates available have serious limitations. The need for an overall study of the staffing requirements of the social services as a whole, excluding education and strictly medical aspects of health has long been felt. The National Council of Social Service undertook a 'Survey of Manpower demand forecasts for the Social Services' in 1963 and these can be studied in the published report.[16]

In the medical sphere the number of medical social workers needed in the hospital services in England and Wales was estimated in 1951 as between 2,500 and 3,000, requiring at least 150 new medical social workers each year.[17] The Institute of Medical Social Workers reported that in the year 1962–63 the number of medical social workers then in employment was 1,278; less than half the maximum estimated as required twelve years previously. In 1951 also the number of psychiatric social workers required was estimated as 1,500, compared to an existing figure of 331; and a 'still larger number' of mental welfare officers was said to be needed.[18] But it was reported in 1962 that the limited number of psychiatric social workers available in hospitals and local authority mental health services was a severe drawback to the development of effective liaison between the two.[19] To this one might add that it must also have been a severe drawback to the proper care of patients.

In 1955 the number of teachers in special schools for maladjusted children was estimated as needing to rise from 120 to 240, and the staff of child guidance services should, it was said, rise to 140 full-time psychiatrists, 280 educational psychologists and 420 psychiatric social workers.[20] This may be regarded as the most unrealistic estimate of all time. In 1962 there was on average one consultant psychiatrist available for about 100,000 of the population.[21] In 1956 the number of health visitors required was estimated as 11,500 compared to approximately 6,000 then employed in England and Wales and 1,500 employed in Scotland.[22] At the end of 1961 the equivalent of approximately 5,200 whole-time health visitors were employed by local health authorities in England and Wales who planned to expand this number to the equivalent of 7,600 by 1972.[23] These figures exclude Scotland and the school health service and it is impossible, therefore, to compare them with the estimate of need made in 1956.

In 1959 the need for social workers in local authority health and welfare services, including Scotland, over a ten-year period and on the assumption that everything possible would be done to economise in the use of staff, was estimated as calling for a rise from 3,155 to 5,550—5,700, or on average a rise of 500—515 a year.[24] By March 1967 the number achieved was 1,967. The estimate included social workers in the mental health services, care and after-care services, services for the elderly and the handicapped, social work with families and in the home help service. Clearly some of these overlap with earlier estimates, and the achievement of the objective would effect the demand for and work of health visitors in particular.

In 1960 the Committee on the Youth Service in England and

Wales (the Albemarle Committee) proposed an increase from 700 to 1,300 full-time youth leaders in 1966,[25] and in reply to a question in the House of Commons on January 19, 1967, the Secretary of State for Education and Science said that this provisional target had been reached.

In 1962 it was estimated that the number of probation officers in England and Wales needed to increase from 1,749 to 2,750.[26] This estimate was raised to 3,474 by 1969 at the Conference of Principal Probation Officers in 1964. According to the report on the Work of the Probation and After-Care Department for 1962 to 1965[27] the number of established officers rose to 2,417 by the end of 1965 and the aim was to achieve 3,500 by 1970. In 1964 at the Annual Conference of the Association of Child Care Officers it was estimated that the child care services would require a minimum of 550 to 600 new entrants a year, having regard to the new demands made by the Children and Young Persons Act, 1963. Answering a question on March 13, 1967, the Minister of State, Home Office, said that the Home Secretary had approved proposals made by the Central Training Council in Child Care to expand the annual output of qualified students from approximately 280 in 1966 to 675 in 1969.

The Working Party on the Youth Employment Service[28] estimated in 1965, without regard to any developments in the service, that 130 to 150 recruits would be needed each year due solely to the inevitable reduction of the 1,340 then in employment as a result of retirement and other movements of staff.

To sum up: The separate estimates, made between 1951 and 1965, of the number of field work staff needed in the social services, excluding doctors, nurses and teachers, other than those in special schools for the maladjusted, amount to:

Medical social workers in hospital	2,500 to 3,000
Psychiatric social workers	1,500
Mental welfare officers	1,500 plus
Teachers in special schools for maladjusted children	240
Staff of child guidance clinics (including full-time psychiatrists, educational psychologists and psychiatric social workers)	840
Health visitors	11,500
Local authority health and welfare services	5,500 to 5,700

Probation officers	2,750
Youth leaders	1,300
Child care officers	550 to 600 new entrants per year
Youth employment officers	130 to 150 new entrants per year

Disregarding certain double counting in this list; that some of the figures include Scotland and others do not; and the effect of achieving a full complement of staff in one field of work upon needs in another, these estimates as they stand amount to a minimum of 29,500 people. This figure, it is true, is considerably less than the additional teachers required, but it takes no account of the needs of voluntary bodies many of whom are known to be in a state of chronic under-staffing. This was illustrated by the case of the Family Service Units which reported its inability in 1965 to provide additional units, with the approval and support of local authorities in Glasgow, Preston and elsewhere, because of the absence of senior staff.

Likewise Norman House, the first of its kind to cater for the needs of homeless ex-prisoners, stated in its Annual Report for 1965–66 that its staffing situation was critical, the demand far exceeding the supply, particularly of trained workers. So acute was the problem it was anticipated, unless it was solved, that the movement would collapse or the quality of the work would be so reduced that provision would become no more than shelter.

The figures quoted also omit the demand for residential staff. This was estimated, so far as Homes for old people and children were concerned, in the report of the Williams Committee, referred to in Chapter Nine. A particular problem of creating and maintaining the status of those employed in residential posts is involved here, together with the difficulty of creating conditions of work that are compatible with a person's own family and social life.

Whatever the imperfections of the estimates, and all the reports that make them recognise difficulties in reaching a figure, one thing is clear. The full complement of staff required to man the social services properly is most unlikely to materialise in the foreseeable future. This is particularly so in view of the high marriage and birth rates which mean that no longer can there be the same dependence on woman power that there has been hitherto. This long-term shortage is no new discovery. As early as 1951 Younghusband pointed out that it was impossible to form any adequate picture of social work in Britain without taking into account the desperate shortage of social workers in relation to demand.[29] In 1960 Rodgers and Dixon advised that for social work 'the best basis to any plan for the recruitment, training and employment of professional personnel is to assume that you will not get as many people as you would like'.[30] In 1962 Donnison emphasised that the manpower problem was the most intractable of any, and that the health and welfare services would break down in any local government system which failed to recruit, train, and economically deploy growing numbers of staff.[31] In April 1964 there was an inconclusive debate in the House of Lords on a motion calling attention to the 'need for a further study of the welfare services to ensure that the best use is made of the limited number of people involved'; that is, of trained staff available now and in the future.[32]

In October 1964 Rodgers' study of the careers of men and women completing social science courses in British Universities in 1950, 1955, and 1960 showed that:

'In spite of some increase in the numbers of men and women completing professional training courses . . . the wastage due to marriage among the younger women has defied all efforts to increase significantly the proportion of trained to untrained workers throughout the various services.'[33]

The plans for health and welfare services drawn up by the 146 local health and welfare authorities in England and Wales for the ten years 1962–72 showed an estimated overall increase of 45 per cent in the staffs to be employed, including health visitors who were to rise to 7,607 (excluding the school health service); home helps to rise from 25,478 to 37,083; home nurses to rise from 7,704 to 9,790; midwives from 5,261 to 6,509; and social workers to rise from 2,943 to 4,879.[34] It is impossible, however, to be assured of the relevance or reality of the individual or overall figures put forward by the authorities. What they are related to, whether they are realistic, and whether they will be put into effect, is anybody's guess and little confidence can be placed in them.

Even were the plans realistic in themselves and the numbers proposed reasonable, employment rests not only upon recruitment of persons but upon giving them the necessary knowledge and skills to carry out their work. In other words, responsibility for ensuring that sufficient training facilities are available for those it is proposed to employ must rest upon or be assumed by someone before paper plans for numbers of persons to be employed make sense.

All in all it becomes increasingly important that such staff as there are, or become available, should be used where their skill is needed most, and that they should be deployed to the best advantage both between different services and different parts of the country. These trite observations serve, however, to do little more than raise unanswerable questions. Who is to decide, and on what grounds, where staff and their skill are needed most? And if and when this is decided who is to assure, and how, that staff go where that need is? There will inevitably be differences of opinion on these questions because they involve competing claims —of the sick, the disabled, the homebound, the maladjusted, the child, the family, the old, the subnormal and others. And there has never been direction of labour in this country other than during the war and it is unlikely and undesirable that it should be introduced in the employment of staff in the social services. Nor has anyone suggested that it should be. Certain devices are used to encourage an even distribution of manpower but no more.

Doctors have been encouraged under the national health service to go to under-doctored areas by scales of remuneration providing inducement to practise in the less attractive areas. In addition a Medical Practices Committee was set up under the National Health Service Act to regulate the succession to existing practices or the opening of new practices within the service. This committee can withhold consent to go to practise in a particular area if there are already enough doctors in the service in that area. But there is still an uneven distribution, the midlands and the north being particularly in need. The Standing Advisory Committee of the Central Health Service Council took the view in 1963 that more should be done to distribute doctors more evenly throughout the country, not only by the work of the Medical Practices Committee, but by greater financial incentives to practise in under-doctored areas and the provision of premises by local housing authorities in those areas.[35] Some deployment of teachers is achieved by a quota system imposed by the Department of Education and Science which no local education authority may exceed. But apart from these instances staff in the social services are left to go as and where they will, seeking employment in the place and with the employing body which, for whatever reason, attract them most.

The shortage and uneven distribution of trained staff is likely to be a very long term, even if not a permanent feature of the social services. It accounts in many instances for the employment of untrained staff, undesirable though this may be. If a local authority has a statutory duty, as it has, to appoint child care officers what is it to do if there is an insufficient number of professionally qualified persons? The answer is to be found in the fact that in March 1966 there were not only 334 (12·5 per cent) unfilled posts but 39·6 per cent of the 2,341 child care officers then employed were without qualifications of any kind.[36] The situation was even more serious in residential work in which in 1963 82 per cent of the child care staff employed at that time and 98 per cent of staff in Homes for old people had no qualifications.[37] In August 1964 39·7 per cent of local authority mental health workers and 40·3 per cent of their social welfare workers had less than what were regarded as desirable qualifications.[38]

The same situation faces probation committees in the appointment of probation officers. Although the situation has considerably improved since 1960, when 56 per cent of all probation officers were appointed without training, it was still the case in 1965 that 18 per cent of those appointed were untrained and there was no hope that a date could be given after which appointment of untrained people should be forbidden.[39] And whereas the Ministry of Health has long recognised that unqualified persons should not be appointed as, nor be called medical social workers in hospitals, this has not prevented the employment there of welfare assistants without professional qualifications, some of whom undertake work carried hitherto or elsewhere by the medical social worker, albeit at a lower salary.

The overall shortage of staff and qualified staff in particular is one reason why the student, when he moves from theory into practice, will find that services do not always work as well or as swiftly as he may hope or have been led to expect. It is one reason, though not necessarily the only one, why some people have to wait to get into hospital whilst others have to wait to get out. It is one reason why old people cannot get places in residential Homes, or not until they are in desperate straits. It is one reason why the sensitive, patient, individual care they should have when they are admitted is too often lacking, and likewise why children in Homes often do not have the regular continuous attention of one person which their emotional and mental health demand. It is one reason why the domiciliary meals or home help services can be given only one or two days a week instead of the four, five or six days on which they may be needed. It is one reason why those referred to family case work agencies may have to wait for an appointment or why there is delay in a disabled person getting some form of aid for the handicapped. Above all, shortage of staff can and does make nonsense of 'community care'; the term that has come to mean care of people in their own homes rather than in hospitals or other residential institutions. The distinction is not a very satisfactory one and it has been frequently criticised since it was first used.*

Shortage of staff may well be the major cause of the *cri de cœur* uttered by a young medical social worker in her first year of employment:

'I am in a disheartened state about the social services. There are terrible delays in the follow up of discharged patients. Those who do the home visiting are so small in number and not only that but they are so often untrained.'

'I am baffled', said another, 'by the way social provisions vary from area to area.'

This was written in 1962. But in 1967 it was still said of community care:

'What they [doctors and administrators] sometimes fail to do is to realise what their policy is likely to mean in practice; what they rather

* See, for example, Richard M. Titmuss, *Commitment to Welfare*, Chapters VI and IX, George Allen and Unwin Ltd., 1968.

often fail to do is to consider whether early discharge is the best thing for the family. . . . At present, taking Britain overall, it is impossible to judge the success of community care because, except in a limited number of areas, it can hardly be said to exist.'[40]

No student should rest comfortably in the belief that what appears on the statute book or in the text-book or the departmental memorandum on local services (or any other) will be found fully implemented in the field and manned by an adequate number of trained and competent staff. Should he do so he will be bound to be quickly and deeply disillusioned once he works outside the walls of the university or technical college.

Successful home or domiciliary care depends on there being a sufficient number of qualified staff available to advise, assist, and support the people concerned and their families. Without them the ex-hospital patient, the discharged prisoner, the foster child, the infirm old person, the disabled man or woman, whether they are living at home, in lodgings or hostels, will be subject to severe strain, quite possibly to the point of breakdown, whether their own or that of some member of the family or group with whom they are. A letter from one who has faced such strain confirms this:

'It seems to me that there is a great need for an organised service to take an interest in and to advise people who are discharged from hospital after very prolonged treatment and left with a greater or lesser degree of disability. As a parent I am left with a feeling of helpless inexperience in the matter and the exquisitely competent and kind treatment in hospital is exchanged for an existence in a vacuum for the ex-patient.'

The concept of community or home care is imaginative and humane but without qualified staff to make it a reality it may well be less desirable than good institutional care and it will have the added disadvantage that human need may be hidden. And those who rely on the expansion of voluntary good neighbour schemes must not only remember the skilled nature and the extent of the work involved but also that those for whom care is needed may well not wish a neighbour to know all their family troubles. There is an important place for the voluntary worker within the social services but it is not one that replaces the need for trained and qualified staff. That this is recognised by many organisations is shown in the emphasis increasingly laid upon the wisdom of voluntary workers having some form of training to equip them for the service they are able and willing to give. The Younghusband Working Party, for example, agreed on the importance of selection for particular types of voluntary work and said: 'We think that if voluntary workers are asked to give regular time, and to take appropriate responsibility there then exists an obligation to equip them to do the job competently. Training is essential if voluntary workers are to give their service knowledgeably and acceptably and training can help them to feel an integral part of the service.'[41]

Certain voluntary bodies have for some time offered or required training for their voluntary workers, whether through their local branches or otherwise. These include the Family Planning Association, the National Old People's Welfare Council, the Family Welfare Association, Citizens' Advice Bureaux, and Youth Service Organisations. The setting up of the Aves Committee, referred to in Chapter Nine, was another sign of the recognition of the need for selection and training of voluntary workers.

A parallel on the statutory side is contained in the Justices of the Peace Act, 1959, which required the provision of instruction for Justices and laid an obligation on those appointed to a juvenile court panel after January 1, 1966, to complete an appropriate course of training within a year of appointment.

Enough has been said now about shortages of staff of all kinds as one of, if not the major problem of the social services. But one last observation may be made. The shortage is not caused by a fall in supply but by an increase in demand for staff on the part of employing bodies, particularly local authorities. There are more people employed in the social services today than ever before including those in executive and administrative positions and those in the professions, and the demand for the last is steadily increasing. The employment of professional workers has long been a feature in certain of the social services—the teacher in the education service—the doctor, nurse and health visitor in the health service. But it has developed further and extensively of recent years, until today there are professional personnel in medical social work, psychiatric social work, probation work, child care, personnel management, family case work, moral welfare, house property management, youth work and elsewhere. As many as twenty professional social workers' associations were referred to by Younghusband in a report on social work in Britain in 1951.[42]

This growth of the professions in the social services gave rise to a concern on the part of some who feared that inter-professional jealousies would result; that status-seeking might take precedence over the interest of the patient, student, or client; that in achieving professional standing there would be too much self-concern. Bearing these dangers in mind, it may be helpful to look briefly at the characteristics which are generally agreed denote a profession as such. These are first, recognition and acceptance of a code of ethics which includes offering the highest standard of service within the ability of the practitioner and putting first and foremost the interests of the client, within the limits of the law and the rights of others. (It can be argued that in the long run the best interests of the client must coincide with the law and the rights of others but this is not the place to pursue this argument.)

The code of professional ethics includes rejection of competition, advertisement and self-seeking in the practice of the profession and respect for the confidentiality of the relationship between client and practitioner, which calls for and justifies the trust of the one in the other and without which the service offered cannot be expected to be successful. A profession is characterised also by the requirement that its members reach a minimum standard of knowledge and proficiency before they practise their art or science. Such a standard is achieved by training, is tested by examination, and makes possible reasonable claims for remuneration and conditions of work deemed necessary for the proper pursuit of the service and commensurate with professional standing. Lastly, a profession is characterised by membership of a society or association which may be consulted about training and qualifications, may register practitioners, publish journals, organise conferences, watch over the interests of its members and consider matters of professional practice and etiquette.

In the case of the social work profession there are three additional characteristics which do not apply to all other professions. First, an acceptance of the right of every individual, with the exception of the delinquent, the deranged, or the child, to decide for himself the course of action to be taken, and not to have this decided for or imposed upon him, even if this means his choosing to go to hell in his own way. Second, the acceptance of a person as he is without criticism or condemnation and, third, the pursuit of social policy or social action necessary to remedy economic or environmental ills which affect the welfare of the client. It is not wholly correct as Peyser claimed that 'what really distinguishes social workers as a profession is their *order* of *values . . . human values rank highest*. Wherever he goes he advocates the urgencies of human values and human rights'.[43] So should certain other professions; the doctor, or the priest for example.

If each of the above characteristics was always apparent there would be little need for concern about professionalism in the social services. Indeed Marshall said:

'They [the social services] are inspired by the spirit of professionalism, in the sense that they do not design their work to meet an articulate and effective demand only, but plan it in the light of expert knowledge of the social arts and sciences and of fundamental principles of social welfare formualted on the basis of accumulated human experience.'[44]

This, surely, is desirable.

But honesty compels one to admit that even people of the highest ethical standards sometimes slip and professional jealousies and possessiveness do at times enter to the detriment of the users of services. They are there if a worker is unwilling or refuses to 'hand on a case' to another worker because it is too difficult for him to admit that the second would be able to cope with it better. There is a lowering of standards if and when as Rodgers and Dixon said a 'professional social worker's . . . sense of responsibility for the sound development of the social services generally goes no further than the interests of his profession'.[45] Even if grosser instances of jealousy, possessiveness, or self-interest are absent, any proliferation of professions can give rise to over-specialisation with consequent confusion for a client or patient, for employing bodies, social service personnel, or the public generally. It can result in the personal and social problems of one and the same person or family being dealt with separately by too large a number of workers, who may even take a different view of the right solution to the problems involved.

This should not be taken to imply that even in a perfect world one person could always work effectively and alone with one family towards the solution of all its problems. There are many occasions when it is necessary for two or three different people to visit the same family. No one has suggested, for example, that a health visitor who has a statutory duty to visit a household when a baby is born should also act as a probation officer for a delinquent boy; combining the two functions in one home visit. Nor is it the case that there is necessarily only one solution to a family's problem. There are frequently instances in which a choice of actions is possible and no one can be certain of the outcome of a particular choice. What is important is that a family should not receive visits from different workers about precisely the same problem and be the recipients of conflicting suggestions or advice. This can only result in confusion, irritation, time wastage and frustration. The Porritt Committee instanced the visits of both health visitor and doctor and rightly said:

'It is important, when intimate health advice is being given to individuals or families, that the health visitor and the doctor speak with one voice and give consistent advice.'[46]

In other words both will visit the same home but this should be with an awareness that each is doing so and why. This should be the case wherever more than one visitor is necessary.

A proliferation of professions can also hinder a body of workers as a whole from speaking with a united voice on matters of social policy or provision. This does not mean that there is no room for differences of opinion nor for varying views to be expressed, but a common forum for discussion is essential if a profession is to speak with authority, be listened to with respect, and carry weight in the corridors of power where social policy is made.

The recognition and discussion of these problems was manifest for some time in the field of social work and after long and careful deliberations it was agreed in 1968 to pursue the formation of a National Association of Social Workers to take the place of eight of the previously separate and individual professional organisations. This was a positive and constructive move which augured well for the social work profession but the situation would become sadly confused again if the medical profession were ever seriously to implement the views expressed by the Standing Medical Advisory Committee of the Central Health Services Council on

H

the field of work of the family doctor;[47] views which stemmed from the Porritt Committee. These views maintained that the general practitioner was not only the patient's medical adviser in the prevention and treatment of illness. He was also, it was said, the one who advises on family problems which concern children, adolescents and the aged; who handles difficult school children; advises on family planning and counsels in marital difficulties; interprets to his patient the health and welfare services whose development he is in a position to influence; who secures after-care in the training of recovery or adjustment to handicap and who should control (sic) the activities of other workers who may be dealing with his patients, for example health visitors and social workers. For all this to happen would be for doctoring, social work, welfare work, and public health work to become inextricably confused and to place a tremendous burden on the shoulders of one profession which it is neither trained nor designed to carry.

One aspect of professionalism in the social services which is of importance is that self-employment is rare. The large majority of professional staff in the social services today are in the employ of others; in the main in the statutory services and to a lesser extent in the voluntary organisations. This particular development—from voluntary body to local authority—took place largely between 1945 and 1950.[48] The reasons for the change are clear—the introduction of the national health service, of local authority child care and welfare services, the development of public education, the youth service, the youth employment service, council housing and so forth. In certain fields the self-employed professional remains, but only to a small extent. The doctor, the specialist, or the nurse can take private patients. The teacher can give private lessons. But they are comparatively few in number, and the fee-charging, private case-work service has not developed in this country as it has to some extent in America and elsewhere. Even the professional services of the lawyer can now be obtained free or at reduced fees in certain circumstances under the Legal Aid and Advice Act, to which reference is made in Chapter Twelve.

The reduction in self-employment by professional people, by reason of the development of statutory services, is of some importance because, amongst other things, it is essential that employment by statutory authorities should not be accompanied by any surrender of the professional ethic. There must be the same regard for confidentiality; the same first concern for the interests of the client; the same relationship of trust; and the same giving of the highest standard of service possible. The medical profession has been the one to express the greatest anxiety on these scores, with the fear that the so-called doctor–patient relationship under a national health service would be undermined. They saw the only safeguard to their professional freedom, and successful opposition to any system which could leave them at the mercy of party politics, in the encouragement of private practice as an alternative to which both doctors and public alike could turn.[49] But doctors have no monopoly of professional freedom and if social workers, nurses, and health visitors, for example, can maintain professional standards without claiming a right to private practice why not also the medical practitioner?

To conclude: It may perhaps be said that those who fear the growing importance of the professional in the social services who, like the administrator, will become more not less important in policy making and social practice, can take comfort from Marshall who regarded the professions as being weaned today from excessive individualism, adapting themselves to new standards of social service. 'The professions', he said, 'are being socialised [that is humanised] and the social and public services are being professionalised. . . . In spite of all their faults it rests with [the professions] more than with anyone else, to find for the sick and the suffering democracies a peaceful solution to their problems.'[50] And the same may be said of the sick and suffering individual.

CHAPTER ELEVEN

Avoidance of Conflict

It was pointed out in the last chapter, somewhat tritely, that the serious shortage of staff in the social services calls in particular for their employment in those areas where their skills are needed most. It is equally clear that it calls also for the closest co-operation between staff at all levels and in all services. This requires knowledge and appreciation by each member of the staff of the purpose and role of every other member. So obvious is this that it should go without saying. Unfortunately, however, there is a body of evidence to show that co-operation, knowledge, and appreciation of each other's purpose and role, are often lacking amongst those who staff the social services, though such lack is not of course peculiar to them.

By co-operation is meant a close, continuous, informed and harmonious working relationship between two or more persons who are employed for the achievement of the same end or purpose, though not necessarily employed by the same body. Co-operation is essentially inter-personal, whereas co-ordination, to which attention is turned in the second half of this chapter, is inter-service. People co-operate. Services are co-ordinated. The first is active, the second passive. This simple difference is not always kept clear and co-operation and co-ordination are spoken of as though they were identical. Thus one most interesting and useful article began:

'Some of us have been feeling recently that this topic of co-ordination and co-operation in social work has become a little stale. Everyone agrees it is a good and necessary thing but the suggestions made to explain why it is only partially successful seem to have been for the most part superficial.'[1]

This passage should of course read '*they* are good and necessary things'. Many other instances could be given of the common confusion between co-operation and co-ordination and the student is advised, therefore, always to ask himself which a speaker or author is in fact talking or writing about. Co-operation denotes absence or control of competitiveness, possessiveness, jealousy, rivalry, ignorance and self-satisfaction; all traits which are found in or between people. Co-ordination denotes absence of duplication, omissions, overlapping and delays in provision; all faults which are found within or between services. Unless this distinction is kept clear, confusion is bound to occur and understanding of the causes and solutions to the problems arising from the absence of co-operation and co-ordination will be rendered more difficult than they already are. For different devices or procedures are required to cure the one or the other.

Even if co-operation and co-ordination are not spoken of as identical they are often linked together as inseparables. It is certainly desirable they should be but this is not inevitable. People can and do co-operate even though services are unco-ordinated, although the lack of co-ordination may well render their co-operation more difficult. And services can be co-ordinated without their staff being co-operative. Again it is important to keep the distinction between the two states of affairs clear. An example from within the social services may help.

If an old lady—Mrs A—is discharged from hospital unexpectedly because the bed she occupies is urgently required for an emergency case, and the news of her discharge is not sent to the public health department of the local authority in time for arrangements to be made for her home to be ready for her and for regular domestic help to start at once, she will arrive to a cold, unstocked house and an unaired, unmade bed. She will suffer from a lack of co-ordination between services. The domiciliary services, that is to say, did not begin when the hospital service left off. If, on the other hand, news of Mrs A's discharge is received by the public health department in time for arrangements to be made for domiciliary help to begin without delay, but on the day in question the home help has 'words' with the home help organiser and flounces off without telling the organiser that she is not going to Mrs A, then she, Mrs A, will suffer from lack of co-operation. Timely arrangements were made for the domiciliary services to begin, but these failed to materialise because one member of the staff let another one down.

Again, if, in the first instance, the ambulance driver on arrival at Mrs A's empty house acts on his own initiative and calls on a neighbour for help and the neighbour says she will look in and do what she can, then Mrs A will suffer from lack of co-ordination between services but one that is softened by co-operation between people. But if the neighbour says it is nothing to do with her and what is the Welfare State for anyway, then Mrs A will suffer from both lack of co-ordination and of co-operation.

Co-operation and co-ordination are essentials, as the example of Mrs A shows, because people suffer if either is absent and since the social services are there, amongst other things, to prevent or mitigate suffering, they have failed if they do not do this. Though the absence of co-operation between people may well be encouraged by unco-ordinated services or the structure of services which separate staff from one another, physically or functionally, it is also due to the frailty of human nature. People frequently do not co-operate with each other because they misunderstand each other, do not like or do not trust one another. They are prejudiced or jealous or feel threatened by another person. They are forgetful, careless, or irresponsible, and fail to pass on information, or they fear criticism or loss of status if they do. It may even be that people simply do not want to co-operate. 'It often seems less trouble to get on with your own job without bothering about what the other man is doing (except to criticise him) or how you can fit in with him.'[2] To this observation of Hope-Wallace it can be added that it may not only seem less trouble to get on with one's own job, it often *is* less trouble. Co-operation in many instances requires an effort.

Whatever the cause or causes of lack of co-operation it is found at times amongst and between all kinds of personnel; of statutory and voluntary services; in administrative and field work; amongst salaried and voluntary workers. For example, of administration and administrators Wheare said:

'An outstanding defect of committee administration is the isolation in which committees tend to work, insulating themselves from the activities of other committees and refusing to co-operate with them. . . . Chairmen and committee members develop these self-contained, self-sufficient and self-important attitudes as well, and resent attempts by others to encroach upon their authority. . . . There is nothing peculiar to local government about this of course. Central departments are often at war with each other; departmental jealousies and territorial disputes are a regular feature of central administration, and ministers are expected and urged by their officials to fight for the department.'[3]

In the report of one investigation in the social work field, Smith and Bate remarked that it was noteworthy that health visitors, school welfare officers and the N.S.P.C.C. had sent no cases, in a four-month period, to a special case committee set up for consultative purposes, although they each had heavy case loads and were in touch with families in difficulties over long periods.[4] This referred to the year 1950–51 and it may well be thought that since then, with the development of local authority services and greater familiarity with the principles and practice of social work, the position must have improved. But Rodgers and Dixon's study of social services in a northern town, made over the years 1957–59, still found many instances of lack of effective co-operation. For example, school nurses had little contact with other departments and were vague about referring cases. There was little contact between officers of the then National Assistance Board and other workers. General practitioners knew very little about the work of maternity and child welfare or what health visitors did or who they were, and an approved school after-care visitor showed no signs of talking to the probation officer. Co-operation that required not only a passing on of information but a decision upon action appeared to be particularly difficult.[5]

Another study undertaken in 1958–59 of old people's welfare in London also provided evidence of lack of co-operation, in some boroughs at least. One social worker, for example, never wrote to the secretary of the old people's welfare committee because she never received a reply. Club leaders in several boroughs were said to cut themselves off from or not to be interested in the activities of other workers. The organiser of one large and well-established club virtually refused all contacts with the old people's welfare committee.[6]

The report of the Younghusband Working Party, 1959, referred to instances of lack of co-operation found during their investigations. There was, for example, the observation of one witness: 'We find considerable resistance in the different branches of field work to co-operation with each other.' There was the case in which none of the workers concerned with a family with multiple problems had even met or discussed these or suggested a case conference to work out a long-term plan and means of co-operation with each other. In one area it was clear that some of the workers, seen by the Working Party's field investigators, had never met each other face to face before, although employed by the same authority, and some officers in the health and welfare departments had 'only the vaguest understanding of the powers and responsibilities of the children's department'. The Working Party even 'came across instances in which it was a matter of pride to keep information from another department rather than work in co-operation with it'.[7] The report of the Ingleby Committee on Children and Young Persons, 1960, expressed the opinion that failure or delay on the part of those first making contact with a family at risk in calling in further help, was due to inter-service rivalries and failure to analyse the different processes of help involved.[8] That is to say, co-operation between people was absent.

Jefferys, in a study of the work of staff employed in the statutory and voluntary welfare services in an English county in 1960–61, found that general practitioners often remained unaware of the range of social services that could assist their patients.[9] Such ignorance is bound to result in lack of co-operation. One cannot co-operate with staff of a service one does not know exists.

In gathering together in this way evidence of lack of co-operation between staff in the social services it is easy to give the impression that it is the rule rather than the exception. This is unlikely to be the case. Were it so the social services would be in a parlous state which, whatever their deficiencies, they are not. It is certain that as many or more instances of the presence as the absence of co-operation could be found if it were the intention to emphasise these. But non-co-operation, like vice, has greater news value than co-operation or virtue. The only justification for drawing attention to it is that it is a constant danger and every effort should be made by all concerned to avoid it. This is not primarily because it causes confusion, waste of time, money and energy, nor because refusal to co-operate is a stupid form of behaviour for intelligent people to indulge in, but because the welfare of the individual, family or group, may and will suffer if staff are or remain at loggerheads with one another or are ignorant or unaware of each other's work. All things may not always work together for good for those who co-operate, but they are more likely to do so than for those who are quarrelsome, critical or uninformed. It is pertinent, therefore, to consider the means by which co-operation can be encouraged.

In the first place co-operation depends upon an attitude of mind and a quality of person. The desire and the will to co-operate, to work closely in harmony with others, must be there. As Jones emphasised: 'The effective care of the patient (and client) will depend on the fostering of suitable mental attitudes among those responsible for his well-being.'[10] Some people clearly are or have become more co-operative by nature or intent than others and this quality is one to be looked for by interviewing committees in all applicants for posts in the social services. How they are to recognise it is perhaps a question for the social psychologist to answer. It is clear, at least, there is little if anything to be gained by asking an applicant, although this is often done, whether he is able to work as a member of a team, as no one in his senses is likely to reply: 'No, I quarrel with everyone whom I meet.' But every effort, including an effort on the part of the person concerned, should be made to discover whether the would-be social servant is of a co-operative nature or not.

Apart from an attitude of mind and a quality of person, co-operation can be encouraged by certain devices instituted for the use of those who staff the social services. One of these is the case conference, which is not to be confused with the co-ordinating committee to which attention will be turned later. The case conference was used in Chapter One as an example of a method in social administration, when that term is used to refer to a process directed to the promotion of social welfare. The possible composition of a case conference and the way in which it functions and proceeds was outlined there and will not be repeated here. It may be helpful, however, to quote from the report of the Younghusband Working Party:

'A case conference provides the setting for a limited number of workers involved in the case under consideration to assess the total situation or need, to work out a concerted plan of action and to carry it into operation with each other, and with the person or family involved.'[11]

Implicit in this observation is the assumption that the assess-
H*

ment, the plan of action, and the operation will be carried through without acrimony or competition, without professional jealousy, and without fear of loss of face. For these ideals to become actual it is essential for those who are gathered together, to meet as equals under a skilled but democratic chairman, and not as leader and led, or master and servant. Each must be free to contribute to the discussion, to make suggestions, or offer alternative proposals. Any feeling of superiority or inferiority will at once undermine the effectiveness of the case conference. It is essential also for those who compose the conference to have a sufficiently common background of knowledge, training and experience to enable them 'to speak the same language' and to understand what each person present is about. A common cause of failure of the case conference is that each of its members does not in fact have a sufficient grasp of the principles and practices of all its other members—the health visitor of the case worker, or the school welfare officer of the child care officer, for example. Nothing is more conducive to failure in co-operation than a suspicion on the part of one person that another one simply does not know what he is talking about, or the belief that a speaker is merely using jargon or trying to practise an esoteric art of little value in everyday life. Excellent examples of problems of this nature are given in the article quoted at the beginning of this chapter, although the case conference from which they were taken was there mistakenly called a co-ordinating committee.[12]

Where there is no common background of knowledge, training and experience, co-operation is rendered very difficult indeed and in these circumstances the case conference may not be the right device to use. With the haphazard development of social services and the appointment at various points of time of men and women with different or no qualifications or training to staff them, it would be unreasonable always to expect common backgrounds at the present juncture. Therefore and even without a case conference the closest contact between all concerned is essential, with the fullest exchange of information, short of breaking the principle of confidentiality. Even if the case conference is too advanced there can at least be regular meetings of staff together and reports be given of such events as an anticipated eviction, with the consequent danger of family separation, or the discharge of hospital patients, or the admission of a person to a residential home. If one worker does not even know such things are to take place he cannot be expected to co-operate with another who does, in order to prevent or solve the personal problems that are involved. And to call a conference or make a report after children are received into care, or an infirm aged person is languishing in an empty house, is to open the stable door after the horse has collapsed in its stall.

Who should call a case conference and when is, therefore, of some importance. Divided responsibility, here as elsewhere, is no one's responsibility. The best arrangement and the one generally followed is for a chief officer of the local authority—the medical officer of health—the chief welfare officer—the children officer—or the town clerk—to be made responsible for calling a conference at the request of any worker whenever he or she feels a need for one to be held or recalled. It should not follow necessarily, however, that he who calls the conference takes the chair. This should be filled by whoever has the greatest knowledge and skill to fit him for this post. It is questionable that the family doctor can best mobilise and co-ordinate the health and welfare services, as was suggested by a sub-committee of the Standing Medical Advisory Committee of the Central Health Services Council in relation to mentally subnormal persons living in the community.[13] The doctor is not an administrator. He has few, if any, facilities for calling conferences. He is in touch with only some of those staffing the social services, and he is concerned too intimately with the treatment of his patients to have the time to organise meetings of others, although it may be extremely useful for him to attend a case conference which concerns one of his patients, and he should feel free at any time to ask that one should be held.

Case conferences are a familiar part today, although not a universal one, in many social service settings. They are found in the hospital between psychiatrists, nurses, psychiatric social workers and other hospital staff; in the child guidance clinic between psychiatrists, educational psychologists and psychiatric social workers; in local authority health, welfare or children departments between the child care officers, health visitors, school welfare officers and case workers from voluntary agencies. They are occasionally found in old people's welfare. Taking the social services as a whole, however, they are still the exception rather than the rule. This is not necessarily a bad thing for they can be costly in time and effort and a need to extend their use unduly could be a symptom of something amiss with social service provision as a whole.

However great the value of co-operation, in whatever way it may be achieved, its importance must not be over-estimated. It alone will not solve all the problems of administration in the social services. For example, it is not the case, as the Ministry of Health appeared to suggest, that active co-operation between general practitioner, health visitor and social worker will necessarily discover and uncover the problems of all solitary old people.[14] More than co-operation is necessary for the achievement of this end, although co-operation is certainly an essential. Co-ordination of services is of equal importance and to this attention is now turned.

Co-ordination may be defined as a close, interlocking connection or combination of different services, departments or agencies, or between different parts or sections of the same service, department or agency, in order that an agreed and common policy may be pursued by all concerned as swiftly, smoothly and economically as possible, and in order that there may be no gaps, no overlapping, and no duplication. Lack of co-ordination may be due to the complicated structure of the service or services or it may be due to several bodies being responsible for different parts of the same service. It may arise out of a failure to co-operate. It may be because, as the National Council of Social Service pointed out: 'The fact is that, while the need for some kind of co-ordination is widely recognised, nobody wants to be co-ordinated by someone else!'[15]

The clearest example of the problem of co-ordination and the one most frequently criticised, is to be found in the division of the national health service with its tripartite structure, placing responsibility upon three different organs of administration, under the overall responsibility of the Minister of Health. These organs are the regional hospital boards responsible for the hospital services, the local health authorities responsible for preventive and domiciliary health services and the executive councils concerned with the provision of medical, dental, pharmaceutical and supplementary ophthalmic services. It is because of this tripartite structure and division of responsibility that people can and do pass from the purview of one section of the service and its staff to another; from the psychiatric social worker in the hospital, for example, to the mental welfare officer of the local authority on discharge; from the medical social worker in the geriatric unit to the Homes admission officer of the local welfare authority. This adverse view of the present structure is shared by the medical profession itself: 'Our review has convinced us that a major fault with the National Health Service is its present tripartite administration, for this has led to difficulties in co-ordination and co-operation.'[16]

The problem of old people of like condition, some admitted to hospital and some to Homes, or old people exchanged by hospital and Home to free beds in the one or the other, or looked upon by both hospital and Home as the responsibility of the other, has many times been posed as an example of acute lack of co-ordination. The only solution some critics have long said is for one body to be made responsible for the health service as a whole so that the hospital and the domiciliary health services are not divided. At one time the Ministry of Health did not regard this as necessary. It was held to be enough clearly to define the responsibilities of hospitals and local authorities for different categories of people, and this the Ministry attempted to do. The categorisation was given in full in the report of and upheld as valuable by the Guillebaud Committee on the Cost of the National Health Service although it had itself earlier observed:

'We regard the division between the hospital and local authority services for the care of the aged as one of the most serious divisions in the whole service.'[17]

It is this division that would seem to lie at the heart of the problem, for definitions of categories can rarely, if ever, be so precise that the same person falls clearly and for ever into only one of them. Human needs are too complex and too varied for this and to co-ordinate services, not to categorise people, is the only satisfactory answer as and when they fall across the boundaries of different human needs, as they inevitably will. The problem remains, however, as to who is to co-ordinate a service and how.

Few people other than those in the medical profession itself, and possibly not all of them, would be likely to accept the rather startling answer offered by the sub-committee of the Standing Medical Advisory Committee of the Central Health Services Council, to which reference has already been made, who said that it is the family doctor who can best co-ordinate the health and welfare services. The Committee expressed this view most precisely in relation to the mental health services of which it observed: 'All the services provided by clinics, hospitals, local authorities, employment officers and voluntary workers, exist to support the family doctor and should be co-ordinated through him.'[18] But services do not exist to support the doctor. They exist to support the patient. That the doctor should have regard to the social problems of his patient is unquestionable, but this does not necessarily support the view that he should be the head of what is called a domiciliary team.

One person as the leader of a team might facilitate co-ordination but the provision of social services in this country, including statutory and voluntary, central and local services, do not lend themselves to this kind of organisation. Even if they did, the doctor as the leader of a team, having direct access to those dealing with his patients and the ability to consult with them, is one thing. To share in 'the control of their activities',[19] is another, and one unlikely to commend itself to social workers or many others. This view appears to be borne out by a somewhat cryptic observation in the report of the Seebohm Committee that one 'factor in poor collaboration (in the social services) is the common assumption that the doctor must be the leader in any team of which he is a member'.[20]

Other instances under the national health service where lack of co-ordination has been found lie in the fields of convalescent treatment and the maternity services. Convalescent treatment can be provided both by the hospital and the local health authority, although in the second case the provision is called recuperative holidays—a distinction with little difference. The hospital makes no charge for the services it provides, the local authority does. The same home may be used by the two authorities but on different terms. The confusions and inefficiencies resulting from this dual service were revealed and discussed in a report of a

Ministry of Health Working Party in 1959,[21] but the divided responsibility still remains.

So far as the maternity services are concerned responsibility is shared by the local health authority, the hospital, and the general practitioner under contract with an Executive Council, under the National Health Service, to provide maternity medical services. Thus a woman may go to her family doctor for examination and care before and after childbirth, or attend the local authority ante- and post-natal clinic and be served by its health visitor, midwife or home nurse, or she may go to the clinic of the hospital in which she may in due course have her baby. The Guillebaud Committee concluded on the evidence it received that as a result the maternity services were in a state of some confusion, impairing their usefulness, and that the position should be reviewed.[22] Such a review was undertaken and it was agreed in 1959 that there was need for a greater degree of planned co-ordination of the activities of all persons carrying out maternity care. Since then efforts have been made to achieve this end by the arrangement, in some areas at least, of regular meetings between representatives of the three parties concerned to agree upon procedure for the booking of maternity beds, introduce better order in the provision of maternity care and agree upon plans to serve the best interests of the user of the services.

In 1967 the Minister of Health announced that a review of the administrative structure of the medical and related services was being undertaken which would include a consideration of whether the three types of authority, hospital boards, executive committees, and local authority services, achieved the degree of integration needed then and in the future. Tentative proposals for changes were to be submitted in the form of a Green Paper that could be considered with the report of the Royal Commission on Local Government in England and Wales (the Maud Commission) and the report of the Committee on the Local Authority and Allied Personal Social Services (the Seebohm Committee), and this Green Paper appeared in 1968 with the proposals referred to in Chapter Eight.

Services other than the national health service in which the need for co-ordination is clearly to be seen, are those in respect of deprived and delinquent children, welfare services for the old, and the rehabilitation and welfare services for the disabled. To a lesser extent the need is apparent in the youth service and the youth employment service. The need for co-ordination arises in each of these instances because more than one body has either been given or has taken upon itself at different points of time responsibility for providing the service or part of the service concerned. Thus in the case of deprived and delinquent children there is not only the local authority children department and the juvenile court, but also voluntary bodies concerned to prevent cruelty, provide substitute homes, approved schools, or casework services. The health, welfare, housing and education departments of the local authority may also be involved. It was pointed out in Chapter Six that it is often a matter of chance into which category —deprived or delinquent—a child at risk may ultimately fall. He may become delinquent because he is first deprived or he may be deprived because he is first delinquent. It may be that one child in a family has committed an offence and is on probation with a condition of residence, and another, because the family is too large for the housing accommodation it occupies, is deprived and in the care of the local authority, whilst a third is beginning to truant from school and showing symptoms of becoming one or the other.

It is clearly of great importance in such instances that the probation, the child care and the school welfare services should be closely co-ordinated. The efficacy of a probation order with a condition of residence depends, for example, on the local authority or a voluntary body having a vacancy in a suitable probation hostel or home. And the probation officer will need to know that another child in the family is in care and the third is truanting from school. In short, welfare of the child is shared at the present time by more than one service and it is essential they should be co-ordinated if the child is not to suffer.*

A similar situation arises in the case of physically and mentally handicapped children and young people. A report of a Working Party set up by the British Council for the Rehabilitation of the Disabled on the Handicapped School Leaver, and a report to the Carnegie United Kingdom Trust on Handicapped Children

* The provisions of the Children and Young Persons Bill (1969) materially affect this situation.

and their Families both referred to the lack of adequate co-ordination between individual services for such children and young people. As a result a Joint Circular of the Department of Education and Science (9/66) and the Ministry of Health (7/66) was sent to local authorities in March 1966, after consultation with the then Ministry of Labour and appropriate Advisory Committees, on 'The Co-ordination of Education, Health and Welfare Services for physically and mentally handicapped children and young people'. This invited all education, health and welfare authorities to review their practices in relation to these groups and to join with hospital authorities and executive councils for the area to review the situation in consultation with voluntary organisations providing similar services.

One step that followed was the formation of a Joint Council for the Education of Handicapped Children; an attempt to secure closer co-operation between the organisations concerned. That such an achievement takes time is illustrated by the fact that having explored various ways of co-ordinating activities locally and nationally the Council planned to have a joint conference in 1970. Even the preliminaries to better co-ordination were expected to take four years.

Another step was the setting up of a working party by the Inner London Education Authority which made a number of recommendations that serve as examples of what can be done to improve the situation. The recommendations included the preparation of a register of handicapped children and young persons; the medical officer of health to be appointed as a nominated officer to co-ordinate all the services a particular child might need; welfare and mental welfare officers to be consulted about the future of a handicapped child as early as possible and be told of his progress throughout his school life; the preparation of pamphlets setting out all the services available for handicapped children and the provision of centres where parents could obtain information; and, finally, the Minister of Health to introduce a national 'at risk' notification form to help in the exchange of information between hospitals, general practitioners and local authorities.

In the case of old people an even larger number of organisations may become involved in their welfare than in that of the child.

There may be the Department of Health and Social Security to ensure maintenance of income; the local authority health and welfare departments to ensure the provision of domiciliary health and welfare services; the housing department to provide suitable housing accommodation; the hospital to provide in-patient treatment in illness; the old people's welfare committee and other voluntary bodies to organise visiting, clubs, holidays, workshops and any other activity they have the means and the mind to do, and the residential Home for the more infirm. If ever there were an instance in which co-ordination is needed, and has been repeatedly called for, but has as yet in many areas eluded its pursuers, it is in the field of old people's welfare. As a result one old person may enter a Home because domiciliary welfare services are inadequate, another old person may have several visitors whilst her neighbour has none, and another may wait till she is dying for a one-roomed flatlet and then it is too late for her to benefit.

In the case of the disabled person, rehabilitative treatment for the injured can be provided both by the hospital and by the Department of Employment and Productivity. The Department can also provide training courses and sheltered employment for the disabled as can the local welfare authority, as was seen in Chapter Seven. There are also numerous voluntary organisations concerned with the disabled, the majority of them interested in one form of disability only. Indeed more than twenty national voluntary organisations for the disabled have been formed since 1900. The need for co-ordination of all these services is self-evident. It has long been recognised by the Minister of Health but it is questionable that it has yet been achieved.

The Committee of Inquiry on the Rehabilitation and Resettlement of Disabled Persons (Tomlinson Committee) recommended in 1956 that, so far as those able to engage in remunerative employment were concerned—that is those who could undertake more than work of a diversionary or therapeutic nature—the provision of sheltered employment whether in workshops or at home and whether for the blind or other disabled persons, should be transferred from the local welfare authorities to be administered by the Ministry of Labour and National Service as it then was under the Disabled Persons (Employment) Act.[23] This, however, has not happened and the confusing duplication of services remains.

The dual responsibilities of the Department of Employment and Productivity and of local education authorities for the youth employment service, and of local education authorities and voluntary bodies for the youth service were referred to in Chapter Six and no more is added here. They serve only as two more instances calling for co-ordination of services. Advice of this nature is easy to give and is frequently given. It is not, however, so easy to follow and attention can be drawn to instances of failure to co-ordinate as it can and has been to instances of failure to co-operate. For example, Shapiro pointed out that in a children department:

'there may be a finance section, a court section, an admission section and so on . . . it may happen . . . that a caseworker, attempting to re-habilitate a family and slowly establishing an effective relationship with difficult parents, calls one day to find that, through the action of another section of her own Department, and quite unknown to her, the father has been prosecuted and imprisoned for non-payment of parental contributions'.[24]

In the study of old people's welfare referred to earlier there was, in addition to the instances of non-co-operation, the case of the voluntary organisation which appointed a member of staff to develop work with the old in one part of a borough without consulting or informing the staff of an already well-established and active old people's welfare committee who then found work in that area duplicated. In another borough a newly appointed member of a public health department undertook visiting of old people well known to and already visited by the organiser of the old people's welfare committee, without informing her of the reason or intention of doing so, thus confusing her and the old people involved.[25] In a National Council of Social Service study of services for the handicapped in 1958 it was found that centrally at all events, progress towards co-ordination was disappointing. The situation, with its possibilities of dispersal of effort, over-lapping and waste of resources, gave ground for anxiety. There was a strong impression that in most areas co-ordination lagged far behind the development of services themselves.[26] Visiting of the same family by several workers may also be an example of failure to co-ordinate services. The Younghusband Working

Party observed: 'The difficulty is not so much multiplicity of visiting as multiplicity of independent unco-ordinated visiting.'[27] Whether or not all these are examples of the exceptional rather than the general is beside the point. The point is to avoid lack of co-ordination altogether. The devices designed to promote this end are, therefore, of importance.

The first of these was the brainchild of voluntary service when it gave birth to the National Council of Social Service in 1918. This constituted an initial attempt to bring some sort of rational order into a confused field. The original motive for establishing the Council, as was the case with the Charity Organisation Society [now Family Welfare Association] in 1896, arose from the need to co-ordinate charitable effort in the pecuniary meaning of that term; in other words to avoid confusion, chaos, overlapping, and indiscriminate begging. This limited purpose quickly broadened out until the National Council and the local Councils of Social Service which it encouraged, became the media by which any or all voluntary and statutory agencies could come together for purposes of discussion, mutual assistance and co-operation, and the promotion of new services in conjunction not competition with one another. In examining the intent and value of such co-ordinating bodies Beveridge spoke of the difficulties with which they will almost inevitably be faced:

'Of course, the way to co-ordination of the spirit of service is hard. Any organisation which attempts it will run into storms. It will appear from time to time as the critic as well as the friend of other organisations, as an additional hurdle to be surmounted on the way to some cherished aim. It will be accused of being more interested in co-ordination than in getting anything done. Its officers will be told that they are becoming another bureaucracy, indistinguishable from the civil servants with whom they deal, If, in addition to promoting co-ordination, it undertakes directly any work of its own, it will appear as the competitor instead of the friend and ally of other agencies.'[28]

Anyone who has attempted or been connected with attempts to co-ordinate voluntary social services, whether national or local, is likely to endorse all that Beveridge says. Co-ordination is no easy task. Claims couched in terms of freedom and independence often win the day over those couched in terms of unity and concord. The ideal, of course, is to have both but ideals often founder on the rocks of reality.

In 1936 an effort to co-ordinate the numerous parts of the voluntary youth service came with the establishment of the Standing Conference of National Voluntary Youth Organisations, whose purpose is to provide a consultative body to discuss matters of common interest, to make joint representations or recommendations to statutory or other bodies, and to act as a clearing-house for the exchange of information and a medium for representation on outside bodies. The establishment of the National Old People's Welfare Committee (now Council) in 1940, was with the intention of bringing together in consultation, national voluntary organisations working for the welfare of old people with representatives of appropriate government departments, old people's welfare committees and individuals with special experience, to study and promote measures for their wellbeing, and to encourage similar effort locally throughout the country. The pursuit of co-ordination was as much part of this intention as the promotion of services. In 1962 the National Bureau for Co-operation in Child Care was set up to become an information centre and clearing-house for those engaged in work concerned with the welfare of children and to improve the quality of the services provided. The first Annual Report of the Bureau for the year 1963–64 included in its list of members no less than thirty-two national voluntary societies and associations of professional workers, each concerned entirely with some aspect of the care of children. With so large a number of organisations and so many different staff the importance of the 'principal aim of the Bureau to help improve lines of communication between different professional disciplines' cannot be over-estimated. The Bureau is concerned also to carry out research on a national scale.

It was in 1950 that the State joined forces with the co-ordinative efforts of voluntary bodies and another co-ordinating committee was born. Concern about children neglected or ill-treated in their own homes, who strictly speaking fell outside the scope of the Children Act, 1948, had been frequently expressed. Finally, a working party of officials of the Home Office, the Ministry of Education and the Ministry of Health was set up to examine the situation. On its report the Government concluded that there was no immediate need for additional statutory powers, or for an enquiry by a departmental committee. The need, they said, was for the fully co-ordinated use of existing statutory and voluntary services, which could be achieved by setting up co-ordinating committees in every local authority area. History has subsequently shown that this diagnosis, as many believed at the time, was incorrect. Ten years later, in 1960, a committee of enquiry *was* set up (the Ingleby Committee). It *did* recommend additional statutory powers, and these *were* included in the Children and Young Persons Act, 1963. In other words the co-ordinating committees recommended in 1950 did not achieve all the Government hoped of them. Nevertheless the majority of local authorities do now have and use them.

The purpose of these co-ordinating committees in child care was set out in a Joint Circular from the Home Office, Ministry of Health and Ministry of Education on 'Children Neglected or Ill Treated in their own Homes', of July 31, 1950. There were to be regular meetings, called by a designated officer, of officials of the local authority and other statutory services and of representatives of voluntary organisations, at which 'significant cases of child neglect and all cases of ill-treatment coming to the notice of any statutory or voluntary service in the area, reported to the designated officer, were to be brought forward so that, after considering the needs of the family as a whole, agreement might be reached as to how the local services could best be applied to meet those needs.'[29]

There is a certain ambiguity in the wording of the last part of this statement which may well explain how it came about that in many cases co-ordinating committees came to be used as case conferences. Such misuse may account for and possibly justify the opposition which has on occasion been shown in a refusal to submit cases, or the observation of disgruntled workers that they get nowhere, do nothing or are a waste of time. The Younghusband Working Party attempted to rectify the confusion by pointing out the difference, as they saw it, between a case conference and a co-ordinating committee. The functions which they ascribed to the first have been given earlier in this chapter. The functions of the second they said were 'to work out and operate a plan for co-operation in general terms and to consider general questions of principle or policy'.[30] It is to be hoped that this effort to clear up the confusion did not come too late; in other words that the mistaken use of co-ordinating committees as case conferences has not become a permanent feature of social administration.

One further device designed to promote co-ordination is that known as 'the joint appointment'. This is neither more nor less than the appointment of one person to give his or her services to two bodies concurrently, part to one and part the other, or to two departments of the same authority. There are, for example, many areas in which the chief medical officer of the health committee is also the principal school medical officer of the education committee, or the chief welfare officer of the welfare committee. Health visitors may be appointed also as school nurses or nurses in the ante- and post-natal maternity and child welfare clinics. Such joint appointments can further co-ordination between different departments of the same authority.

It is possible also for a hospital to appoint onto its staff a psychiatric social worker to act also as a mental welfare officer of the local health authority. Or a local health authority may appoint a mental welfare officer to serve part-time on the staff of the hospital. Or the medical officer for mental health in the employ of the local authority can also be employed as medical superintendent of a local hospital. In these ways one and the same person will be concerned, in consultation with the general practitioner and under the medical officer of health, with initial proceedings in providing care and treatment of the mentally ill, will maintain contact with the patient whilst in hospital, or attending an out-patient clinic under the psychiatrist, and will continue after-care in consultation again with the general practitioner on discharge from hospital. Co-ordination of the mental health services of the hospital, the local authority, and the doctor will be furthered through such appointments, one staff member carrying continued responsibility for the social care of the pre-hospital, the in-hospital and the ex-hospital patient.

Whereas, as Jones said: 'The problem of continuity of care is at its most acute in relation to patients discharged from mental hospitals',[31] joint appointments need not be confined to the mental health field. Nevertheless and even with the encouragement of the Minister of Health, they are relatively few in number. One obstacle in their extension is the irrational difference that is to be found at the present time in rates of salaries. The local authority mental health officer, the psychiatric social worker and the medical social worker are all appointed on different scales, the more highly qualified person often receiving a lower salary. It is understandable, therefore, if illogical, that there should be some reluctance on the part of an employing body faced with a higher salary bill than its opposite number, to make appointments, in the hope that these will be made at someone else's expense. The solution to this particular problem, which would also be an act of professional justice, would be for the rate for the job to be paid whether the job is in the service of the local authority, hospital or elsewhere. The anomaly of salary scales runs right through the field of employment of social workers.

If the distinction between and the examination of co-operation and co-ordination that have been pursued now in this chapter, seem to the student of social administration somewhat remote and academic it can only be repeated that they are of practical importance because they affect the lives of individual people. People benefit from their presence. They suffer from their absence. The importance of understanding the causes of their absence and appreciating the means of their promotion does not lie in mere tidy-mindedness on the part of the bureaucrat nor the desire for clarity on the part of the teacher. It lies in the welfare and well-being of people to whose comfort or convenience, safety or satisfaction, they minister. No social servant is worth his salt, therefore, until and unless he is willing to co-operate. No services are satisfactory until and unless they are co-ordinated.

Certain important questions remain. Is it, it may be asked, always and only to co-operation that one must look to overcome those frailties of human behaviour that imperil working relationships—possessiveness, forgetfulness, rivalry and so on—that were instanced at the opening of this chapter? Is it always and only to co-ordination that one must look to avoid the undesirable features of duplication, gaps, or overlapping in services? May it rather not be that these faults are encouraged by or arise merely because there are too many services directed to the same person, and whose staff are employed by different bodies? Would not amalgamation or merger of services be a better answer to the problems that have been posed than the pursuit of co-operation and co-ordination which so often prove so elusive? Or could not their administrative structure be changed to avoid divided responsibility in the first place?

The answer to these questions is both 'No' and 'Yes'. Some separate provisions or services will always be necessary in certain areas of need and these will continue to demand co-operation between staff and co-ordination between services. For example, the separation of cash-paying services from local authority welfare services will continue to require that visiting officers of the Department of Health and Social Security work closely with local authority welfare officers in the case of families where both financial and social problems arise. But in other instances complete reorganisation may be necessary, as suggested, for example, in the Green Paper on the administrative structure of medical and related services in England and Wales and in the report of the Seebohm Committee.

So far as voluntary social service organisations are concerned if these were to ask themselves if each of their separate provisions were really necessary, in the light of what other voluntary organisations and local authorities now do, there might well be some diminution in numbers through amalgamation. The need for co-operation between present separate staff and co-ordination between separate services would be reduced accordingly. No doubt the questioner had some such possibility in mind when he asked the Minister of Health if he did not agree that the existence of the National Old People's Welfare Council, the National Corporation for the Care of Old People, the National Benevolent Fund for the Aged and the National Trust for the Welfare of the Elderly, was a proliferation of national voluntary organisations that was giving ground for concern.[32] That the Government had already had a similar point in mind is suggested by the observation of the Chancellor of the Duchy of Lancaster, in speaking of the review of the social services in general, when he said that studies of the work and needs of the many voluntary services were to be undertaken because there was no room for competition, but every room for co-operation, and the Government wanted to make the best use of the voluntary services.[33]

One move towards this end was made in 1966 when the British

Council for the Rehabilitation of the Disabled, the Central Council for the Disabled and the National Fund for Research into Crippling Diseases set up a joint committee to review their work and objects. The immediate aim was to see how far and to what extent the three bodies could be more closely associated and how collaboration for the physically handicapped could be encouraged and provided. In view of the existing multitude of voluntary bodies concerned in one way or another with the care and welfare of the disabled, referred to earlier in this chapter, such association or collaboration is much to be desired.

That such a wise and welcome development as a merger can take place is to be found in the case of the erstwhile Central Association for Mental Welfare, the Child Guidance Council and the National Council of Mental Hygiene which, after careful consideration, united with one another in 1946 to form the National Association for Mental Health, because, as Rooff said, they saw 'the advantages to the mental health service of co-ordination of all branches at a national level'.[34] Co-ordination in this instance was achieved by amalgamation or merger.

The same is true of the Children's Aid Society and Dr Barnardo's which, after working in close co-operation for many years, finally united with one another in 1966 thus achieving satisfactory amalgamation after separate even if connected lives since their establishment in 1856 and 1866.

In short it is important not to place the value of co-operation and co-ordination so high that the advantages of union are overlooked. The cry for the first two can become so loud that the ears are stopped against hearing or heeding the case for the third. One may have great respect for those in the field of old people's welfare of whom Kemp said: 'Against the background of administrative chaos (largely centrally determined and tolerated) it was very impressive to find what a great volume of practical help was being given and how well the absurd machinery was working.'[35] But it would be infinitely better to clear away administrative chaos by the creation of administrative machinery that was not absurd.*

* For an illustration of co-operation and co-ordination in casework practice see: Anthony Forder, *Social Casework and Administration*, X, Faber and Faber, 1966.

CHAPTER TWELVE

Advice and Protection for the Citizen

It should have been evident in all the preceding chapters that the study and practice of social administration gain their greatest importance and purpose where there is the belief that all people, without exception, are of individual worth and merit. It is only in this belief that the provision of comprehensive, all-inclusive social services is justified; that the identification and search for solutions of social problems of the minority as well as the majority are intelligible; and that efforts to strengthen family life, further educational opportunity, or improve environmental conditions for everyone are desirable. It is fitting, therefore, that the examination of aspects of social administration which has taken place here, should draw to a close with the individual citizen in the centre of the picture. What follows places him there, for it comprises a consideration of those parts of the machinery of administration that are designed to inform him of his rights and protect him against ignorance, error, omission, or injustice.

The very extension of the social services which are provided for the benefit of the citizen, or through him of society as a whole, has brought with it growing dangers of confusion, feelings of inadequacy, violation of conscience or of privacy. Or at worst there may come the terrifying sensation of a Kafka novel; of grappling ineffectively with distant officials, complex regulations, innumerable papers and complicated procedures. As the relationship between citizen and State becomes both closer and more complex it is necessary, in the words of the report of the Committee on Administrative Tribunals and Enquiries (the Franks Committee): 'To seek a new balance between private right and public advantage, between fair play for the individual and efficiency of administration . . . to consider afresh the procedures by which the rights of individual citizens can be harmonised with wider public interests.'[1]

To achieve these ends the citizen must know what services are available to him and how best to use them; be assured that he and his dependants are receiving that to which they are entitled; and be aware how he may appeal against what is, or what appears to him to be, an error of judgment or an act of injustice. These are not goals that are easily reached. They require not merely the ability on someone's part to read, write and understand, but the initiative to act, the determination to pursue and the courage to combat. Not everyone who has a grievance has the skill and personal qualities necessary to write to a member of parliament or to the press. It is true that the John Hilton Bureau, which began as personal advice given through the medium of the B.B.C. and then became a column in *The News of the World*, has now developed a specialist service dealing with thousands of queries a week. But the paper's readers are a minority group, as are trade union members who can get help from their unions.

It is in all probability still the case, as the National Corporation for the Care of Old People said in 1964, and it may always be so, that 'we', that is to say those who are in a position to have and make use of the latest information, 'all tend to over-estimate what the general public knows about the social services and about what help is available to them to meet various needs and this can result in failure to discover in time those who require assistance. To plan the services ahead is essential but to educate the public in their use is equally important.'[2]

Everyone certainly can approach a chief officer at the town hall or a minister of State, if he is dissatisfied about the care or education of his child, or the payment of his pension. But such action may be beyond the competence or courage of the less educated, experienced, or privileged person. Pressure or even a fight may be necessary to win the day and not all have the knowledge or determination to act so vigorously. And it is idealistic to observe, as did the Minister of Health in the Green Paper referred to in Chapter Eight on the administrative structure of medical and related services in England and Wales, that if Area Health Boards were set up they would be expected, as the responsible local managers of the health services, to deal promptly with complaints from members of the public about the services provided for them or their relatives.[3] Of course they would have been, but reliance on such an expectation alone would be administratively naïve. Safeguards must be specifically built in to social legislation and be provided independently of it.

Included in the safeguards today are the Citizens' Advice Bureaux and their statutory counterpart, the local authority information and advice centres; the explanatory document or handbook; the specialist information service; the legal right of appeal and appeals tribunals; the legal aid and advice scheme; and finally the Parliamentary Commissioner for Administration whose functions are similar to those of the Ombudsman in Scandinavia; a name which is often given colloquially to the Parliamentary Commissioner in this country.

Citizens' Advice Bureaux, which are sometimes mistakenly believed to be part of a statutory service provided by the local authority, were established as voluntary bodies in 1939 at the outbreak of war and on the initiative of the National Council of Social Service; 'to make available to the individual accurate information and skilled advice on many of the personal problems that arise in daily life; to explain legislation; to help the citizen to benefit from and to use wisely the services provided for him by the State, and in general to provide counsel to men and women in the many difficulties which beset them in an increasingly complex world.' Behind this almost Biblical language the intention of the Citizens' Advice Bureaux was seen to be, as their name implies, the provision of a service of information and advice, particularly in relation to the many and complex personal and social problems arising out of war-time conditions and regulations. They were, and in the main still are, manned by volunteers provided with a manual of full and up-to-date information, prepared for their use by a central secretariat. They are accessible without charge to all who are anxious to obtain answers to any questions arising from daily life, whether related to landlord or tenant, government or governed, birth or death, marriage or divorce, sickness or health, schooling or leisure.*

The Government made use of the bureaux in their early days as a means of disseminating information and interpreting new legislation and war-time regulations. Their value at that time was beyond question and it was clear at the end of the war that they

* For a fuller examination see: M. E. Brasnett, *The Story of the C.A.B.* National Council of Social Service, 1966.

could serve a useful purpose in years of peace also. They were, therefore, established on a permanent footing and became eligible for grant under Section 134 of the Local Government Act, 1948, which empowers local authorities:

'to make, or to assist in the making of arrangements whereby the public may on application readily obtain... information concerning the services available within the area of the authority provided by the authority or by other authorities or by Government departments and other information as to local government matters affecting the area'.

The use of the words 'readily obtain' should be noted here. There is no merit, as the Editor of *Case Conference* once pointed out, 'in making people ferret round for information which they can easily be given'. There may be merit in students being required to seek information for themselves at the source, although even this may have a limit, but to cause the user of a social service to go to and fro seeking or failing to find answers to reasonable and relevant questions is both inefficient and unkind.

The major drawback in relying upon the Citizens' Advice Bureaux to meet the need for advice and dissemination of information is that people cannot always 'readily obtain' information from them. They are not evenly distributed throughout the country nor are they necessarily open each and all day where they are available. They suffer in short from two of the common disadvantages of the voluntary organisation. Their existence is uncertain and their distribution is uneven, rural areas in particular being poorly served. Annual Reports of the National Council of Social Service showed that out of a total of 427 bureaux in Great Britain in 1962–63 there was a heavy concentration in London, Manchester and Glasgow; that some counties had no bureaux at all; and that others were thinly served by one or two bureaux only.[4] The number of bureaux grew to 463 in 1965–66 but they were still situated mainly in the larger towns and cities throughout the country, and it was estimated that a further two hundred were needed in England and Wales.[5] Fourteen new bureaux were set up in 1966–67.

The limitation in number and distribution do not detract from such value as the bureaux now have; although no enquiry has ever been made into the precise nature or extent of that value.

The limitations serve but to show what still remains to be done if all citizens are to have equality of opportunity in obtaining advice and information.

The Information and Advice Centres which can be provided by local authorities under the Local Government Act, 1948, are not as yet large in number and they do not fill the gaps left by the Citizens' Advice Bureaux. This is one of the disadvantages of permissive legislation. Local authorities may not use it. In all, in too large a part of the country face to face question and answer cannot easily be put and received by a person who is puzzled and perplexed by the demands or complexities of his daily life. In a highly industrialised, swiftly moving, densely populated, and necessarily regulated society, these may well be neither few in number nor slight in importance.

If all people could read and write with ease and could understand all that they read, this might not be too serious a matter. But this is not so. Nor unfortunately is it true, as Townsend said of the old, that there is little to stop people 'writing a letter, making a telephone call or even going along in person to the appropriate office',[6] to make a request or seek advice. There are many things which may stop them. There are numbers of people alive today who left school at twelve and who have had no formal education since. There are those whose limited abilities are such as always to handicap them in fields where literacy or verbal fluency is essential. There are those whose education has been broken by accident, illness, war-time evacuation, or other misfortune. There are those whose family life and background are such that they have never been encouraged to develop or use the initiative or abilities they possess. For these and others easy means of obtaining first hand, clear, and accurate information about the social services is vitally important and the approach cannot always be left to the user of the service.

For those who can read and are of good intelligence and education the printed word may be appropriate but this still often leaves much to be desired in clarity or conciseness. Social service departments have taken trouble in many instances to inform the citizen of his rights through the publication of printed leaflets, memoranda and so forth, the Department of Health and Social Security being particularly active in this respect. But depart-

mental jargon can and does creep in, and that which is designed
to inform, may tend in fact to confuse. Examples illustrating this
tendency are to be found in Gowers' book, written 'for those who
use words as tools of their trade, in administration or business'.[7]
The following is one:

'With reference to your letter of the 12th August, I have to state in
answer to question 1 thereof that where particulars of a partnership
are disclosed to the Executive Council the remuneration of the individual partner for superannuation purposes will be deemed to be such
proportion of the total remuneration of such practitioners as the proportion of his share in the partnership profits bears to the total proportion of the shares of such practitioner in those profits.'

This Gowers thought meant merely: 'Your income will be taken
to be the same proportion of the firm's remuneration as you used
to get of its profits.'[8] The student may try out his own ability to
interpret on the following extract from the Explanatory and
Financial Memorandum which accompanied the National Insurance Bill, 1959, relating to graduated retirement pensions:

'Graduated benefit will normally take the form of an increase of the
main retirement pension, and will in general be payable at the same ages
and on the same conditions, for example as to retirement. It will be
at the rate of 6d. for each unit of graduated contributions paid by the
employed person. Such units will initially be £7. 10s. od. for men and
£9 for women, being increased proportionately as and when contributions are increased under Clause 1 (2). Half the graduated benefit not
drawn at pensionable age owing to postponed retirement will be treated
as an additional employee's contribution (i.e. corresponding to a joint
contribution by employer and employee equal to the full amount of
such benefit) towards increased graduated benefits on ultimate
retirement.'

An example of a specialist information service was one sponsored in 1964 by the Disabled Living Activities Group of the
Central Council for the Disabled. This was to make available
information on the care of the disabled, whether in the community
or in hospital, designed for the benefit of the disabled themselves
and those professionally concerned with their care. Such schemes
are useful and desirable and one small piece of evidence contained
in the Annual Report of the Family Welfare Association for
1965–66 suggested that users were becoming increasingly aware

of services available to them. In that year 40 per cent of the Association's clients sought help on their own initiative. This was an increase of 6 per cent over the previous year and 12 per cent over the previous two years. Clearly no conclusion can be drawn from these figures but that even one body found greater direct user approach was encouraging.

The view that the provision of information and advice for the citizen still leaves much to be desired, however, was borne out by the recommendation of the Ingleby Committee on Children and Young Persons that there should be some centre or body to which not only parents, but others as well, might know they could turn for advice and assistance: 'Some door on which they can knock, knowing that their knock will be answered by people with the willingness to help them.' The Committee later referred to such a centre as a 'family advice centre' or 'family bureau' which would be a central point of reference both for the various local authority services and for members of the public.[9]

No provision was made for the establishment of such centres or bureaux under the Children and Young Persons Act, 1963, which followed the report of the Ingleby Committee, but Circular No. 204/1963 of September 17, 1963, of the Home Office to local authorities on Section 1 of the Act, expressed the hope that authorities would:

'give further consideration to the possibility of creating in the large local authority areas a "family advice centre" as examined by the Ingleby Committee, to serve as a central point of reference for members of the public who are in need of advice or assistance on the welfare of children. It is important', the Circular continued, 'not only that advice and assistance should be available, but that it should be known to be available, and that those who are in need of help and advice may be encouraged to seek it and may be enabled to discover where it can be obtained either by the attendance of social case-workers in existing Citizens' Advice Bureaux or by local authority officers being ready. Such centres will also be of value in assisting families or individuals where no question arises of children going into care and where indeed no children may be involved.'

In a written reply to a question in the House of Commons on January 21, 1965, the Home Office stated that by June 30, 1964, sixty-nine local authorities had set up family advice centres and

I

that thirty others were using offices of their children departments for that purpose. A further twenty seven had plans for such centres in hand.* Whatever the final outcome of this development, however, or even if the user of a service is fully informed and aware of his rights, or indeed just because he is aware of his rights, there will still be occasions when doubts arise as to whether justice has been done. It is necessary, therefore, to examine social legislation to see whether a right of appeal is written into it. Such examination shows many and various ways of ensuring that this is so.

First, if any person is dissatisfied about an award or a decision in respect of the payment of a Family Allowance, appeal may be made under Section 5 of the Family Allowances Act, 1945; first to the Minister of Pensions and National Insurance, now the Department of Health and Social Security, and second from him to one or more referees selected from a panel of persons appointed by the Lord Chancellor to act in this capacity. Decisions of the referee or referees are final, except that questions of law as such can always be referred to the courts. Under Section 43 of the National Insurance Act, 1946, there is provision for the determination of any claims arising in connection with the provisions of that Act. These are to be determined first by an Insurance Officer appointed for that purpose, second by reference to a Local Tribunal, presided over by a lawyer, and third by appeal to a National Insurance Commissioner appointed by the Crown, who must be a barrister or advocate of not less than ten years' standing, or by a Tribunal presided over by such a Commissioner. The decision at this third stage is final. In 1967 there were some 200 National Insurance Local Tribunals throughout the country dealing with approximately 40,000 appeals a year. Similar procedure applies to appeals in respect of the industrial injuries scheme. There is also right of appeal against decisions of the Industrial Injuries Medical Boards which are set up under the National Insurance (Industrial Injuries) Act and are concerned with purely medical matters and assessment of disablement. Such appeals may be made to a Medical Appeal Tribunal whose decision is final.

Under Section 14 of the National Assistance Act, 1948, pro-

* For a study of a sample of Family Advice Services organised by Children Departments in England see: Aryeh Leissner, *Family Advice Services*, The National Bureau for Co-operation in Child Care, 1967.

vision was made for any aggrieved person to appeal to a District Appeal Tribunal against any decision in respect of a grant or supplementary pension. The same right of appeal was continued in the Ministry of Social Security Act, 1966, in respect of decisions reached by the Supplementary Benefits Commission which replaced the National Assistance Board. Under Section 42 of the National Health Service Act, 1946, a Tribunal is set up consisting of a chairman who must be a practising barrister or solicitor of not less than ten years' standing and two other members. Their function is to enquire into any instances of a doctor, pharmacist, dentist, or optician, against whom a complaint has been made, according to prescribed and complex procedure, that his continued inclusion in the service would be prejudicial to its efficiency. The Tribunal may direct that the person concerned shall be removed from the list of those practising in the service, but in such case there is right of appeal to the Minister of Health who has final authority to confirm or revoke the decision in favour of the practitioner.

This procedure does not protect a patient personally nor does it give him any redress if he believes himself to be aggrieved, or to have suffered from or by any treatment he has or has not received, except that which may come to him from the knowledge that judgment has been sought and given. It is the efficiency of the service which is being protected in this instance, although clearly if this is safeguarded the patients' interests are promoted at the same time. If, however, there is a case for damages arising from carelessness or neglect these have to be sought through the courts, not through the National Health Service Tribunal.

Section 3 of the Mental Health Act, 1959, provides for the establishment of a Mental Health Review Tribunal in the area of every regional hospital board. These Tribunals, which are independent bodies composed of legal, lay, and medical members, replaced the Board of Control that existed previously. They deal with any written applications or references made by or in respect of patients who are affected by the Act. Since this includes provisions relating to those who may be compulsorily admitted to or detained in hospital or nursing homes for observation or treatment, and to those placed under guardianship in their own interests or for the protection of others, the right of appeal and review of such cases is of particular importance. The Council on Tribunals (to which further reference is made shortly) in its report for the year ended December 31, 1963, gave particular attention to the work of the Mental Health Review Tribunals on submissions made by the National Council for Civil Liberties and referred the points at issue to the Tribunals concerned.[10]

The last Appeal Tribunals to which reference is made are the Independent Schools Tribunals, set up under the Education Act, 1944. These Tribunals each consist of a chairman drawn from a legal panel appointed by the Lord Chancellor and two other members drawn from an educational panel appointed by the Lord President of the Council. Their purpose is to determine any complaints referred to them which have been served by the Secretary of State for Education and Science upon any school registered under the Act, on the grounds that its premises are in whole or in part, unsuitable for a school; that the accommodation provided is inadequate; that efficient and suitable instruction is not being provided; or that the proprietor or any teacher employed is not a proper person to be the proprietor of or a teacher in an independent school.

The Tribunal, after considering the evidence, may order the complaint to be annulled; or the school to be struck off the register unless the requirements are carried out; or disqualify the whole or part of the premises for use as a school; or disqualify the proprietor or teacher concerned from being a proprietor or teacher. Disqualification of a person can be removed by the Secretary of State for Education and Science if he is satisfied on application that a change of circumstance merits this. If, however, he refuses to remove a disqualification the person concerned may again appeal to the Tribunal. From this there is no further right of appeal, except to a court on a point of law. Since a decision can affect the whole professional life of a man or woman it is clearly of extreme importance that justice should be done.

All the instances outlined above relate to appeals which are heard by specially appointed persons or tribunals. The practice and procedure should throughout be characterised by what the Committee on Administrative Tribunals and Enquiries (the Franks Committee) referred to as openness, fairness and impartiality.[11] As well as their informality, the hearing of appeals by

tribunals, boards, referees or commissioners, relieves the courts of
what would otherwise be a grave burden of work and has the
advantage of 'cheapness, accessibility, freedom from technicality,
expedition and expert knowledge of [a] particular subject.'[12] To
be fully satisfied, however, those who make appeals must understand procedure, be capable of preparing, presenting and arguing
a case, be clear about the way in which a decision is reached, and
in due course that that decision is a fair one.

It was to further these ends that the Franks Committee recommended that at the discretion of the chairman legal representation
should be allowed before all tribunals and referees. The Government accepted this recommendation and as from 1958 the right
to legal representation has been acceded where it is clear an
applicant's case cannot be presented satisfactorily without the
assistance of a lawyer. It is still the exception, however, for an
applicant to seek legal representation.

Tribunals are now normally held in public which safeguards
the principle of openness, but it is the exception rather than the
rule that any member of the public attends other than interested
parties and the press. There is always the right of appeal to a
court on a point of law.

The Tribunals and Inquiries Act, 1958, which was passed
following the report of the Franks Committee, set up a Council
on Tribunals to keep them under review, to report annually on
their constitution and working, and to consider and report on any
matter of special importance relating to them which might be
referred to it. There are now some 35 to 40 categories and over
2,000 individual tribunals which are the concern of the Council
on Tribunals. Clearly not all of these relate to the social services.
But as in other fields the tribunals in the social service field
constitute:

'The everyday procedure whereby the citizen can contest the decision
of authority. He can, for example, appeal against the denial of national
insurance benefit, challenge his income tax assessment, object to a
proposal by a local authority to purchase his house compulsorily or
appeal against the refusal of planning permission to build himself a
new one.' In these and other areas it is the task of the Council or
Tribunals, 'To act as a watchdog for the ordinary citizen and to see that
he gets fair play'.[13]

In its Annual Reports the Council has concluded that the tribunals are in general working well. It regards the system of settling conflicts between government departments and private individuals as reasonable, efficient, and just. Complaints from the general public about tribunals have been few in number.*

In addition to those situations in which the machinery of appeal tribunals applies, there are others affected by social legislation which are not so covered. They are to be found in the education service, the child care service, and the welfare services. It is important to know whether and what protection is afforded to the citizen in these instances. All social legislation, but particularly that which includes compulsions or the exercise of discretionary powers by statutory officials, involves the possibility of maladministration, the miscarriage of justice, or a violation of conscience. Against these the citizen must have proper protection or redress.

To achieve these the Education Act, 1944, for instance, provides firstly, under Section 25(4), that a parent may withdraw his child from attendance at religious worship or instructions in the school if he so wishes, whether to worship or receive such instruction elsewhere, or not to worship or receive it at all. Secondly, the Act recognises in principle, under Section 78, that children should be educated in accordance with the wishes of their parents. There is the proviso here, however, that such wishes shall be compatible with the provision of efficient instruction and training and the avoidance of unreasonable public expenditure, and honesty compels the admission that in any dispute between a local education authority and a parent on these issues the odds are weighted in favour of the authority. Nevertheless a general right of complaint to the Secretary of State for Education and Science is conceded under Section 68 of the Act. This empowers him, if satisfied on complaint that any local education authority, or the managers or governors of any county or voluntary school, have acted or propose to act unreasonably with respect to any of the powers or duties given to or laid upon them by the Act, to direct them in the way that appears to him to be expedient. By this means parents have,

* For a fuller examination of Administrative Tribunals see: (i) Harry Street, *Justice in the Welfare State*, Stevens and Sons, 1968, and (ii) Kathleen Bell, *Tribunals in the Social Services*, Routledge and Kegan Paul, Ltd., 1968.

for instance, successfully fought proposals to close separate grammar schools and provide one comprehensive school in their stead. If, however, the decision of the Secretary of State is in favour of the local education authority no further appeal is possible, other than through a court of law.

The same safeguards apply to handicapped children as to normal children. Parents, that is to say, can appeal to the Secretary of State for Education and Science if they think that a local education authority has unjustifiably required the attendance of a child at a special school, under Section 34 of the Education Act. The number of such appeals is small in relation to the total of some 60,000 children in special schools. But the serious nature of the decision made by the education authority is such that every care should be taken to ensure that both the health and welfare of the child, and the rights of the parent, are considered carefully and impartially.

The Children Act, 1948, contains certain provisions similar to those of the Poor Law Act, 1930, when in force. These empower a local authority to assume by resolution parental rights over a child in their care where it appears to them that the child either has no parent or guardian, that the parent or guardian is incapable of caring for him by reason of a permanent disability, or is of such habits or mode of life as to be unfit to have the care of the child. The important difference between the Children Act and the Poor Law Act is that under the former any parent or guardian whose rights are affected by the resolution must be told, if he has not already consented in writing to the passing of the resolution, that he can lodge an objection to it within one month. If he does lodge an objection the resolution must lapse unless, on application by the local authority to a juvenile court, a court order is issued that it shall remain in force. If this is the case it so remains until the child reaches the age of eighteen, unless it is rescinded by the local authority as appearing to be for the benefit of the child. It remains open, however, to the parent or guardian whose rights are affected to apply to a court at any time to have the resolution determined. The court may so determine or it may make an order requiring the local authority to allow the child to be under the control of the parent or guardian for a fixed period or until it directs othere wise. In these ways an attempt is made to balance the rights of parents to have the care and control of their own child and thf rights of a child to protection against inability, irresponsibility, or incompetence on the part of the parents; protection which may require that temporarily or permanently someone should act in their stead.

Powers of compulsory removal of a person from his home are also conferred upon a local authority by Section 47 of the National Assistance Act, 1948. This applies to any person who is suffering from grave chronic disease or is aged, infirm or physically incapacitated and is living in insanitary conditions unable to devote proper care and attention to himself and not receiving it from any other person. The intention of removal in such cases is solely to secure that proper care and attention are given somewhere by someone. But removal by compulsion inevitably involves violation of a person's right to choose where and how he should live. Even in extreme cases this should be done only after the most serious consideration. The Act, therefore, requires that it should be done only after a medical officer of health has satisfied himself, after thorough enquiry and investigation, that it is in the interests of the person concerned, or is necessary to prevent injury to the health of or serious nuisance to other people.

Certification must be made by the medical officer of health in writing and application to remove must be made by the local authority to a court which, if satisfied on the evidence given of the allegation in the certificate, may order the removal of the person concerned to a hospital or elsewhere. In the first place this is for a period not exceeding three months and subsequently by extension as the court may determine. The court may revoke an order if it appears expedient to do so on application by or on behalf of the person concerned, at any time after the expiration of six weeks from the making of the order.

Study of the annual reports of medical officers of health reveals that compulsory removal is rare and on the face of it that every effort is made to provide care and attention in some other way. But how far the threat of taking a case to court is used, which even if benevolent in intent is a form of blackmail, one cannot tell. The right of self-determination is, however, often respected even longer than some might think is humanely desirable; to the extent, for example, of permitting two sisters in their eighties to live for years on their own choosing in the extreme dirt and discomfort of a hen house.

It is one thing, however, to leave people undisturbed in conditions which they have chosen, to which they are used, and which they do not wish to change. It is quite another to run the risk that they may be neglected or exploited by others. One of the unhappiest features of poor communal or institutional provision, whether it is in respect of children, old people, the disabled, the sick, or the prisoner, is the loss of individuality, of morale, of independence, and of personality as a whole. It is essential, in so far as it can be achieved, that those living in residential homes should be protected not only against more obvious neglect, inefficiency, or physical discomfort, but also against lack of understanding, affection, and the satisfaction of other emotional needs. These are the intentions of those sections of the Children Act, 1948, for instance, that empower the Secretary of State to make regulations relating to the conduct of residential homes for children. With these both voluntary bodies and local authorities must comply in order to secure the welfare of children living in them, and voluntary homes for children must also be registered and open to inspection. Clearly even the wisest and most humane regulations and the most careful and frequent inspection cannot guarantee that no child in a home will ever suffer from some human limitation or error on the part of those who are in charge. But a continuous effort to this end should be made.

Similar provisions as for children homes are made under the National Assistance Act for the registration and inspection by the local authority of voluntary and private homes for disabled persons and the old, and for the Minister of Health to make regulations as to their conduct. Registration of a home can be refused or cancelled if it is held that the person in charge is not fit to run it; that the premises, staffing, or equipment are inadequate; or if the services and amenities do not meet the needs of the residents. Proper regulation and inspection of voluntary and private homes for the old and disabled do, however, present particular problems. These homes, unlike children homes, can be run for profit and if residents are or appear to be satisfied with what they receive for the payment they make what justification is there for interference? There is the problem also of definition.

I*

What is a residential home as distinct from a nursing home, guest house, private hotel, or residence letting furnished rooms, one or two of which happen to be occupied by an old or a disabled person? As a result of these difficulties, and of staff shortages, standards and frequency of inspection by local authorities vary. And unfortunately there are reasons to believe, at least so far as homes for the old are concerned, that all is not well in this area in which the dependent and the weak so clearly need protection. Townsend, for example, cited six cases of homes which had not been inspected for at least five years.[14] And he instanced a case in which a manageress of one home, sent to prison for embezzling residents' money, opened another home elsewhere after her discharge.[15]

In addition to these difficulties, ignorance of legal requirements has yet to be overcome. It was still the case, even in 1964, more than fifteen years after the insertion of the protective clause in the National Assistance Act, that it was not generally known that local welfare authorities were responsible for registering all homes for old people and even those people who started homes of their own were not always aware of the fact that these should be registered by the appropriate local authority before they could admit residents.[16]

Another provision for the protection and advice of the citizen is that which is rendered necessary by the cost involved in appealing to, or taking action through a court of law to secure the enjoyment of a legal right or obtain redress of grievance. Such cost may be beyond the means of the person concerned and should this be so it is clear that justice requires that assistance should be available. This was first provided under the Legal Aid and Advice Act, 1949, which followed the report of the Committee on Legal Aid and Legal Advice in England and Wales (the Rushcliffe Committee).[17] The Act provided for the establishment of a scheme to afford legal aid and advice for the benefit of persons of limited means to be known as 'assisted persons', whose eligibility was to be determined by the amount of their disposable income.

The income limits fixed by the Act were extended by the Legal Aid Act, 1960, which made available legal aid on a sliding scale to those with disposable incomes between £250 and £700 a year.

If disposable income is below £250 per annum legal aid is available free of charge or contribution from the assisted person. Disposable income above £700 p.a. removes entitlement to assistance. Those whose disposable incomes fall between the limits are required to make some contribution towards the cost of litigation. The maximum of such contribution is one-third of the amount of disposable income by which it exceeds £250. The provisions are designed to ensure that no one is financially unable to prosecute a just and reasonable claim, or defend a legal right, whilst allowing at the same time for counsel or solicitors, who are freely chosen by the assisted person from a panel of those taking part in the scheme, to be remunerated for their services.

A Legal Aid Fund, financed by the State, is administered by the Law Society through area and local committees, which are responsible for ascertaining that a prospective litigant has reasonable grounds for taking, defending, or being a party to proceedings. Any proceedings held to be vexatious, frivolous, or discreditable or in which the costs are likely to be out of all proportion to the amount or importance of the claim, are refused as not proper ones to be brought at the public expense. So also are those of such a simple nature as would not ordinarily require the employment of a solicitor. The scheme is limited to proceedings in courts other than the coroner's court. Certain specified types of proceedings are excluded. These are actions for libel, slander, breach of promise of marriage, enticement, and seduction. But the large majority of proceedings normally brought to the courts are covered.

The provision of legal advice, as distinct from actual assistance in litigation, is a development of the poor man's lawyer scheme which is a voluntary service given by members of the legal profession working from centres provided by voluntary organisations. Since 1959 oral advice, at a small charge, on any legal question, including help in preparing applications to appeal tribunals, has also been obtainable through legal advice centres as part of the statutory legal aid and advice scheme. It is available to anyone over the age of sixteen who satisfies the income restrictions.

Generally satisfactory though the arrangements and provisions for protecting the citizen may now appear to be it must be remembered that people frequently do not know they can appeal, complain, or obtain legal assistance. And it is far from certain that officers concerned, if and when a query over any decision arises, make it clear to the person involved that he may do so and how he can set about it.

Nor is there always a right of appeal; for example, if the provision of a car for a disabled person is rejected by the Minister of Health, or if a medical officer of health will not authorise the use of a domiciliary laundry service, or a senior welfare officer refuses residential accommodation to an elderly person. Patients have no formal channel of complaint if they are dissatisfied about the nursing received or conditions experienced in hospital, unless there happens to be a complaints committee set up voluntarily by the hospital management committee itself. There is no right of appeal by students on decisions of local education authorities or central departments as to the amount of grant, if any, awarded towards the cost of courses of further education or professional training. All these decisions are at the discretion of a particular person or department but a refusal to aid may leave the person concerned with a sense of grievance or injustice that should not be left unexamined.

It is because of a sense of grievance or injustice or a general dissatisfaction about the standard of service offered that various forms of mutual protection societies have developed of recent years amongst consumers of the social services. Thus there has been formed 'The Mother Care for Children in Hospital Association'; a body of mothers concerned about rules of visiting children in less progressive hospitals, or the limited part they have been permitted to play in nursing or staying with their own children when in hospital. Armed with the report of the Committee on The Welfare of Children in Hospital (the Platt Committee),[18] they fight a battle to improve the hospital care given to their children.

Then there is 'The Association for Improvements in the Maternity Services' formed by women who have been dissatisfied with the service they themselves received at home or in hospital. Both these two Associations have undertaken fact-finding surveys to support their case for improved services. There is also 'The Home and School Council' formed in 1967 by parents concerned to improve and expand, in co-operation with local education authorities, the educational facilities for children in State schools and to promote the participation of parents in the educational system.

Another recently formed body is 'Mothers in Action'; a group of unsupported mothers joining together to achieve a better status for themselves and their children, by achieving changes in the law relating to illegitimate children and the payment of maintenance allowances, and more and better accommodation in homes, day nurseries, and housing.

Such societies as these are not merely self-help societies. Their intention is to improve State services and achieve what they regard as proper provision for themselves, for others, and for their own children. Their formation is an indication that the users of particular services are not truly thankful for what they have or believe they are about to receive, and is evidence of a failure to obtain satisfaction through the more usual channels of request or complaint.

Self-help groups also arise out of dissatisfaction that a service does not exist which those concerned believe should exist. One such is the recently formed National Council for the Single Woman and her Dependants. This Council is concerned to improve the economic position, particularly by changes in income tax allowances, of single women who have the care and responsibility of elderly dependent relatives or mentally or physically handicapped brothers or sisters. By reason of present demographic trends the single woman is decreasing proportionately in number but her dependent relatives are not. Thus a group emerges whose particular needs are emphasised by changes in the social structure but to whom little special attention has as yet been paid other than by its own members.

There is similarly the Disablement Income Group which was started in 1965 by two young housewives, both of whom suffered from disseminated sclerosis. The main objective of this group is the provision of a State pension for all disabled persons regardless of national insurance contributions. It is their belief that not only is this justified on grounds of financial need but to avoid institutional care which would be unnecessary if disabled persons could afford adequate domestic help or aids in the home which they too often have to go without at the present time.*

It has never been suggested that neglect of duty or maladministration are common features of the civil service in this country, but it was said of government departments, in a report by 'Justice', the British Section of the International Commission of Jurists, that:

'There appears to be a continuous flow of relatively minor complaints, not sufficient in themselves to attract public interest but nevertheless of great importance to the individuals concerned, which give rise to feelings of frustration and resentment because of the inadequacy of the existing means of seeking redress.'[19]

Of local government 'Justice' made a more serious charge:

'The opinion was expressed by several persons of experience in public affairs whose responsibility and judgement in these matters command respect, that there was probably a serious amount of maladministration in local government, and certainly considerably more than in the central government departments.'[20]

Not only was it because these charges were felt to carry weight but also because the powers of the State are now so wide and varied and because certain areas of public provision are not served by formal machinery of appeal, that 'Justice' recommended that a permanent office of Parliamentary Commissioner for Administration should be set up, to receive and investigate complaints of maladministration against government departments, and to draw attention to any deficiencies in the law discovered in his investigations.

A Parliamentary Commissioner for Administration, with broadly the functions proposed by 'Justice', was appointed under the Parliamentary Commissioner Act, 1967, but with important limitations in his powers. Large areas of work in the social services were excluded; the hospitals, the administration of justice, and all local government services, about which 'Justice' made more serious complaints than it did about central government. It should, however, be noted here that the Maud Committee on the

* For a fuller account of the concern of this group see: *Nine Points from the Disabled*, Jane Owtram—Case Conference—Vol. 13, No. 1, May 1966.

Management of Local Government expressed the hope that a Parliamentary Commissioner would *not* be introduced into local government, at least until his working was much better understood. One or two local authorities have taken action themselves, however, by giving to one of their own officials the duty of investigating residents' complaints against the council, for example the London Borough of Haringey. Finally, Ministers have discretion to prohibit the disclosure of information by the Parliamentary Commissioner for Administration if the public interest or safety of the State are held by them to make this necessary. Continued vigilance is necessary, therefore, to ensure that the citizen is assured of his rights and of redress if necessary.

With this warning the present examination of social administration ends. It has been concerned with the meaning of the term, with its relation to the social sciences as a whole, with social policy and the Welfare State, with social research and the social services, and with their administration and staffing. Throughout, whether explicitly or implicitly, the importance of the individual has been emphasised and judgments of value have been accepted as an inevitable and proper part of the whole field of study.

The end in view has been not merely to inform the student but to further his appreciation that the learning of social administration, whether pursued by reading in the library or by practice in the field, is not a dull or mundane affair. It is concerned with the life of all citizens, their hopes and aspirations, their fears and tribulations, their needs and their good. Mastery of social administration, as a subject of study and as a process directed towards human welfare, is essential to the development of health and happiness of individuals, families, and society as a whole. If the student does not grasp this either his teaching or his own understanding is at fault. He should find in the subject an exercise for his intellect, a furthering of his imagination, and a clarification of his ethical or moral values.

There may be no one 'right' answer to many of the questions he will ask or be asked as he proceeds in his study or practice. What is required is that he overcomes ignorance, avoids prejudice, rejects self-interest, and continues to learn with interest and enthusiasm.

REFERENCES

CHAPTER ONE

1. John J. Clarke. *Social Welfare*, p. 4. Pitman and Sons Ltd., 1953.
2. D. V. Donnison. 'The Teaching of Social Administration', *The British Journal of Sociology*, Vol. XIII, No. 3, September 1961.
3. Richard M. Titmuss. 'Social Administration in a Changing Society' in *Essays on the 'Welfare State'*, p. 14. Allen and Unwin Ltd., 1958.
4. T. S. Simey. *Principles of Social Administration*, p. 1. Oxford University Press, 1937.
5. D. V. Donnison, op. cit. (2).
6. Julia M. Parker, 'Pinning down a Subject', Review, *New Society*, May 19, 1966.
7. G. D. H. Cole. *British Social Services*, p. 1. Longmans, Green and Co., Ltd. for the British Council, 1959.
8. Emmeline W. Cohen. *English Social Services*, p. 3. Allen and Unwin Ltd., 1949.
9. The National Council of Social Service. *Voluntary Social Services*, p. 4. Revised Edition, 1966.
10. The National Council of Social Service. *Public Social Services*, p. 7. Twelfth Edition, 1965.
11. Walter Hagenbuch. *Social Economics*, p. 179. James Nisbet and Co. Ltd. and Cambridge University Press, 1958.
12. David C. Marsh. *The Future of the Welfare State*, p. 15. Penguin Books Ltd., 1964.
13. R. M. Titmuss. 'The Social Division of Welfare' in op. cit. (3) p. 40.
14. Political and Economic Planning. *Report on the British Social Services*, p. 10, 1937.
15. M. Penelope Hall. *The Social Services of Modern England*, p. 3. Routledge and Kegan Paul Ltd., Sixth Edition, 1963.
16. R. M. Titmuss op. cit. (13), p. 40.
17. Iain Macleod and J. Enoch Powell. *The Social Services—Needs and Means*, p. 1. Conservative Political Centre, 1952.
18. R. M. Titmuss, op. cit (13).
19. A. F. Young. *Social Services in British Industry*, p. xiii. Routledge and Kegan Paul, 1968
20. Desmond G. Neill. *The Unfinished Business of the Welfare State*, p. 12. The Queen's University of Belfast, 1958.
21. D. V. Donnison. 'Can Administration Be Taught?' Review Article, *Case Conference*, Vol. 7, No. 7, January 1961.

CHAPTER TWO

1. J. R. Hicks. 'Economic Theory and the Social Sciences' in *The Social Sciences—Their Relations in Theory and in Teaching*, pp. 129–130. Le Play House, 1936.
2. George Simpson. *Man in Society*, p. 11. Random House, New York, 1962.
3. A. L. Rowse. *The Use of History*, p. 16. English Universities Press, 1946.
4. G. M. Trevelyan. *English Social History*, pp. vii–viii and ix–x. Longmans, Green and Co. Second Edition, 1946.
5. D. V. Donnison. *The Development of Social Administration*. An Inaugural Lecture, The London School of Economics and Political Science, 1962.
6. A. L. Rowse, op. cit. (3), p. 16.
7. Lionel Robbins. *An Essay on the Nature and Significance of Economic Science*, p. 16. Macmillan and Co. Ltd., Second Edition, 1935.
8. George Schwartz. 'Wealth and Welfare' in *The Future of the Welfare State*, p. 23. Conservative Political Centre No. 178, 1958.
9. J. Enoch Powell, 'A Policy of Sewage' in op. cit. (8), p. 47.
10. Report of the Committee on Higher Education, 1961–1963, 'Higher Education', p. 201, para. 612. Cmnd. 2154. H.M.S.O., 1963.
11. *Ibid.*, p. 199, para. 601.
12. Arthur Seldon. *Pensions in a Free Society*, p. 36. Institute of Economic Affairs, 1957.
13. Margaret Cole. *Servant of the County*, p. 164. Dennis Dobson, 1956.
14. Morris Ginsberg. *On the Diversity of Morals*, pp. xiii, 163/164. Heinemann Educational Books Ltd., 1956.
15. Morris Ginsberg. 'The Problems and Methods of Sociology' in *Reason and Unreason in Society*. Heinemann Educational Books Ltd., 1960.
16. T. H. Marshall. 'Introduction' in *The Teaching of Sociology to Students of Education and Social Work*. The Sociological Review Monograph No. 4, p. 7. The University College of North Staffordshire, 1961.
17. The National Institute for Social Work Training, Series 2. *Introduction to a Social Worker*, p. 102. Allen and Unwin, Ltd., 1964.
18. The Ministry of Health. 'Report of the Sub-Committee of the Standing Medical Advisory Committee of the Central Health Services Council', *The Field of Work of the Family Doctor*, p. 48, para. 178. H.M.S.O., 1963.
19. Gunnar Myrdal. 'The Relation Between Social Theory and Social

Policy', *The British Journal of Sociology*, Vol. IV, No. 3, September 1953.

20. Desmond G. Neill, op. cit. (20 Chap. 1), p. 18.
21. Richard M. Titmuss. *The Irresponsible Society*, p. 19. Fabian Tract 323. The Fabian Society, 1960.
22. G. D. H. Cole. 'Sociology and Social Policy', *The British Journal o, Sociology*, Vol. VIII, No. 2, June 1956.
23. William A. Robson. *The Welfare State*, p. 18. L. T. Hobhouse Memorial Trust Lecture No. 26. Oxford University Press, 1957.
24. F. Lafitte. 'Sociology and Welfare' in op. cit. (16), p. 54.
25. D. V. Donnison, op. cit. (2 Chap. 1).

CHAPTER THREE

1. Arthur Seldon, op. cit. (12 Chap. 2), pp. 14 and 37.
2. H. L. Beales. *The Making of Social Policy*. L. T. Hobhouse Memorial Trust Lecture No. 15. Oxford University Press, 1945.
3. R. M. Titmuss. 'War and Social Policy' in op. cit. (3 Chap. 1), p. 77.
4. R. M. Titmuss. *Problems of Social Policy*, p. 506. H.M.S.O. and Longmans, Green and Co., 1950.
5. A. MacBeath, *Can Social Policies be Rationally Tested?* L. T. Hobhouse Memorial Trust Lecture No. 27. Oxford University Press, 1957.
6. Maurice Milhaud. *The Historical Development of Social Policy*, Institute of Social Studies Publications on Social Change, No. 7, 1958.
7. Walter Hagenbuch, op. cit. (11 Chap. 1), p. 205.
8. F. Lafitte. *Social Policy in a Free Society*. An Inaugural Lecture. University of Birmingham, 1962.
9. T. H. Marshall. *Social Policy*, p. 7. Hutchinson University Library, 1965.
10. Geoffrey Howe. 'Reform of the Social Services' in *Principles in Practice*, p. 61. The Conservative Political Centre on behalf of the Bow Group. C.P.C. No. 223, 1961.
11. Maurice Milhaud, op. cit. (6).
12. R. M. Titmuss, op. cit. (21 Chap. 2).
13. R. M. Titmuss, op. cit. (13 Chap. 1).
14. F. Lafitte, op. cit. (24 Chap. 2), p. 54.
15. F. Lafitte, op. cit. (8).
16. D. V. Donnison, op. cit. (5 Chap. 2).
17. Barbara N. Rodgers *et al. Comparative Social Administration*, p. 12. George Allen and Unwin Ltd., 1968.
18. D. V. Donnison, op. cit. (21 Chap. 1).

19. Kathleen Jones. 'Introduction'; Nesta Roberts, *Mental Health and Mental Illness*, p. 2. Routledge and Kegan Paul, 1967.
20. R. M. Titmuss, op. cit. (4), p. ix.
21. Invalid Children's Aid Society, *Today's Invalid Child*, 1966.
22. Geoffrey Howe, op. cit. (10) p. 63.
23. Report of the Inter-departmental Committee on Social Insurance and Allied Services, p. 6, para. 8. Cmd. 6404. H.M.S.O., 1942.
24. T. H. Marshall. *Sociology at the Crossroads*, pp. 320 and 322. Heinemann Educational Books Ltd., 1963.
25. R. M. Titmuss, op. cit. (21 Chap. 2), p. 17.
26. F. Lafitte, op. cit. (24 Chap. 2), p. 53.

CHAPTER FOUR

1. T. H. Marshall, op. cit. (24 Chap. 3), p. 245.
2. David C. Marsh, 'Preface' in op. cit. (12 Chap. 1).
3. T. H. Marshall, op. cit. (24 Chap. 3), p. 289. See also op. cit. (9 Chap. 3). Chapters 6 and 7.
4. Alan Peacock. *The Welfare Society*, p. 11. Unservile State Papers No. 2, The Liberal Publication Department on behalf of the Unservile State Group, 1960.
5. Peter Goldman, 'Preface' in op. cit. (8 Chap. 2), p. 7.
6. Mark Abrams. *Social Surveys and Social Action*, p. 126. William Heinemann Ltd., 1951.
7. Maurice Bruce. *The Coming of the Welfare State*, pp. 17 and 293. B. T. Batsford Ltd., 1961.
8. Labour Party Publication. *The Welfare State*, Discussion Pamphlet No. 4, 1952.
9. Kingsley Martin. *Socialism and the Welfare State*, Fabian Tract No. 291, Fabian Publications Ltd., 1952.
10. T. H. Marshall, op. cit. (24 Chap. 3), Chapter XII.
11. *Ibid.*, Chapter XIII.
12. Una Cormack. *The Welfare State*, Loch Memorial Lecture, 1953, Family Welfare Association.
13. D. L. Hobman. *The Welfare State*, John Murray, 1953.
14. William A. Robson, op. cit. (23 Chap. 2).
15. Arthur Seldon, op. cit. (12 Chap. 2).
16. Desmond G. Neill, op. cit. (20 Chap. 1).
17. Alan Peacock, op. cit. (4), p. 11.
18. Timothy Raison. 'Principles in Practice' in op. cit. (10 Chap. 3).
19. Richard M. Titmuss. 'The Welfare State—Images and Realities', *The Social Service Review*, Vol. XXXVII, No. 1, March 1963. University of Chicago.

20. George Schwartz. 'Wealth and Welfare' in op. cit. (8 Chap. 2), p. 20.
21. S. E. Finer. 'Voluntary Social Service in the Changing Welfare State' in *Social Service*, Vol. XXIX, No. 1, Summer 1955.
22. The Editor. 'Towards a Welfare Society' in *Social Service*, Vol. XXVII, No. 4, March/May 1955.
23. 'Editorial.' *Social Service*, Vol. XXVI, No. 1, June/August 1952.
24. David Howell. 'Expanding Prosperity' in op. cit. (10 Chap. 3).
25. T. H. Marshall, op. cit. (24 Chap. 3), p. 287.
26. M. Penelope Hall, op. cit. (15 Chap. 1).
27. Audrey Harvey. *Casualties of the Welfare State*. Fabian Tract 321. The Fabian Society, 1960.
28. *Responsibility in the Welfare State;* Report of the Birmingham Social Responsibility Project. The Birmingham Council of Christian Churches, 1961.
29. Political and Economic Planning. *Family Needs and the Social Services*, pp. 33–34. Allen and Unwin Ltd., 1961.
30. Brian Abel-Smith. *Freedom in the Welfare State*. Fabian Tract 353. The Fabian Society, 1964.
31. Pauline Gregg. *The Welfare State*. George G. Harrap & Co., Ltd., 1967.
32. Arthur Seldon, op. cit. (12 Chap. 2), p. 14.
33. William A. Robson, op. cit. (23 Chap. 2), p. 18.
34. Godfrey Hodgson. 'Education on Demand' in op. cit. (10 Chap. 3), p. 39.

CHAPTER FIVE

1. G. D. H. Cole, op. cit. (22 Chap. 2).
2. C. A. Moser. *Survey Methods in Social Investigation*, p. 6. Heinemann Educational Books Ltd., 1958.
3. Julian Huxley. 'Science, Natural and Social' in *Science and Man*, Ed. Ruth Nanda Anshen. Harcourt, New York, 1942.
4. Mark Abrams, op. cit. (6 Chap. 4), p. 127.
5. D. T. Wilkins. *Survey of the Prevalence of Deafness in the Population of England, Scotland and Wales, 1948*. The Social Survey, Report (New Series), No. 92.
6. Parliamentary Debate (Hansard). House of Lords Official Report, Vol. 257, No. 65. Wednesday, April 22, 1964.
7. D. V. Glass. 'The Application of Social Research', *The British Journal of Sociology*, Vol. 1, No. 1, March 1950.
8. Pendleton Herring. 'Research on Government, Politics and Administration' in *Research for Public Policy*. Brookings Dedication Lecture. The Brookings Institution, Washington, 1961.

9. G. D. H. Cole, op. cit. (22 Chap. 2).
10. D. V. Glass, op. cit. (7).
11. Letter to the Editor. *Case Conference*, Vol. 10, No. 4, September 1963.
12. Barbara Wootton. *Social Science and Social Pathology*, p. 317. Allen and Unwin Ltd., 1959.
13. O. R. McGregor. 'Social Research and Social Policy in the Nineteenth Century', *The British Journal of Sociology*, Vol. VIII, No. 2, June 1957.
14. Board of Education. *The Education of the Adolescent*. Report of the Consultative Committee, H.M.S.O., 1927.
15. Board of Education. *Curriculum and Examinations in Secondary Schools*. Report of the Committee of the Secondary School Examinations Council. H.M.S.O., 1943.
16. Royal Commission on Marriage and Divorce Report 1951–55. Cmd. 9678. H.M.S.O., 1956.
17. O. R. McGregor. *Divorce in England*, pp. 176 and 181. William Heinemann Ltd., 1957.
18. Royal Commission on Population Report. Cmd. 7695. H.M.S.O., 1949.
19. Ministry of Education. '*15 to 18*'. A Report of the Central Advisory Council for Education (England). H.M.S.O., 1959.
20. John Greve. *The Housing Problem*. Fabian Research Series 224. The Fabian Society, 1961.
21. David Donnison, *et al. The Ingleby Report*. Fabian Research Series 231. The Fabian Society, 1962.
22. The Care of Children Committee Report. Cmd. 6922. H.M.S.O., 1946.
23. Ministry of Education. Report of the Committee on Maladjusted Children. H.M.S.O., 1955.
24. Pauline V. Young and Calvin F. Schmid. *Scientific Social Surveys and Research*, pp. 47 and 53. Prentice-Hall, Inc., New York, 1939.
25. Ministry of Education. *Half our Future*. A Report of the Central Advisory Council for Education (England). H.M.S.O., 1963.
26. Report of the Committee on Higher Education, op. cit. (10 Chap. 2).
27. Department of Education and Science, *Children and their Primary Schools*. A Report of the Central Advisory Council for Education (England). H.M.S.O., 1966.
28. Ministry of Pensions and National Insurance. *Financial and other Circumstances of Retirement Pensioners*. H.M.S.O., 1966.
29. Ministry of Social Security. *Circumstances of Families*. H.M.S.O., 1967.

30. D. V. Donnison. *The Government of Housing*, page 351. Penguin Books, 1967.
31. D. V. Glass. op. cit. (7).
32. Report of the Committee on Local Authority and Allied Personal Social Services, p. 146, para. 473. Cmnd. 3703. H.M.S.O., 1968.

CHAPTER SIX

1. Barbara N. Rodgers *et al.*, op. cit. (17 Chap. 3), p. 85.
2. Peter Townsend. 'Poverty, Socialism and Labour in Power' in *Socialism and Affluence*, p. 40. Four Fabian Essays. Fabian Society, May, 1967.
3. The Committee on Local Authority and Allied Personal Social Services, op. cit. (32 Chap. 5), pp. 20 and 152, paras. 39 and 495.
4. Joan F. S. King (Ed.). *New Thinking for Changing Needs*. Association of Social Workers, 1963.
5. Bleddyn Davies. *Social Needs and Resources in Local Services*, p. 34. Michael Joseph, 1968.
6. Arthur Seldon, op. cit. (12 Chap. 2), pp. 36–37.
7. Parliamentary Debate (Hansard). House of Lords Official Reports, Vol. 257, No. 65. Wednesday, April 22, 1964.
8. Ministry of Health. Final Report of the Departmental Committee on Maternal Mortality and Morbidity. H.M.S.O., 1932.
9. Ministry of Health. Report on an Investigation into Maternal Mortality. H.M.S.O., 1937.
10. Royal College of Obstetricians and Gynaecologists. Report on a National Maternity Service, 1944.
11. Joint Committee of the Royal College of Obstetricians and Gynaecologists and the Population Investigation Committee. *Maternity in Great Britain*. Oxford University Press, 1948.
12. Ministry of Health. Report of the Maternity Services Committee. H.M.S.O., 1959.
13. Neville R. Butler and Dennis G. Bonham. *Perinatal Mortality*. The First Report of the 1958 British Perinatal Mortality Survey under the auspices of the National Birthday Trust Fund.
14. Lena M. Jeger, Ed. *Illegitimate Children and their Parents*, pp. x–xi. National Council for the Unmarried Mother and her Child, 1951.
15. J. E. Spence. 'Early Days in School Health Work', *Public Health*, May 1950.
16. Report of the Chief Medical Officer of the Department of Education and Science. *The Health of the School Child 1964 and 1965*. H.M.S.O., 1966.

17. The Medical Services Review Committee. *A Review of the Medical Services in Great Britain*, p. 93, para. 344. Social Assay, 1962.
18. G. A. N. Lowndes. *The Silent Social Revolution*, p. 3. The Clarendon Press, Oxford, Third Edition, 1947.
19. Board of Education, op. cit. (14 Chap. 5).
20. Board of Education. Report of the Consultative Committee on Secondary Education. H.M.S.O., 1938.
21. Board of Education, op. cit. (15 Chap. 5).
22. Ministry of Education. *Early Leaving*. A Report of the Central Advisory Council for Education (England). H.M.S.O., 1954.
23. Ministry of Education, op. cit. (19 Chap. 5).
24. Ministry of Education. op. cit. (25 Chap. 5).
25. Department of Education and Science, op. cit. (27 Chap. 5).
26. The Committee on Higher Education, op. cit. (10 Chap. 2).
27. G. A. N. Lowndes, op. cit. (18), p. 248.
28. Ministry of Labour and National Service. Report of the Committee on the Juvenile Employment Service. H.M.S.O., 1945.
29. National Youth Employment Council. A Report on the Work of the Youth Employment Service, 1962–65, paras. 47 and 57. H.M.S.O., 1965.
30. Ministry of Education, op. cit. (25 Chap. 5).
31. Ministry of Labour Central Youth Employment Executive. *The Future Development of the Youth Employment Service*. Report of a Working Party of the National Youth Employment Council. H.M.S.O., 1965.
32. A. E. Morgan. *Young Citizen*, p. 12. Penguin Books, 1943.
33. L. J. Barnes. *Youth Services in an English County*. Report prepared for King George's Jubilee Trust, 1945.
34. L. J. Barnes. *The Outlook for Youth Work*, p. 125. Report prepared for King George's Jubilee Trust, 1948.
35. King George's Jubilee Trust. *Citizens of Tomorrow*. Odhams Press Ltd., 1955.
36. Ministry of Labour and National Service. Seventh Report of the Select Committee on Estimates—Session 1956–57. 'The Youth Employment and Youth Services Grants'. H.M.S.O., 1957.
37. Ministry of Education. Report of the Committee on the Youth Service in England and Wales. Cmnd. 929. H.M.S.O., 1960.
38. Home Office. Report of the Committee on Children and Young Persons. Cmnd. 1191. H.M.S.O., 1960.
39. Scottish Home and Health Department and Scottish Education Department. *Children and Young Persons in Scotland*. Cmnd. 2306. H.M.S.O. 1964.

40. The Care of Children Committee, op. cit. (22 Chap. 5).
41. Scottish Home Department. Report of the Committee on Homeless Children. Cmd. 69. H.M.S.O., 1946.
42. Leo Silberman. *Analysis of Society*, p. 120. William Hodge and Co. Ltd., 1951.
43. Home Office. *The Child, the Family and the Young Offender*. Cmnd. 2742. H.M.S.O., 1965.
44. Labour Party. *Crime, a Challenge to us all*. Report of the Longford Committee, 1964.
45. Scottish Education Department and Scottish Home and Health Department. *Social Work and the Community*. Cmnd. 3065. H.M.S.O., 1966.
46. Home Office. *Children in Trouble*. Cmnd. 3601. H.M.S.O., 1968.
47. Home Office. *Children in Care in England and Wales*. March 1967. Cmnd. 3514. H.M.S.O., 1968, and March 1968. Cmnd. 3893. H.M.S.O., 1969.

CHAPTER SEVEN

1. Arthur Seldon, op. cit. (12 Chap. 2), p. 11.
2. B. Seebohm Rowntree. *Poverty: a study of town life*. Macmillan and Co. Ltd., Second Edition, 1902.
3. A. L. Bowley and A. R. Burnett-Hurst. *Livelihood and Poverty*. G. Bell and Sons Ltd., 1915.
4. G. Seebohm Rowntree. *Poverty and Progress*. Green and Co. Ltd., 1941.
5. Royal Commission on Population, op. cit. (18 Chap. 5), p. 206.
6. The Inter-departmental Committee on Social Insurance and Allied Services, op. cit. (23 Chap. 3), p. 7, para. 11.
7. The Royal College of Obstetricians and Gynaecologists and the Population Investigation Committee, op. cit. (11 Chap. 6), p. 206.
8. B. Seebohm Rowntree and G. R. Lavers. *Poverty and the Welfare State*, p. 42. Longmans, Green and Co. Ltd., 1951.
9. Peter Townsend. 'The Meaning of Poverty', *The British Journal of Sociology*, Vol. XIII, No. 3, September 1962.
10. Brian Abel-Smith and Peter Townsend. *The Poor and the Poorest*. Occasional Papers on Social Administration. Number 17, 1965.
11. Ministry of Social Security. *Circumstances of Families*. H.M.S.O., 1967.
12. R. M. Titmuss, op. cit. (13 Chap. 1), pp. 44–50.
13. Walter Hagenbuch, op. cit. (11 Chap. 1), pp. 121–122.
14. A. L. Bowley and Margaret H. Hogg. *Has Poverty Diminished?* P. S. King and Son Ltd., 1925.

15. D. C. Jones *et al*. *The Social Survey of Merseyside*. Hodder and Stoughton Ltd., 1934.
16. Clara D. Rackham. 'Unemployment Insurance' in *Social Security*. Editor, William A. Robson, p. 133. Allen and Unwin Ltd., Second Edition, 1945.
17. B. Seebohm Rowntree and G. R. Lavers, op. cit. (8), p. 45.
18. Ministry of Social Security. Annual Report 1966. Cmnd. 3338. H.M.S.O., 1967.
19. The National Assistance Board. *Reception Centres for persons without a settled way of living*. Report to the Minister of National Insurance, p. 8, para. 13. H.M.S.O., 1952.
20. Philip O'Connor. *Britain in the Sixties—Vagrancy*, p. 185. Penguin Books, 1963.
21. The Medical Services Review Committee, op. cit. (17 Chap. 6), p. 158, para. 607.
22. The Inter-departmental Committee on Social Insurance and Allied Services, op. cit. (23 Chap. 3), p. 39, para. 81.
23. Report of the Inter-departmental Committee on the Rehabilitation and Resettlement of Disabled Persons, p. 7, para. 12. Cmd. 6415. H.M.S.O., 1943.
24. Report of the Committee of Inquiry on the Rehabilitation Training and Resettlement of Disabled Persons. Cmd. 9883. H.M.S.O., 1956.
25. *Health and Welfare—The Development of Community Care*. Plans for the Health and Welfare Services of the Local Authorities in England and Wales. Cmnd. 1973. H.M.S.O., 1963.
26. Peter Marris. *Widows and their Families*, p. 129. Routledge and Kegan Paul, 1958.
27. The National Assistance Board. Report for the year ended December 31, 1965. Cmnd. 3042. H.M.S.O., 1966.
28. The National Assistance Board. Report for the year ended December 31, 1955, p. 5. Cmd. 9781. H.M.S.O., 1956.
29. The Inter-departmental Committee on Social Insurance and Allied Services, op. cit. (23 Chap. 3), p. 134. para, 347.
30. Margaret Wynn. *Fatherless Families*, p. 24. Michael Joseph Ltd., 1964.
31. Ministry of Health. *Housing Act, 1935*. Report on the Overcrowding Survey in England and Wales 1936, p. xiii. H.M.S.O., 1936.
32. The Royal College of Obstetricians and Gynaecologists and the Population Investigation Committee, op. cit. (11 Chap. 6), p. 58.
33. J. W. B. Douglas and J. M. Blomfield. *Children under Five*, Chap. VI. Allen and Unwin Ltd., 1958.

34. National Assistance Board. *Homeless Single Persons*. H.M.S.O., 1966.
35. John Greve, op. cit. (20 Chap. 5).
36. D. V. Donnison, op. cit. (30 Chap. 5), pp. 78 and 372.
37. Political and Economic Planning, op. cit. (29 Chap. 4), p. 204.
38. John Greve, op. cit. (20 Chap. 5), pp. 16 and 20.
39. Peter Townsend. *The Last Refuge*, p. 430. Routledge and Kegan Paul, 1962.
40. Peter Townsend and Dorothy Wedderburn. *The Aged in the Welfare State*. Occasional Papers on Social Administration. Number 14. G. Bell and Sons Ltd., 1965.
41. Jeremy Tunstall. *Old and Alone*. Routledge and Kegan Paul, 1966.
42. F. Lafitte, op. cit. (24 Chap. 2), p. 11.

CHAPTER EIGHT

1. W. J. M. Mackenzie. 'Local Administration of the Social Services' in *The Future of the Welfare State*, p. 48, op. cit. (8 Chap. 2).
2. Ministry of Health, Department of Health for Scotland. Report of the Working Party on Social Workers in the Local Authority Health and Welfare Services, p. 36, para. 173. H.M.S.O., 1959.
3. W. J. M. Mackenzie, op. cit. (1), p. 48.
4. The Working Party on Social Workers in the Local Authority Health and Welfare Services, op. cit. (2), p. 298, para. 1035.
5. Political and Economic Planning. *Mental Subnormality in London*, p. 78. PEP, 1966.
6. Barbara N. Rodgers and Julia Dixon. *Portrait of Social Work*, p. 94. The Oxford University Press, 1966.
7. Ministry of Housing and Local Government. *Management of Local Government*. Report of the Committee, Vol. 1, pp. 121–122, paras. 433–435.
8. T. H. Marshall. 'Voluntary Action', in *Sociology at the Crossroads*, op cit. (24 Chap. 3), p. 331.
9. *Ibid.*, p. 233.
10. The Care of Children Committee, op. cit. (22 Chap. 5), p. 71, para. 229.
11. Local Government Commission for England. Report No. 1. *Report and Proposals for the West Midlands Special Review Area*, p. 16, para. 34. H.M.S.O., 1961.
12. Deborah Paige and Kit Jones. *Health and Welfare Services in Britain in 1975*, p. 14. National Institute for Economic and Social Research. Cambridge University Press, 1966.

13. D. V. Donnison. 'Health, Welfare and Democracy in Greater London', p. 6. *Greater London Papers No. 5*, London School of Economics and Political Science, 1962.
14. Royal Commission on Local Government in Greater London, 1957–60 Report. Cmnd. 1164. H.M.S.O., 1960.
15. *Ibid.*, p. 59, para. 221.
16. D. V. Donnison, op. cit. (13), pp. 18–20.
17. F. M. G. Willson. *The Organisation of British Central Government 1914–1964*, p. 15. Allen and Unwin Ltd., Second Edition, 1968.
18. Ministry of Health. *National Health Service*. The Administrative Structure of the Medical and Related Services in England and Wales. H.M.S.O., 1968.
19. F. M. G. Willson, op. cit. (17) p. 178.
20. Committee on Higher Education, op. cit. (10 Chap. 2), p. 250, para. 784.
21. The Inter-departmental Committee on Social Insurance and Allied Services, op. cit. (23 Chap. 3), p. 145, para. 385.
22. Report of the Committee on the Law and Practice relating to Charitable Trusts, p. 178, para. 723. Cmd. 8710. H.M.S.O., 1952.

CHAPTER NINE

1. Royal Commission on Population, op. cit. (18 Chap. 5).
2. Report of the Royal Commission on Capital Punishment 1949–53. Cmd. 8932. H.M.S.O., 1953.
3. Royal Commission on Marriage and Divorce, op. cit. (16 Chap. 5).
4. Report of the Royal Commission relating to the Law on Mental Illness and Mental Deficiency, 1954–57. Cmnd. 169. H.M.S.O., 1957.
5. Royal Commission on Local Government in Greater London, op. cit. (14 Chap. 8).
6. First Report of the Public Schools Commission. H.M.S.O., 1968. Report of the Royal Commission on Medical Education, 1965–1968. Cmnd. 3569. H.M.S.O., 1968.
7. Report of the Royal Commission on Medical Education 1965–1968. Cmnd. 3569. H.M.S.O., 1968.
8. Report of the Royal Commission on Local Government in England. Cmnd. 0000. H.M.S.O., 1969.
9. Hugh McD. Clokie and J. William Robinson. *Royal Commissions of Inquiry*, p. 123. Stanford University Press, 1937.
10. Report of the Committee on Administrative Tribunals and Enquiries. Cmnd. 218. H.M.S.O., 1957.

11. The Inter-departmental Committee on Social Insurance and Allied Services, op. cit. (23 Chap. 3).
12. The Inter-departmental Committee on the Rehabilitation and Resettlement of Disabled Persons, op. cit. (23 Chap. 7).
13. Board of Education. Report on the Public Schools and the General Educational System. H.M.S.O., 1944.
14. Board of Education. Report of the Committee on Teachers and Youth Leaders. H.M.S.O., 1945.
15. Ministry of Labour and National Service. Report of the Committee on the Juvenile Employment Service. H.M.S.O., 1945.
16. The Care of Children Committee, op. cit. (22 Chap. 5).
17. Reports of the Committees on Medical Auxiliaries. Cmd. 8188. H.M.S.O., 1951.
18. Report of the Committee on Social Workers in the Mental Health Services. Cmd. 8260. H.M.S.O., 1951.
19. Report of the Departmental Committee on the Adoption of Children. Cmd. 9248. H.M.S.O., 1954.
20. Report of the Committee on the Economic and Financial Problems of the Provision for Old Age. Cmd. 9333. H.M.S.O., 1954.
21. Ministry of Education, op. cit. (23 Chap. 5).
22. Report of the Committee of Enquiry into the Cost of the National Health Service. Cmd. 9663. H.M.S.O., 1956.
23. The Committee of Inquiry on the Rehabilitation Training and Resettlement of Disabled Persons, op. cit. (24 Chap. 7).
24. The Committee on Administrative Tribunals and Enquiries, op. cit. (10).
25. Report of the Committee on Homosexual Offences and Prostitution. Cmnd. 247. H.M.S.O., 1957.
26. The Committee on the Youth Service in England and Wales, op. cit. (37 Chap. 6).
27. The Committee on Children and Young Person, op. cit. (38 Chap. 6).
28. Report of the Departmental Committee on the Probation Service. Cmnd. 1650. H.M.S.O., 1962.
29. Report of the Committee on Housing in Greater London. Cmnd. 2605. H.M.S.O., 1965.
30. Department of Education and Science. *Service by Youth*. Report of a committee of the Youth Service Development Council. December 1965. H.M.S.O., 1966.
31. Ministry of Housing and Local Government. *Staffing of Local Government*. Report of the Committee. H.M.S.O., 1966.
32. Ministry of Housing and Local Government, op. cit. (7 Chap. 8).

33. The Committee on Local Authority and Allied Personal Social Services, op. cit. (32 Chap. 5).
34. Ministry of Labour and National Service. Report of the Working Party on the Employment of Blind Persons. H.M.S.O., 1951.
35. Ministry of Health, Department of Health for Scotland, Ministry of Education. *An Inquiry into Health Visiting*, Report of a working party on the field of work, training, and recruitment of health visitors. H.M.S.O., 1956.
36. The Working Party on Social Workers in the Local Authority Health and Welfare Services, op. cit. (2 Chap. 8).
37. Ministry of Labour and National Service. Report of the Working Party on Workshops for the Blind. H.M.S.O., 1962.
38. Ministry of Labour Central Youth Employment Executive, op. cit. (31 Chap. 6).
39. K. C. Wheare. *Government by Committee*, p. 253. The Clarendon Press, Oxford, 1955.
40. Ministry of Health, op. cit. (18 Chap. 8).
41. Ministry of Education. *School and Life*. A First Enquiry into the Transition from School to Independent Life. A Report of the Central Advisory Council for Education (England). H.M.S.O., 1947
42. Ministry of Education. *Out of School*. The Second Report of the Central Advisory Council for Education (England), H.M.S.O., 1948.
43. Ministry of Education, op. cit. (22 Chap. 6).
44. Department of Education and Science, op. cit. (27 Chap. 5).
45. Political and Economic Planning. *Advisory Committees in British Government*, p. 22, PEP, 1960.
46. Ministry of Housing and Local Government. *Living in Flats*. Report of the Flats Sub-Committee of the Central Housing Advisory Committee. H.M.S.O., 1952.
47. Ministry of Housing and Local Government. *Unsatisfactory Tenants*. Sixth Report of the Housing Management Sub-Committee of the Central Housing Advisory Committee. H.M.S.O. 1955.
48. Ministry of Housing and Local Government. *Moving from the Slums*. Seventh Report of the Housing Management Sub-Committee of the Central Housing Advisory Committee. H.M.S.O., 1956.
49. Ministry of Housing and Local Government. *Homes for today and tomorrow*. H.M.S.O., 1961.
50. Home Office. *The After-Care and Supervision of Discharged Prisoners*. Report of the Advisory Council on the Treatment of Offenders. H.M.S.O., 1958.

51. Home Office. *The Treatment of the Young Offender*. Report of the Advisory Council on the Treatment of Offenders. H.M.S.O. 1959.

52. First and Second Reports of the National Advisory Committee on the Employment of Older Men and Women. Cmd. 8963 and Cmd. 9628. H.M.S.O., 1953 and 1955.

53. Ministry of Health, Department of Health for Scotland, Central Health Services Council. *The Welfare of Children in Hospital*. H.M.S.O., 1958.

54. Ministry of Health, Department of Health for Scotland. *The Pattern of the In Patients Day*. Report of the Standing Nursing Advisory Committee of the Central Health Services Council. H.M.S.O., 1961.

55. K. C. Wheare, op. cit. (39), p. 167.

56. Political and Economic Planning, op. cit. (45), pp. 1–2.

57. The Care of Children Committee, op. cit. (22 Chap. 5), p. 6, para. 7.

58. The Working Party on Social Workers in the Local Authority Health and Welfare Services, op. cit. (2 Chap. 8), p. 2, para. 11.

59. The Committee on Local Authority and Allied Personal Social Services, op. cit. (32 Chap. 5), p. 194, para. 637.

60. Political and Economic Planning, op. cit. (45), p. 63.

61. David Donnison *et al.*, op. cit. (21 Chap. 5), p. 6.

62. K. C. Wheare, op. cit. (39), p. 253.

63. National Institute for Social Work Training, *Caring for People*, George Allen and Unwin, 1967.

64. The Medical Services Review Committee, op. cit. (17 Chap. 6), paras. 76–80; 88–89; 105; 276; 350; 353; 440; 447; 469.

65. Harold J. Laski. 'The Committee System in Local Government' in *A Century of Municipal Progress 1835–1935*. Edited by H. J. Laski *et al.*, p. 97. Allen and Unwin Ltd., 1935.

66. Margaret Cole, op. cit. (13 Chap. 2), p. 54.

67. Ministry of Housing and Local Government, op. cit., (7 Chap. 8), p. 53, paras. 203–204.

68. Sir John Maud, K.C.B., and S. E. Finer. *Local Government in England and Wales*, p. 125. The Oxford University Press, 1953.

69. David Hobman. *A Guide to Voluntary Service*, p. 6. H.M.S.O., 1964.

70. Rosalind G. Chambers. 'A Study of Three Voluntary Organisations' in *Social Mobility in Britain*, p. 404. Edited by D. V. Glass. Routledge and Kegan Paul, 1954.

71. S. and B. Webb. *Methods of Social Study*, p. 45. Longman's, Green and Co., Ltd., 1932.

72. C. Northcote Parkinson. *Parkinson's Law*. p. 1. John Murray (Publishers) Ltd., 1958.

73. Hugh McC. Clokie and J. William Robinson, op. cit. (9), p. 156.
74. Lord Beveridge. *Power and Influence*, Chapters XIV and XV. Hodder and Stoughton, 1953.
75. Beatrice Webb, *Our Partnership*. Edited by Barbara Drake and Margaret I. Cole, Chapters VII and VIII. Longmans, Green and Co. Ltd., 1948.

CHAPTER TEN

1. Richard M. Titmuss. 'The Administrative Setting of Social Service: Some Historical Reflections', *Case Conference*, Vol. 1, No. 1, May 1954.
2. David Donnison *et al.*, op. cit. (21 Chap. 5), p. 9.
3. Local Government Commission for England, op. cit. (11 Chap. 8), p. 18, para. 43.
4. Local Government Commission for England. Report No. 2, May 1961, p. 11, para. 45. H.M.S.O.
5. A Fabian Group. *The Administrators—The Reform of the Civil Service*. Fabian Tract 355. The Fabian Society, 1964.
6. Ministry of Social Security. Annual Report 1966. Cmnd. 3338. H.M.S.O., 1967.
7. Sir Geoffrey S. King, K.C.B. *The Ministry of Pensions and National Insurance*, pp. 11 and 98. Allen and Unwin Ltd., 1958.
8. Ministry of Housing and Local Government, op. cit. (31 Chap. 9), p. 84, para. 251(e).
9. The Committee on Local Authority and Allied Personal Services, op. cit. (32 Chap. 5), pp. 189 and 194, paras. 618 and 636.
10. The Care of Children Committee, op. cit. (22 Chap. 5), pp. 145–146, paras, 441–446.
11. Richard M. Titmuss, op. cit. (1).
12. Ministry of Housing and Local Government, op. cit. (7 Chap. 8), p. 62, para. 245.
13. Sir John Maud, K.C.B., and S. E. Finer, op. cit. (68 Chap. 9), Chapter 7.
14. C. Northcote Parkinson, op. cit. (72 Chap. 9), p. 14.
15. Department of Education and Science. *The Demand for and Supply of Teachers 1965–68*. Ninth Report of the National Advisory Council on the Training and Supply of Teachers. H.M.S.O., 1965.
16. National Council of Social Service. *A Survey of Manpower demand forecasts for the Social Services*. N.C.S.S., 1966.
17. The Committees on Medical Auxiliaries, op. cit. (17 Chap. 9).
18. The Committee on Social Workers in the Mental Health Services, op. cit. (18 Chap. 9).

19. Ministry of Health. *On the State of the Public Health*. The Annual Report of the Chief Medical Officer of the Ministry of Health for the Year 1962. H.M.S.O., 1963.
20. The Committee on Maladjusted Children, op. cit. (23 Chap. 5).
21. Ministry of Health, op. cit. (19).
22. Ministry of Health, Department of Health for Scotland, Ministry of Education, op. cit. (35 Chap. 9).
23. Ministry of Health, op. cit. (25 Chap. 7).
24. The Working Party of Social Workers in Local Authority Health and Welfare Services, op. cit. (2 Chap. 8), Table 28.
25. Ministry of Education, op. cit. (37 Chap. 6).
26. The Departmental Committee on the Probation Service, op. cit. (28 Chap. 9).
27. Home Office. Report on the Work of the Probation and After-Care Department 1962 to 1965. Cmnd. 3107. H.M.S.O., 1966.
28. Ministry of Labour, op. cit. (34 Chap. 9).
29. Eileen L. Younghusband. *Social Work in Britain*, pp. 2–3. Carnegie United Kingdom Trust, 1951.
30. Barbara N. Rodgers and Julia Dixon, op. cit. (6 Chap. 8).
31. D. V. Donnison, op. cit. (13 Chap. 8), pp. 11–14.
32. Parliamentary Debates (Hansard) House of Lords Official Report, Vol. 257, No. 65, Wednesday, April 22, 1964. H.M.S.O.
33. Barbara N. Rodgers. *The Careers of Social Studies Students*. Occasional Papers on Social Administration, No. 11, p. 39. The Codicote Press, 1964.
34. Ministry of Health, op. cit. (25 Chap. 7).
35. Ministry of Health, op. cit. (18 Chap. 2).
36. Ministry of Housing and Local Government, op. cit. (31 Chap. 9), p. 48, para. 145.
37. The Committee on Local Authority and Allied Personal Services, op. cit. (32 Chap. 5), p. 173, para. 564.
38. Ministry of Housing and Local Government, op. cit. (31 Chap. 9), Table 3/3, p. 19.
39. Home Office. Report on the Work of the Probation and After-Care Department 1962–1965, pp. 15–16, para. 42. Cmnd. 3107. H.M.S.O., 1966.
40. Nesta Roberts. Mental Health and Mental Illness, pp. 49 and 74. Routledge and Kegan Paul, 1967.
41. The Working Party on Social Workers in the Local Authority Health and Welfare Services, op. cit. (2 Chap. 8), p. 305, para. 1059.
42. Eileen L. Younghusband, op. cit. (29).

43. Dora Peyser. *The Strong and the Weak*, p. 122. Angus and Robertson Ltd., 1951.
44. T. H. Marshall. 'The Recent History of Professionalism in relation to Social Structure and Social Policy' in op. cit. (24 Chap. 3), p. 161.
45. Barbara N. Rodgers and Julia Dixon, op. cit. (6 Chap. 8), p. 22.
46. The Medical Services Review Committee, op. cit. (17 Chap. 6), p. 71.
47. Ministry of Health, op. cit. (18 Chap. 2).
48. Eileen L. Younghusband, op. cit. (29), Chapter 1.
49. Ministry of Health, op. cit. (18 Chap. 2).
50. T. H. Marshall, op. cit. (44) pp. 163 and 170.

CHAPTER ELEVEN

1. Olive Stevenson. 'Co-ordination Reviewed', *Case Conference*, Vol· 9, No. 8, February, 1963.
2. J. Hope-Wallace. 'The Case Worker, the Welfare Officer and the Administrator in the Social Services' in *The Boundaries of Casework*, p. 90. The Association of Psychiatric Social Workers, 1956.
3. K. C. Wheare, op. cit. (39 Chap. 9), p. 196.
4. Winifred P. Smith and Helen A. Bate. *Family Casework and the Country Dweller*. Edited by A. V. S. Lochhead. The Family Welfare Association, 1953.
5. Barbara N. Rodgers and Julia Dixon, op. cit. (6 Chap. 8).
6. Kathleen M. Slack. *Councils, Committees and Concern for the Old*, Chapter III. Occasional Papers on Social Administration, No. 2. The Codicote Press, 1960.
7. The Working Party on Social Workers in the Local Authority Health and Welfare Services, op. cit. (4 Chap. 8), pp. 311–317, paras, 1078–87 and 1091–93.
8. The Committee on Children and Young Person, op. cit. (38 Chap. 6), p. 17, para. 37.
9. Margot Jeffreys, 'The Organisation of Community Health and Welfare Services', *Social Work*, Vol. 22, Nos. 2–3.
10. Kathleen Jones. 'Co-operation and Casework in the Mental Health Services'. *Case Conference*, Vol. 1, No. 2, June 1954.
11. The Working Party on Social Workers in the Local Authority Health and Welfare Services, op. cit. (4 Chap. 8), p. 307, para. 1065.
12. Olive Stevenson, op. cit. (1).
13. The Ministry of Health, op. cit. (18 Chap. 2), p. 9, para. 21 (iii).
14 *Ibid.*, p. 12, para. 29.

K

15. The National Council of Social Service. *Help for the Handicapped*, 1958, p. 102.
16. The Medical Services Review Committee, op. cit. (17 Chap. 6), p. 158, para. 608.
17. The Committee of Enquiry into the Cost of the National Health Service, op. cit. (22 Chap. 9), pp. 216–217, paras. 644–645 and p. 201, para. 611.
18. Ministry of Health, op. cit. (18 Chap. 2), p. 21, para. 68.
19. *Ibid.*, p. 38, para. 137.
20. The Committee on Local Authority and Allied Services, op. cit. (32 Chap. 5).
21. Ministry of Health. *Convalescent Treatment*. The Report of the Ministry of Health Working Party. H.M.S.O., 1959.
22. The Committee of Enquiry into the Cost of the National Health Service, op. cit. (22 Chap. 9), p. 212, para. 637.
23. The Committee of Inquiry on the Rehabilitation Training and Resettlement of Disabled Persons, op. cit. (24 Chap. 7), pp. 49 and 51, paras. 201 and 207.
24. Pauline C. Shapiro. 'The Case Worker, the Welfare Officer and the Administrator in the Social Services' in op. cit. (2), p. 80.
25. Kathleen M. Slack, op. cit. (6).
26. The National Council of Social Service, op. cit. (15), pp. 92 and 101.
27. The Working Party on Social Workers in the Local Authority Health and Welfare Services, op. cit. (4 Chap. 8), p. 319, para. 1100.
28. Lord Beveridge. *Voluntary Action*, p. 150. Allen and Unwin Ltd., 1948.
29. Home Office. Sixth Report on the Work of the Children's Department, Appendix IX. H.M.S.O., 1951.
30. The Working Party on Social Workers in the Local Authority Health and Welfare Services, op. cit. (4 Chap. 8), p. 307, para. 1065.
31. Kathleen Jones, op. cit. (10 Chap. 11).
32. Parliamentary Debates (Hansard). House of Commons Official Report, Vol. 709, No. 87, Monday, March 29, 1965, Column 1175.
33. Parliamentary Debates (Hansard) House of Commons Official Report, Vol. 706, No. 61, Friday, November 19, 1964, Columns 1597–8.
34. Madeline Rooff. *Voluntary Societies and Social Policy*, p. 122. Routledge and Kegan Paul Ltd., 1957.
35. Robert Kemp, T.D., M.D. 'Old-Age—a Regret'. *The Lancet*, Saturday, November 2, 1963.

CHAPTER TWELVE

1. The Committee on Administrative Tribunals and Enquiries, op. cit. (10 Chap. 9), p. 2, para. 5.
2. National Corporation for the Care of Old People, Seventeenth Annual Report for the Year Ended September 30, 1964.
3. Ministry of Health, op. cit. (18 Chap. 8).
4. The National Council of Social Service. 44th Annual Report, 1962–63, p. 29.
5. The National Council of Social Service. 47th Annual Report, 1965–66, p. 17.
6. Peter Townsend, op. cit. (39 Chap. 7), p. 231.
7. Sir Ernest Gowers. *The Complete Plain Words*, p. iii. H.M.S.O., 1954.
8. *Ibid.*, p. 31.
9. The Committee on Children and Young Persons, op. cit. (38 Chap. 6), p. 9, para. 14.
10. The Annual Report of the Council on Tribunals for the year ended December 31, 1963, Section iii. H.M.S.O., 1964.
11. The Committee on Administrative Tribunals and Enquiries, op. cit. (10 Chap. 9), p. 5, para. 23.
12. *Ibid.*, p. 9, para. 38.
13. The Second Report of the Council on Tribunals for the year ended December 31, 1960, p. 2, para. 6. H.M.S.O., 1961.
14. Peter Townsend, op. cit. (39 Chap. 7), p. 174.
15. *Ibid.*, p. 215.
16. National Corporation for the Care of Old People, op. cit. (2).
17. Report of the Committee on Legal Aid and Legal Advice in England and Wales, Cmd. 6641. H.M.S.O., 1945.
18. Ministry of Health Central Health Services Council, *The Welfare of Children in Hospital*. H.M.S.O., 1958.
19. Justice. *The Citizen and the Administration—The redress of grievances*, p. 37. Stevens and Sons Ltd., 1961.
20. *Ibid.*, Appendix A, p. 87, para. 6.

INDEX

Abel-Smith, B., Poverty Study, 130

Abrams, Mark, quoted, 63, 66, 79

'Administrative Tribunals and Enquiries', see Franks Committee

'Adolescent, Education of', see Hadow Committee

Adoption Act (1950), 162

'Adoption of Children', see Hurst Committee

Advisory Bodies to Central Government Departments, 187–92

Advisory Committees, Women on, 190

Aged Poor, Royal Commission on (1895), 151

Albemarle Committee on 'The Youth Service in England and Wales', 117, 118, 214–15

Albemarle Working Party on 'The Future Development of the Youth Employment Service', 115, 215

Allen of Hurtwood, Lady, 121

Appeals Machinery in the Social Services, 258–60

Approved Schools, Central Advisory Committee, 188

Area Health Boards, 170, 252

Assistance Board, 99, 176. See also National Assistance Board and Unemployment Assistance Board

Aves Committee on 'Voluntary Workers in the Social Services', 194, 222

Barnes, L. J., quoted, 116–17

Bate, Helen A., quoted, 231

Beales, H. L., quoted, 46, 59–60

Beveridge Committee on 'Social Insurance and Allied Services', 57, 128–9, 175–6, 201

Beveridge, Lord, 'Power and Influence', 203

Beveridge, Lord, quoted, 244

Blind, Central Advisory Corporation for Workshops, 186. See also Stewart and Taylor Working Parties

Blind Persons Act (1920), 140, 165

Board of Control (1913–59), 170, 259

Board of Customs and Excise, 176

Board of Trade, 113, 133

Booth, Charles, Survey of Poverty, 82, 134

Bow Group, quoted, 56

Bowley, A. L., Survey of Poverty, 128, 134

Bruce, Maurice, quoted, 63

Capital Punishment, Royal Commission on (1949–53), 181

'Care of Children', see Curtis Committee

Care and Resettlement of Offenders, National Association, 149

'Caring for People', see Williams Committee

Carnegie United Kingdom Trust, 240

'Case Conference', 82, 254

Central After-Care Association, 149

Central Office of Information, 90

Central Statistical Office, 179

Chambers, Rosalind G., quoted, 198

'Charitable Trusts, Law and Practice relating to', see Nathan Committee

Charity Organisation Society, see Family Welfare Association

Child Care, Advisory Council, 187

Child Care, Central Training Council, 188, 215

Child Care, National Bureau for Co-operation, 245

Child Care Officers, Association of, 215

'Child, the Family and the Young Offender', Home Office White Paper, 123, 124

Child Poverty Action Group, 132